Jefferson's
Garden

ALSO BY PETER LOEWER

The Indoor Water Gardener's How-to Handbook
Bringing the Outdoors In
Growing and Decorating with Grasses
Gardens by Design
The Annual Garden
American Gardens
A Year of Flowers
The Wild Gardener
Secrets of the Great Gardeners
Tough Plants for Tough Places
The Evening Garden
The New Small Garden
Seeds
Thoreau's Garden
The Winter Garden
Fragrant Gardens
Solving Weed Problems
Solving Deer Problems
Small-Space Gardening

CHILDREN'S BOOKS
(Illustrated by Jean Jenkins Loewer)
The Inside-Out Stomach
Pond Water Zoo
The Moonflower

*I think this is the most extraordinary
collection of talent, of human knowledge, that
has ever been gathered together at the
White House, with the possible exception
of when Thomas Jefferson dined alone.*

—John F. Kennedy,
addressing Nobel Prize
winners, April 1962

JEFFERSON'S GARDEN

Peter Loewer

Foreword by
PEGGY CORNETT
Director of the Thomas Jefferson Center
for Historic Plants, Monticello

STACKPOLE
BOOKS

Published by
Stackpole Books
5067 Ritter Road
Mechanicsburg, PA 17055
www.stackpolebooks.com

Printed in the United States of America

10 9 8 7 6 5 4 3 2 1

First Edition

Design by Beth Oberholtzer

Frontispiece: Thomas Jefferson, 1805, by Rembrandt Peale.
© Collection of The New-York Historical Society.

Library of Congress Cataloging-in-Publication Data

Loewer, H. Peter.
    Jefferson's garden / Peter Loewer.—1st ed.
        p.   cm.
    Includes bibliographical references and index.
    ISBN 0-8117-0076-3
    1. Gardening—Virginia.   2. Gardens—Virginia.   3. Monticello (Va.)
4. Jefferson, Thomas, 1743–1826—Homes and haunts—Virginia.   5. Jefferson,
Thomas, 1743–1826.   6. Presidents—United States—Biography.   I. Title.
SB451.34.V8 L64   2004
635.9′09755′482—dc21

                                                          2003008242

CONTENTS

FOREWORD

Thomas Jefferson's interest in plants and gardening was an all-encompassing passion that went beyond a patriotic desire to improve the lot of farmers and diversify the country's agriculture. It exceeded his eager pursuit of knowledge about North American flora or his study of botanical nomenclature and natural history. It was more than just a hobby that he dabbled in with his daughters and grandchildren. For Jefferson, the study and accumulation of hundreds of flowers, fruits and vegetables, trees and shrubs, and the physical process of growing them, became a means by which he connected with the world and a way of maintaining and strengthening bonds of friendship for a lifetime. Our present-day fondness for sharing and passing along plants for the sheer pleasure of it is nothing new, and it is safe to say that Jefferson was likely one of America's original enthusiasts.

Peter Loewer vividly describes the historical tales of such garden favorites as amaranths, honesty, hollyhocks, chaste tree, and even hops, all plants known to Jefferson and grown through the ages. In writing this book, Loewer gleaned information from a rich and varied collection of significant garden literature, from Carolus Clusius' 1601 *Rariorum plantarum historia* to Alice Morse Earle's classic 1901 work, *Old Time Gardens*. Yet this is not a book to keep on the shelf as an occasional reference. With each plant's description, Loewer—a seasoned gardener himself—weaves in hints and techniques gained from his first-hand experience and considerable knowledge of the subject. By using Monticello's gardens as his catalyst and muse, he captures the essence of Jefferson's love of gardening, making this timeless activity accessible to the modern gardener and successfully connecting him with a new generation.

Peggy Cornett, Director
Thomas Jefferson Center for Historic Plants
Monticello

ACKNOWLEDGMENTS

In the fall of 1991, the College for Seniors of the University of North Carolina at Asheville asked me to do a presentation on Thomas Jefferson, the gardener. As a result of that assignment, my wife, Jean, and I motored to Charlottesville, Virginia, where we spent a delightful three days, including an entire afternoon and the following morning at Monticello. Since then I have never wavered in my admiration of Jefferson—the man, the architect and designer, and the gardener.

Thanks are due to W. Kirkland Symmes, for the initial contact with Monticello; my wife, Jean, who continues to be the necessary help in maintaining house, garden, and time when I choose to be a writer; Peter Gentling, for advice and counsel; Peggy Cornett, Director of the Center of Historic Plants at Monticello; and my editor at Stackpole, Kyle Weaver, who always has been everything an editor should be.

INTRODUCTION

What better way to begin writing about Thomas Jefferson's garden than to quote Benjamin Franklin:

> There seem to be but three ways for a nation to acquire wealth. The first is by war, as the Romans did, in plundering their neighbors. This is robbery. The second by commerce, which is generally cheating. The third is by agriculture, the only honest way, wherein a man receives a real increase of the seed thrown into the ground, in a kind of continual miracle, wrought by the hand of God in his favor, as a regard for his innocent life and his virtuous industry.

I follow this with Jefferson's famous gardening quote from a letter to Charles Wilson Peale, on August 20, 1811:

> No occupation is so delightful to me as the culture of the earth, no culture comparable to that of a garden. . . . But though an old man, I am but a young gardener.

America in the time of Jefferson and Franklin was a country devoted to the land, to the farm, and generally, to work. It was a country that so understood the importance of agriculture that even today our school year is still based on freeing the family children for seasonal farm work.

Then, too, there were gardens. But unlike his European counterparts, Jefferson designed his garden around the passing seasons. The gardens at Monticello were never meant as tributes to wealth or power. They were a theater alfresco, where he and his family would wander the pathways and observe the natural world. It would be, he said, "the workhouse of nature—clouds, hail, rain, thunder, all fabricated at our feet." But Jefferson's influence on garden design has been limited, and the English garden scheme is still desired by most. With the vagaries of the American climate, however, Jefferson's Monticello garden ideas should be used on a far larger scale.

The two distinguishing characteristics of the garden are twenty oval flowerbeds (possibly the source of the "island beds" made popular in the twentieth century by the English gardener Alan Bloom) and long walkways. Along with a plan for further plantings in the West Lawn, Jefferson wrote his granddaughter Anne in 1807: "I find that the limited number of our flower beds will too much restrain the variety of flowers in which we might wish to indulge, and therefore I have resumed an idea—of a winding walk—with a narrow border of flowers on each side. This would give us abundant room for a great variety."

Documentary evidence suggests that Jefferson grew 105 species of herbaceous flowers. This might sound like a lot of plants, but today there are gardeners with hundreds of species. Nevertheless, in Jefferson's time, and with his duties, to have taken care of that many plants was a distinct achievement. Almost every year, Jefferson received up to 700 species of seeds from Paris, and many probably did survive and find their way to the gardens but were never entered in the logs.

The gardens at Monticello, which is in USDA Zone 7, go through three phases every year. The first is in the spring, with bulbs like tulips making a grand display; the second is mid-May to mid-June, when most of the popular garden perennials are in bloom; and the third phase begins in mid-July and runs to mid-October, when the flowering annuals are able to bloom even in the midst of the summer heat.

When it came to vegetables, Jefferson was responsible for feeding a number of people. His vegetable garden included about 300 varieties, many not known today. In 1811, there were eighty-five separate plantings of vegetables. The rows were tightly packed together then, and there were no grass walkways for maintenance like there are today. The color of the ground is from the high clay content, but so much vegetable matter has been incorporated into the soil that the vegetables grow in a mammoth manner.

Around the garden, Jefferson built a ten-foot-high, three-quarter-mile wooden fence to keep out intruders—animal and human. It contained 300 posts, 900 rails, and 7,500 boards.

My wife, Jean, and I visited Monticello during an early fall recently. The weather was fine and beyond compare, and we wandered the gardens and the pathways. In front of the house were mounds of spider flowers *(Cleome hasslerana)* in full bloom (in cultivation by 1840), accompanied by sunflowers *(Helianthus divaricatus);* spike-tipped celosia *(Celosia cristata* var. *spicata),* an annual in cultivation by 1790; and globe amaranth *(Gomphrena globosa),* which arrived in 1767 and was popular every summer, not only because it withstood the Virginia heat, but also for its use all winter in everlasting bouquets. We stood above the vegetable garden just before sunrise and watched the hyacinth beans waiting for the sun.

In the garden was a pavilion or temple inspired by the Italian architect Palladio. It was modeled after an English orangerie and had windows that became doors so that orange and lemon trees could be moved indoors, but Jefferson built it as an observation room in which to sit and read.

Steps led to the 1,000-foot-long garden wall, which was built without mortar and in places is over eleven feet high. A lone bachelor button grew in the wall.

We walked the vineyard, which was a continual battle for Jefferson since the Old World grape, *Vitis vinifera,* was largely unsuccessful, and the New World grape, *V. labrusca,* produced wine with a distinctly foxy taste.

Dogwoods grew at the edge of the woods and along the path to the cemetery, where Jefferson and his friend Dabney Carr agreed to be buried beneath the great oak that stood there. Carr, who married Jefferson's sister, died in 1773 and was the first to be buried. Looking through the fence, where grew hardy oranges and yuccas, we saw Jefferson's present tombstone, erected in 1883 by the U.S. government. Its base covers the graves of Jefferson, his wife, two daughters, and Gov. Thomas Mann Randolf, his son-in-law.

THE IMPORTANCE OF
SEEDS IN AMERICA

Columbus brought seeds from the Old World to the New on his second voyage, in 1493, carrying wheat, barley, sugarcane, and grapes. The colonists that followed the Spanish armies into Florida, Mexico, and Peru took along seeds of their favorite crops. Because the new arrivals had a tendency to settle in areas that reminded them of home, most of these plants adjusted with ease.

But as the population grew, more seeds were needed. And seeds were reasonably cheap to transport, compared with tubs of dirt with desiccated trees or large bulbs or plants that often required more water than the crew. The Spanish government ordered that all ships sailing for the Indies carry seeds in their cargoes. As a result, almost 150 species and varieties were introduced to New Spain, including lemons, cabbage, turnips, anise, alfalfa, flax, bamboo, daffodils, irises, poppies, and of all things, carnations. The Native Americans helped in the distribution of plants by carrying seeds on their travels; the trading worked two ways, with the Spanish taking back native crops, including corn, tobacco, cotton, chili peppers, squash, and tomatoes. Wild peaches were found by the first settlers of Pennsylvania, probably from the original trees planted a century earlier in St. Augustine, Florida.

In 1611, Jamestown planters brought tobacco from Trinidad. So by the end of the seventeenth century, most of the food and feed crops growing in present-day America were already established. At that time, it was believed that America should be growing cash crops for Europe, and the choices included rice, indigo, cotton, sugar, spices, tea, and mulberry trees for silkworms. But few of the plants introduced from the subtropics could withstand the winters found in most of the settled country.

Then in the 1690s, South Carolina planters brought seeds for rice from Madagascar, and it proved a great success growing on their lowlands around Charleston. In 1745, one Eliza Lucas brought indigo seeds from Antigua, West Indies, and they, too, proved successful.

Just after the end of the American Revolution, seeds of sea-island cotton were introduced from the Bahamas, adding a fourth cash crop to tobacco, rice, and indigo. Unlike regular cotton, the lint of sea-island cotton separated easily from the seed (although this was no longer necessary after Eli Whitney invented the cotton gin in 1793).

On May 14, 1686, a gardener in the hire of William Penn wrote to someone in England about gardening in America: "Trees and Bulbes are shot in five weeks time, some one Inch, some two, three, four, five, six, seven, yea some are eleven Inches. . . . And seeds do come on apace; for those seeds that in England take fourteen days to rise, are up here in six or seven days." The letter concludes with a request: "Pray make agreement with the Bishop of London's Gardiner or any other that will furnish us with Trees, Shrubs, Flowers and Seeds, and we will furnish them from these places."

William Penn had great plans for mapping gardens of beauty in his state, including, unlike most American cities, the city of Philadelphia. There were to be five public squares inside the town proper, with a great square of ten acres in the center. Penn directed that every man's house "be placed, if the Person pleases, in ye middle of its place as to the breath way of it, so that there may be grounds, on each side, for Gardens, or Orchards, or fields, yt may be a greene Country Towne, wch will never be burnt and will always be welcome."

But Philadelphia aside, according to Ann Leighton in *American Gardens in the Eighteenth Century*, in the American colonies, "the seventeenth-century gardens had been almost totally what it is now fashionable to call 'relevant.' They existed to feed, clothe, clean, cure and comfort the settlers."

But America was on the march, and by the eighteenth century, things began to change and reflect what was happening in England and Europe. Both seeds and plants were on the market. In 1728, Pierre Janfroid opened one of the first seed shops in Paris, and in 1769, his successor, Andrieux, issued his first catalog. Ten years later, the Vilmorins married into the family, and since 1799, the firm of Vilmorin-Andrieux et Cie has been selling seeds around the world. Germany saw the seedhouse of L. Spath begin in 1720, and it continued well into the twentieth century.

Many of the seeds imported during the eighteenth century were grown in the gardens of renowned plantsmen like John Bartram of Philadelphia. Bartram's garden was the most widely known of these seed plantations, and it specialized in plants of this continent. While traveling abroad, men like Benjamin Franklin and Thomas Jefferson sent seeds back to Bartram. Franklin, for example, introduced two Scottish crops, rhubarb and kale. And Jefferson risked the death penalty in northern Italy by smuggling back seeds of an upland cotton for South Carolina that the Italians were holding for a monopoly in cotton.

Although seeds were always bought and sold for agricultural purposes, it was not until the rising merchant class of the last few hundred years that seeds for ornamental purposes were actually available at shops.

The following is an advertisement appearing in the July 9, 1763, issue of the *South Carolina Gazette:*

> Thomas Young, Sen. has at present a fine assortment of kitchen garden seeds, several kinds of grass seeds, flower seeds and roots, flower glasses, and some garden tools. Lists of which may be seen at his house near the west end of Broad Street. He will sell no seeds but such sorts as have grown in his garden, and therefore can be warranted good. Those gentlemen or ladies who want flower roots, must call for them soon as most of them are now out of the ground.

In her book *Old Time Gardens,* Alice Morse Earle wrote a great deal about the early sales of seeds in America, including the following:

> The shrewd and capable women of the colonies who entered so freely and successfully into business ventures found the selling of flower seeds a congenial occupation, and often added it to the pursuit of other callings. I think it must have been very pleasant to buy packages of flower seed at the same time and place where you bought your best bonnet, and have all sent home in a bandbox together; each would prove a memorial of the other; and long after the glory of the bonnet had departed, and the bonnet itself was ashes, the thriving Sweet Peas and Larkspur would recall its becoming charms.

An ad in the *Boston Gazette* of February 1719 read:

Garden Seeds. Fresh Garden Seeds of all Sorts, lately imported from London, to be sold by Evan Davies, Gardener, at his house over against the Powder House in Boston; As also English Sparrow-grass Roots, Carnation Layers, Dutch Gooseberry, and Current bushes.

A seedswoman advertised the following list of seeds in a Boston newspaper on March 30, 1760:

Lavender, Palma Christi, Cerinthe or honeywort, loved of bees, Tricolor, Indian pink, Scarlet Cacalia, Yellow Sultans, Lemon African Marigold, Sensitive Plants, White Lupine, Love Lies Bleeding, Patagonian Cucumber, Lobelia, Catchfly, Wing-peas, Convolvulus, Strawberry Spinage, Branching Larkspur, White Chrysanthemum, Nigaella Romano, Rose Campion, Snap Dragon, Nolana prostrata, Summer Savory, Hyssop, Red Hawkweed, Red and White Lavater, Scarlet Lupine, Large blue Lupine, Snuff flower, Caterpillars [plants that looked like pseudo-insects were very popular during the Civil War], Cape Marigold, Rose Lupine, Sweet Peas, Venus' Navelwort, Yellow Chrysanthemum, Cyanus minor, Tall Hollyhock, French Marigold, Carnation Poppy, Glove Amaranthus, Yellow Lupine, Indian Branching Cox-combs, Iceplants, Thyme, Sweet Marjoram, Tree Mallows, Everlasting, Greek Valerian, Tree Primrose, Canterbury Bells, Purple Stock, Sweet Scabiouse, Columbine, Pleasant-eyed Pink, Dwarf Mountain Pink, Sweet Rocket, Horn Poppy, French Honeysuckle, Bloody Wallflower, Sweet William, Honesty, to be sold in small parcels that every one may have a little, Persicaria, Polyanthos, Fifty different sorts of mixed Tulip Roots, Ranunculus, Gladiolus, Starry Scabiouse, Curled Mallows, Painted Lady, topknot peas, Colchicum, Persian Iris, Star Bethlehem.

In the *Boston News-Letter* of April 5, 1764, another seedswoman, named Anna Johnson, advertised a sale at her shop at the Head of Black Harre Lane, leading up from Charlestown Ferry. The list included the following:

A fresh assortment of Garden Seeds, Peas and Beans, among which are, early charlton, early hotspur, golden hotspur, large and small dwarf, large marrowfat, white rouncevals rose and crown, crooked sugar, and grey Pease; large Windsor, early hotspur, early Lisbon, early yellow, six-weeks long podded, and white Kidney Beans; early Dutch, yorkshire, sugar-loaf, battersea, savory, and large winter Cabbage; early and late Colliflower, early orange, scarlet and purple carrots; best smelling

Parsnips; Endive, Cellery; Asparagus, and Pepper; early prickly, long
and short cluster, white and green turkey Cucumber; Thyme and Sweet
Marjoram; Balm, Hyssop and Sage; London short and Salmon Rad-
dish; Lavender; green and white goss, green and white silesia, imperial,
cabbage, tennis-ball, marble, and brown dutch lettice; ripe canary Seeds;
red and white Clover; herd's Grass; red top and tye grass Seeds; also a
Parcel of curious Flower-Seeds.

That's an amazing list when one remembers that apart from the
wealthier inhabitants of the cities, most Americans were working
round the clock, 350 days a year, taking time out only for church,
Easter, and Christmas.

The first seedhouse in America was David Landreth & Son of
Philadelphia, opening in 1780. At first the seed industry grew with
little exuberance, but by 1850, there were forty-five seed firms, most
of them in the East. Seeds for many of the vegetables grown in this
country before the Civil War were brought over by immigrant wives
who saved seed from each year's harvest.

In 1817, Elkanah Watson, one of the founders of the New York
Society for the Promotion of Useful Arts, sent a series of letters to
all the American consuls in Europe, asking for seeds. In answer to one
request, the consul in Valencia, Spain, send back seeds of fourteen
kinds of wheat, one of barley, and one of oats.

Kohlrabi and the rutabaga were introduced to American tables at
the end of the eighteenth century. And with the rise of the merchant
seedhouses, competition began in earnest. U. P. Hendrick wrote in *A
History of Horticulture in America to 1860* about the following incident in
New York:

> A curious dispute arose in New York papers in 1818 between Grant
> Thorburn, an early seedsman, and William Cobbett. The latter, who
> had a seed store in New York in 1818, claimed that he was the intro-
> ducer of the rutabaga and sold better seed at a dollar a pound than
> Thorburn; but Thorburn retorted that his seed was better at the same
> price and that "in the year 1796 a large field of these turnips was grown
> by Wm. Prout on that piece of ground now occupied by the navy yard,
> at the city of Washington." Thorburn was probably right, but the fact
> remains that Cobbett in his *American Gardener* and *A Year's Residence in the
> United States of America* was a great champion of the rutabaga.

Now it was time for the government to get involved. That notice sent to American consuls and asking for seeds was made official in the Congress of 1825, when the consuls were authorized to send home seeds of rare plants. In 1836, the Patent Office was started, with Henry Leavett Ellsworth as director. According to history, he was more interested in agriculture than inventions, and the week he assumed office, he began collecting rare and valuable varieties of seeds. Then the seeds were distributed, with 40,000 packages going out in 1840 and 2,333,474 packets in 1877, some of them being gifts of European governments.

According to Hendrick, "The distribution of seeds became more and more a species of petty graft on the part of congressmen, who used their franking privileges to send them to those who would take them. Instead of rare varieties, the packages often contained packets of the commonest and cheapest seeds that conniving seedsmen could supply."

Billions of seed packets were distributed, most of them seeds of vegetables and flowers, but they also included seeds of sorghum, sugar beets, soybeans, commercial tea, and many more. But continual complaints about poor germination rates led to questions about the reliability of the supply. Some horticulturists questioned the wisdom of selecting seeds for sugar and tea as the most urgently needed crops.

"It was not until well into the twentieth century," continued Hendrick, "that, under the combined forces of farmers, gardeners, seedsmen, and farm and horticultural papers, free seed distribution with its many scandals was brought to a close."

Today's gardeners might wonder about the lure of seeds to the voters, but back then, the farmer ruled supreme, and if a congressman thought enough to send seeds to the bank president's wife, he really must be a grand guy. After all, crop seeds were indispensable to nine out of ten households in the early days of the nation. Most of the seed was homegrown, and seeds for new land were obtained by buying from seedhouses or trading with other farmers.

Patricia M. Tice, in her museum catalog, *Gardening in America*, mentioned that the cost of plants was much higher than the cost of seeds.

Joseph Breck and Sons (then Company) began operations in 1837, and in 1851, Breck published *The Flower Garden; or, Breck's Book of Flowers,* a book about seeds that became so popular that it ran through five editions. At the same time, Fearing Burr (1815–97), a well-known seedsman and writer, published *The Field and Garden Vegetables of America*, a book that contained full descriptions of nearly eleven hundred species and varieties of plants, and included directions for propagation and the uses of vegetables. This book is a treasure trove of information about eighteenth-century farms and gardens, especially since it documents so many cultivars that have now disappeared from commerce.

In 1847, the Landreth Company of Philadelphia bought 375 acres outside of Bristol, Pennsylvania, then hired over 125 employees to run its seed operations. They needed a separate business just to provide paper bags and envelopes. By the middle of the century, Landreth's had a worldwide reputation, and their seeds were planted in every state of the Union—in fact, wherever gardens were maintained. David Landreth was one of the founders of the Pennsylvania Horticultural Society, an organization that has a worldwide reputation and is still located on Walnut Street in Philadelphia.

In 1853, when Commodore Perry lifted the bamboo curtain that surrounded Japan, the Landreth Company sent along a box of seeds and in return received a box of Japanese seeds, an action that was the beginning of importing seeds from Asia and, over the years, so many valuable plants that it would take pages of paper for documentation.

But 1853 was a year of change in the seed business for another reason. One B. K. Bliss, a native of central New York, moved to Springfield, Massachusetts, and opened up the first mail-order seed business in America. Later, the Bliss Company was also the first to print a catalog with colored plates (although some argue that James Vick, a Rochester seedsman and innovator, might have been the first when his 1864 catalog featured a colored lithograph of double zinnias that had been developed only four years earlier). Over the following years, the Bliss Company brought many new garden plants to the American gardener. In 1858, Bliss described 676 varieties of flower seeds alone, and seven years later, the list had grown to 1,612.

Other nurseries, too, began using color in their catalogs. And it became such a popular move that in 1886, when the Ferry Seed Company published its new catalog without colored illustrations, the company felt responsible in printing the following statement on the first page:

> If it seems lacking in brilliantly colored plates of impossible vegetables and glowing descriptions of the superlative excellence of new sorts which are meant to revolutionize garden practice, it is because our aim has been to give in its pages information which will enable our readers to have a good garden, rather than to tempt them to purchase at exorbitant prices a few seeds of some untried novelty liable at least to result in failure and disappointment.

The interest in new seeds and plants was a bottomless pit. England's Thompson & Morgan began producing seed catalogs in 1855. In 1872, Peter Henderson & Co., of New York City, began publishing two catalogs, one just for new plants of that particular year.

In her museum catalog, Tice mentioned a book published in 1877, entitled *History of Monroe County*, that gave an intimate look into James Vick's large Rochester business.

> In addition to the ordinary conveniences of a well regulated seedhouse, there is connected with this establishment a printing office, binder, box-making establishment, and artists' and engravers' rooms, everything but the paper being made in the establishment. The machinery necessary for the various departments is driven by steampower . . . [and] the magnitude of this institution is illustrated from the fact that it occupies a building five stories in height, including a basement 60 feet in width and 150 feet in length, with an addition in the upper story of a large room over an entire adjoining block.
> The first floor is used exclusively as a store for the sale of seeds, flowers, plants, and all garden requisites and adornments, such as baskets, vases, lawn-mowers, lawn-tents, aquariums, seats, etc., etc. . . .
> The second floor is devoted to business offices . . . [and] the mailroom is upon this floor, and the opening of letters occupies the time of two persons, and they perform the work with astonishing rapidity, often opening three thousand in a single day. After these letters are opened they are passed into what is called the registering room, on the same floor, where they are divided into States, and the name of the person ordering and the date of the receipt of the order registered. They are then ready to be filled, and are passed into a large room, called the order room, where over seventy-five hands are employed, divided into gangs, each set or gang to a State, half a dozen or more being employed on each of the larger States. After the orders are filled,

packed, and directed, they are sent to what is known as the post-office
. . . where the packages are weighed, the necessary stamps put on them,
and the stamps cancelled, when they are packed in post-office bags,
furnished by the government, properly labeled for the different routes,
and sent to the postal cars. Tons of seeds are thus dispatched every
day during the busy season.

On the third floor is the German department, where all orders
written in the German language are filled by German clerks; a catalog
in that language is also published. On this floor, also, all seeds are
packed, that is, weighed and measured and placed in paper bags, and
stored ready for sale. About fifty persons are employed in this room,
surrounded by thousands of nicely-labeled drawers.

On the fourth floor are rooms for artists and engravers, several of
whom are kept constantly employed in designing and engraving for
catalogues and chromos [chromos were colored reproductions that
used lithographic stones]. Here, adjoining is the printing office, where
the catalogue is prepared and other printing done, and also the bindery,
often employing forty or fifty hands, and turning out more than ten
thousand catalogues in a day. Here is in use the most improved machin-
ery for covering, trimming, etc., propelled by steam.

The immense amount of business done may be understood by a
few facts: Nearly one hundred acres are employed, near the city, in
growing flower seeds, mainly while large importations are made from
Germany, France, Holland, Australia, and Japan. Over three thousand
reams of printing paper are used each year for catalogues, weighing
two hundred thousand pounds, and the simple postage for sending
these catalogues by mail is thirteen thousand dollars. Millions of bags
and boxes are also manufactured in the establishment, requiring hundreds of reams of paper and scores of tons of pasteboard.

According to Tice, the Shakers at Mount Lebanon, Pennsylvania,
are generally given the credit for the introduction of small packets, or
"papers," of seed, beginning this selling method during the first quarter of the nineteenth century.

Charles Van Ravenswaay noted in *A Nineteenth-Century Garden* (New
York: Universe Books, 1977) that not all of the progress was on the
East Coast. In the early 1870s, E. E. Moore of San Francisco offered
a variety of seeds, including those of native California species, as well
as plants and bulbs.

During the early part of the twentieth century, the seed industry
continued to make progress. Further discoveries were made regarding

crop plants and vegetables. New varieties of rice were introduced for the southern farm. Frank N. Meyer, a young Dutchman, brought back zoysia grass from Asia for the lawns of the burgeoning middle classes.

Interest in seeds continues to this day. But were our country's seed heritage not nurtured by men like Jefferson and the other plantsmen and explorers of the nation's early years, it's quite possible that many of the plants that today we consider commonplace might never have been grown here.

It was Jefferson who said, "The greatest service which can be rendered any country is to add a useful plant to its culture."

THOMAS JEFFERSON, PLANTER AND LANDSCAPE ARCHITECT

We know Jefferson the statesman—delegate to the Continental Congress, ambassador to France, secretary of state under Washington, vice president under Adams, and third president of the United States. We know Jefferson the political philosopher—author of the Declaration of Independence and proponent of the natural rights of man. And there's Jefferson the educator—founder of the University of Virginia—and Jefferson the architect—creator of the rotunda at the university, the Virginia state capitol, and Monticello. Jefferson is also acknowledged to be a talented landscape architect, but his abilities did not spring whole from his forehead like Athena sprang forth from Zeus's head—fully armed.

Jefferson's skills were developed over many years of experience. When he became governor of Virginia, he implemented the move of the capital to Richmond, a move that included his first city-planning document. He also worked on the city of Washington, being indirectly responsible for its location on the Potomac River and setting forth its architectural and landscaping character. And then there was his estate, Monticello, which survives as one of the oldest and best-cared-for examples of the English-type landscape in America.

April 13, 1743, was Jefferson's birthday. He grew up on the family plantation at Shadwell in Albemarle County, Virginia. His father, Peter Jefferson, with the aid of thirty slaves, managed a nineteen-hundred-acre farm, specializing in crops of wheat and tobacco. Like his fathers before him, Peter was a justice of the peace, a vestryman of his parish, and a member of the colonial legislature.

In 1738, Peter Jefferson married Jane Randolph. They had ten children, of which Thomas was the third. Thomas inherited his father's bodily strength and stature, and both were regarded as the strongest men of their county. He also inherited his father's taste for literature, aptitude for mathematics, and leanings toward liberal politics, and he gained a familiarity with the elder Jefferson's abilities as a surveyor and a mapmaker. The Jeffersons were a musical family, and young Thomas practiced the violin. Throughout his life, he always looked for a gardener who could play the French horn so that musical evenings would be assured.

Here's how his grandson Thomas Jefferson Randolf described him:

> His manners were of that polished school of the Colonial Government, so remarkable in its day—under no circumstances violating any of those minor conventional observances which constitute the well-bred gentleman, courteous and considerate to all persons. . . . Mr. Jefferson's hair, when young, was of a reddish cast; sandy as he advanced in years; his eyes hazel. Dying in his 84th year (strangely on July 4, 1826), he had not lost a tooth, nor had one defective; his skin thin, peeling from his face on exposure to the sun, and giving it a tattered appearance. . . .
>
> Mr. Jefferson's stature was commanding—six feet two-and-a-half inches in height; his carriage erect; step firm and elastic, which he preserved to his death; his temper, naturally strong, under perfect control; his courage cool and impassive. No one ever knew him to exhibit trepidation. His moral courage of the highest order—his will firm and inflexible—it was remarked of him that he never abandoned a plan, a principle, or a friend. . . . His habits were regular and systematic. He was a miser of his time, rose always at dawn, wrote and read until breakfast, breakfasted early, and dined from three to four . . . ; retired at nine, and to bed from ten to eleven. He said, in his last illness, that the sun had not caught him in bed for fifty years.

In 1757, when young Jefferson was fourteen, his father died and left him a large estate, along with the wish that his son's education be completed at the College of William and Mary.

He entered the college at the age of seventeen and was described by his peers as being tall, raw-boned, freckled, and sandy-haired, with large hands and feet, and a prominent chin and cheekbones. He was not considered a handsome man, but a man who reflected the sheer health of youth, with a bit of rusticity in his manner.

The young Jefferson soon fell under the influence of Dr. William Small of Scotland, the professor of natural philosophy at the college. Small taught the philosophic systems of the day, with the idea that man is a part and not the whole. Jefferson later wrote, "It was my great fortune, and what probably fixed the destinies of my life that Dr. William Small of Scotland was then professor of mathematics, a man profound in most of the useful branches of science, with a happy talent of communication, correct and gentlemanly manners and an enlarged and liberal mind."

Jefferson also attended many musical soirées, where he played his violin. The lieutenant governor, Francis Fauquier, also performed. George Wythe, a young lawyer at Williamsburg, often attended college functions and also contributed to Jefferson's education.

According to Frederick D. Nichols and Ralph E. Griswold, in *Thomas Jefferson, Landscape Architect,* before his father died in 1757, young Jefferson "knew how to record on a map the shape of the land, the bodies of water, the forests, and the places where people lived in Virginia."

In April 1764, when Jefferson assumed the management of his father's estate, he immediately became a justice of the peace and vestryman. He then turned his attentions to the cultivation of his lands, and throughout his years, he always remained a farmer. In 1767, Jefferson was admitted to the bar of Virginia. He practiced the legal profession for eight years, until the Revolution called. In his *Autobiography* (1821), he wrote, "That one hundred and fifty lawyers should do business together ought not to be expected."

In 1769, using his own plans, Jefferson began construction of Monticello on a mountaintop not far from Charlottesville. Among the books that influenced Jefferson the most when it came to planning the estate was Thomas Whately's *Observations on Modern Gardening,* considered the grand, fundamental, and standard work on English gardening. It featured sixty-seven observations on the gardening art, including the following:

> Gardening . . . is entitled to a place of considerable rank among the liberal arts. It is as superior to landscape painting as a reality to a representation: it is an exertion of fancy, a subject for taste; and being

released now from the restraints of regularity and enlarged beyond the purposes of domestic convenience, the most beautiful, the most simple, the most noble scenes of nature are all within its province.

In 1772, Jefferson married the widow Martha Wayles Skelton, and they moved to the unfinished house. The following year, Martha's father died, thus doubling the size of Jefferson's estate. Martha died on September 6, 1782, leaving her husband and three daughters, the youngest being four months old. Jefferson tried to drown his profound grief by returning to a hectic public life, and in 1785, he succeeded Benjamin Franklin as minister to France.

That he was influenced by what he saw while in France is evident in the view from the front of Monticello, which reaches down to the grounds of the University of Virginia (which Jefferson also designed). Here there are obvious references to Marly, which in 1682 became the official seat of the French government.

As the American minister plenipotentiary in Paris, Jefferson often walked Marly. The natural form of this garden included high banks overhung with steep woods. There were fish ponds tiled in porcelain, and a grand flight of steps led to an all-encircling pergola that linked the chateau with the pavilions that surrounded it. In 1701, Louis XIV, having toured the gardens for a day, declared to all that he could not imagine any further additions to the scene—although for the next thirteen years he continued to adjust the plans.

In 1786, Jefferson was able to tour the grand gardens of England with John Adams and his wife, Abigail, as his companions. Jefferson kept a complete accounting of the visits, including details such as tips given to servants. Adams was the first American minister sent to London, and he asked Jefferson to plan a short visit in order that they could discuss some legal matters referring to shipping and boundaries. They visited sixteen grand estates, the following only a sample. Jefferson often consulted Whately's book as a reference.

Regarding Chiswick in London, a house modeled on Palladio's Villa and including a river with a cascade, a deer house, an avenue of cedars, urns, and sphinxes, plus a banqueting house, Jefferson commented: "A garden of about six acres; the octagonal dome has an ill effect, both within and without; the garden still shows too much of art. An obelisk of very ill effect; another in the middle of the pond useless."

Turning to Hampton Court, with grounds dating back to the reign of Henry VIII (1509–47) and gardens fully developed under the reign of William and Mary (1689–1702), Jefferson noted: "Old fashioned. Clipt yews grown wild."

Next they visited Twickenham, where Jefferson wrote: "Pope's original garden, three and a half acres. This is a long, narrow strip, grass and trees in the middle, walk all around. Now Sir Wellbore Ellis's. Obelisk at the bottom of Pope's garden, a monument to his mother. The house about thirty yards from the Thames; the ground shelves gently to the waterside; on the back of the house passes the street, and beyond that the garden. The grotto is under the street, and goes out level to the water. In the center of the garden a mound with a spiral walk around it. A rookery."

Esher Place, Surrey, was thought to be one of William Kent's masterpieces. Owned by Henry Pelham from 1729 to his death in 1754, it was a landscape park with winding walks and a number of buildings designed to fit into the landscape. The park was broken up for development in the 1930s, and today only the house, pond, and grotto remain. Jefferson observed: "A hollow filled with a clump of trees, the tallest in the bottom, so that the top is quite flat. On the left the ground descends. Clumps of trees, the clumps on each hand balance finely—a most lively mixture of concave and convex. The garden is about forty-five acres, besides the park which joins."

Of Claremont, Surrey, with its development beginning in 1711, its bowling green with serpentine walks through the surrounding woods, and its exotic trees (the rhododendrons and laurels were planted in the 1800s by Queen Victoria), Jefferson said, "Nothing remarkable."

Work on Blenheim Palace, Oxfordshire, was begun on June 22, 1705, and four days after the foundation stone had been laid, the designer Sir John Vanburgh (1664–1726) wrote to the duke of Marlborough: "The garden wall was set agoing the same day with the house and I hope will be done against your Grace's return. . . . The whole gardens will be form'ed & planted in a year." This was an optimistic appraisement, as the first owners did not move into the palace until

1719. Jefferson commented of Blenheim: "Twenty-five hundred acres of which two hundred is garden, one hundred and fifty water, twelve kitchen garden, and the rest park. Two hundred people employed to keep it in order, and to make alterations and additions. About fifty of these employed in pleasure grounds. The turf is mowed once in ten days. In summer about a thousand fallow deer in the park and two or three thousand sheep. The palace of Henry II was remaining until taken down by Sarah, widow of the first Duke of Marlborough. It was a round spot leveled by art, near what is now water and but a little above it. The island was part of the high road leading to the palace. The well is near where the bower was. The water here is very beautiful and very grand. The cascade from the lake, a fine one, except this garden has no great beauties. It is not laid out in fine lawns and woods, but the trees are scattered thickly over the ground, and every here and there small thickets of shrubs, in oval raised bed, cultivated, and flowers among the shrubs. The graveled walks are broad—art appears too much. There are but a few seats in it, and nothing of architecture more dignified. There is no one striking position in it. There has been a great addition to the length of the river since Whately wrote."

Painshill, Surrey, was a garden estate that began as a site with few natural advantages, but the owner Charles Hamilton ultimately developed an estate with great natural and picturesque beauty that wedded local appeal and influence upon other estate designs, notably Stourhead and Stowe. Laid out as partly a park and part pleasure grounds that centered around a lake, Painshill represented a series of crafted scenes both visually beautiful and able to set a distinct mood. Jefferson wrote: "Three hundred and twenty-three acres, garden and park all in one. Well described by Whately. Grotto said to have cost £7000. Whately says one of the bridges is of stone, but both now are of wood, the lower sixty feet high; there is too much evergreen. The dwelling-house built by Hopkins, ill situated; he had not been there in five years. He lived there four years while building the present house. It is not finished; its architecture is incorrect. A Doric temple, beautiful."

About his visits to the English gardens, Jefferson said: "The gardening in that country is the article in which it surpasses all the earth. I mean their pleasure gardening. This, indeed, went far beyond my ideas."

Adams wrote in his diary: "It will be long, I hope, before Ridings, Parks, Pleasure Grounds, Gardens and ornamented farms grow so much in fashion in America. But Nature has done greater Things and furnished nobler Materials there. The Oceans, Island, Rivers, Mountains, Valleys, are all laid out upon a larger Scale."

Jefferson had an extensive collection of gardening books in his library. From these books and his travels, Jefferson learned, from the greatest writers and designers of gardening and nature, all that anyone could ever want to know about the principles and prospects of designing, building, and working a great estate like Monticello. Among his collection were the authors and works discussed below.

For nearly fifty years, Philip Miller (1691–1771) was the gardener to the Botanic Garden at Chelsea. In him, it was said, "the perfect Botanist and Horticulturists were combined." The ninth edition of *The Gardener's Dictionary* was published in 1792 and read not only by Jefferson, but by Washington too.

"In a fine garden," wrote Miller, "the first thing that should present itself to the sight, is a parterre, which should be next to the House, whether in the front or on the sides, as well upon account of the Opening it affords to the House, as for the Beauty with which it constantly entertains the sight from all the windows on that side of the house."

In 1806, Bernard M'Mahon (1775–1816) published *The American Gardener's Calendar: Adapted to the Climates and Seasons of the United States.* It contained a complete account of all the work necessary to be done in the kitchen garden, fruit garden, orchard, vineyard, nursery, pleasure grounds, flower garden, greenhouse, hothouse, and forcing frames for every month of the year, and it ruled the garden roost for fifty years as the definitive American gardening book.

The book opens with an advertisement for his nursery, which announced his intentions to establish a much-needed "repository of seeds of Garden Vegetables, of the Grasses, Grains and roots used in Rural Economy; of plants used in dyeing and other arts, and of useful trees, ornamental Shrubs, etc. . . ." He also solicited American gardeners to send him indigenous plants from their various vicinities "with or without names," which he proposed to exchange for seeds of "culinary vegetables, grasses, fruits or such other kinds as they may desire." Jefferson made M'Mahon chief recipient of plant materials brought back by the Lewis and Clark Expedition. His horticultural interests were very broad, and his seed store became a meeting place for botanists and horticulturists.

In 1768, William Mason (1725–97) published *The English Garden*, in which he wrote: "The first book contains the general principles of the art, which are shown to be no other than those which constitute beauty in the sister art of landscape-painting; beauty which results from a well-chosen variety of curves, in contradistinction to that of architecture, which arise from a judicious symmetry of right lines and which is thus shown to have afforded the principle on which that formal disposition of garden ground, which our ancestors borrowed from the French and Dutch, proceeded: a principle never adopted by nature herself, and therefore constantly to be avoided by those whose business it is to embellish nature."

Sir William Chambers (1726–96) was employed by George III to plan the gardens at Kew, of which he published the *Plans, Elevations and Views* in a 1763 folio edition. Here he discussed the ancient styles of straight lines in city development, then pointed out that in England, "this ancient style is held in detestation, and where, in opposition to the rest of Europe, a new manner is universally adopted, in which no appearance of art is tolerated, our gardens differ very little from common fields, so closely is common nature copied in most of them . . . these compositions rather appear the offspring of chance than design; and a stranger is often at a loss to know whether he be walking in a meadow, or in a pleasure-ground, made and kept at a very considerable expense: he sees nothing to amuse him, nothing to excite his curiosity, nor anything to keep up his attention."

In addition, Jefferson admired Lord Kames, William Hogarth, and Edmund Burke for their books on aesthetics.

In *Gardening and Architecture*, Henry Home, Lord Kames (1696–1782), observed: "Gardening, besides the emotions of beauty by means of regularity, order, proportion, colour, and utility, can raise emotions of grandeur, of sweetness, of gaiety, melancholy, wildness, and even of surprise or wonder . . . in gardening as well as in architecture simplicity ought to be the governing taste. The simplest idea of a garden, is that of a spot embellished with a number of natural objects, trees, walks, polished parterres, flowers, streams, etc."

In 1753, William Hogarth (1697–1764) wrote *The Analysis of Beauty*, where he praised the combining of the beautiful and the useful, commenting, "In nature's machines how wonderfully do we see beauty and use go hand in hand." (Four years later, he was appointed sergeant painter to George II.)

Jefferson had noted that the serpentine curve was behind most of Hogarth's philosophy, and some sixty years later, he wrote: "The plough is to the farmer what the wand is to the sorcerer. . . . We now plough horizontally flowering the curvatures of the hills and hollows. . . . In point of beauty nothing can exceed that of waving lines [and] rows winding along the face of the hills [and] vallies."

Edmund Burke (1729–97) wrote in his 1756 *Essay on the Sublime and the Beautiful:* "Whatever is fitted in any sort to excite the ideas of pain and danger, that is to say, whatever is in any sort terrible, or is conversant about terrible objects, or operates in a manner analogous to terror, is a source of the sublime; that is, it is productive of the strongest emotion which the mind is capable of feeling."

Jefferson himself also wrote several books, including *The Garden and Farm Books*, described by *The Oxford Companion to Gardens* as "the clearest possible record by a layman of the garden materials of the period."

THE GARDENS AND PLANTS OF MONTICELLO

When I visited Monticello, it was an experience I'll never forget. The house was in the top three estates visited (along with FDR's home at Hyde Park and Winston Churchill's Chartwell), and the grounds begged you to just walk and look.

But my view is today's view, so in the interest of historical accuracy, I quote two distinguished French visitors to Monticello in the last two decades of the eighteenth century, who were so impressed by the estate and its setting that they wrote letters about their experiences.

In 1782, the Marquis de Chastellux wrote:

> There was nothing, in such an unsettled country, to prevent him [Jefferson] from fixing his residence wherever he wanted to. But Nature so contrived it, that a Sage and a man of taste would find on his own estate the spot where he might best study and enjoy Her. He called this house Monticello (in Italian, Little Mountain), a very modest name indeed, for it is situated up a very high mountain, but a name which bespeaks the owner's attachments to the language of Italy and above all to the Fine arts, of which that country was the cradle and is still the resort . . . so that it may be said that Mr. Jefferson is the first American who has consulted the Fine Arts to know how he should shelter himself from the weather. . . . Let me describe to you a man, not yet forty, tall, and with a mild and pleasing countenance, but whose mind and attainments could serve in lieu of all outward graces: an American, who, without ever having quitted his own country, is Musician, Draftsman, Surveyor, Astronomer, Natural philosopher, Jurist and Statesman.

In June 1796, the Duc de la Rochefoucauld-Liancourt wrote:

> The house stands on the summit of the mountain, and the taste and arts of Europe have been consulted in the formation of its plan. . . .

Monticello, according to its first plan, was infinitely superior to all other houses in America, in point of taste and the fine arts in books only. His travels in Europe have supplied him with models; he has appropriated them to his design; and his new plan, the execution of which is already much advanced, will be accomplished before the end of the next year, and then his house will certainly deserve to be ranked with the most pleasant mansions in France and England.

At present he is employed with activity and perseverance in the management of his farms and buildings; and he orders, directs, and pursues in the minutest details every branch of business relative to them. I found him in the midst of the harvest, from which the scorching heat of the sun does not prevent his attendance. His Negroes are nourished, clothed, and treated as well as white servants could be. As he can not expect any assistance from the two small neighboring towns, every article is made on his farm: his Negroes are cabinetmakers, carpenters, masons, bricklayers, smiths, etc.

Jumping ahead to more recent times, the following is the description of Monticello by Ann Leighton in *American Gardens in the Eighteenth Century:*

Quite simply, the plan evolves from the leveling of the top of a hill commanding wide view of the valley below and the distant site of the University of Virginia. The level top is oval in shape and allows for a house site on the valley side and an extensive lawn toward other hilltops behind. A drive is designed to wind slowly up and around the site. Terraces on the sides and front are arranged to take care of a vineyard, beds of fruits and vegetables, and a slope of ornamental trees and shrubs over whose flowering tops the wide view may be surveyed. Cultivated fields spread across the valley where the officious foreign visitor lamented the absence of a river. At the back of the house on the lawn side, near the house and cut into the lawn, is an arrangement of oval beds, lying parallel with the house, into which Jefferson liked to put flowers in showy quantities. The lawn, in fact the whole design, is shaped rather like the sole of a shoe with the house for a heel. It forms an elongated loop, within which Jefferson wandered his "roundabout" walk, among sometimes six, sometimes four, large ovals of shrubberies. In his sketched plans these ovals are ranged in an even number opposite each other. Around these his walk made long moderated curves. His ideal plan called for the walk to be bordered on each side by all the flowers sent him or grown by him. It is a handsome plan, reminiscent of a *ferme ornée,* and a pleasant and informal way of enjoying a garden dispersed about a lawn. I have seen a similar walk in a French country mansion of about the same date. Strangely, it seems to be unique in American gardens, even today.

There is a family burying ground, as at Mount Vernon, halfway up the slope at the back of the hill, planned to be planted with melancholy trees and shrubs. There were plans for a deer park or a sort of small wild animal preserve nearby, where some of our native wild animals could be coaxed to show themselves for visitors.

Interestingly, Jefferson arranged for sitting places and viewing places to be, not at strategic intervals about his garden or terraces, but provided for on the top of his outlying mounts on either side of his house, which are not designed as mounts *per se* but to disguise underground accommodations. A little office building commands the level on the side of the entrance drive. The top of the other level is equipped with seats for commanding the view.

Finally, I talked with Nancy St. Clair Talley, former chair of the restoration committee as well as former president of the Garden Club of Virginia, which has done work on the grounds of Monticello since 1927. She gave me some background on the site itself.

Monticello has become hallowed grounds to America. Jefferson both worked out the ideas he wrote in his journals and performed the plantation duties. Moreover, we can enjoy the land and the gardens of Monticello not only because of Jefferson's genius, but also because of the vision and energy of many who followed him.

Today when you visit this great site, it's difficult to believe that in 1831, only five years after Jefferson's death, a local apothecary named James T. Barclay bought the house and 552 acres for $4,500, less the value of his own home. He established at Monticello an unsuccessful silkworm farm; it failed within two years.

In 1836, Uriah Phillips Levy of the U.S. Navy acquired the house and restored it. When he died in 1862, he left the property to the "People of the United States." Uriah's nephew, Jefferson Monroe Levy, gained clear title to Monticello in 1879, repaired the years of neglect since his uncle's death, and finally sold Monticello to the Thomas Jefferson Memorial Foundation for $500,000 in 1923.

That year, the foundation was established in New York under the leadership of Stuart Gibboney, a lawyer and a native Virginian. The foundation leaders proved to be energetic fund-raisers, a quality more and more necessary in working with public lands today. Not only did they approach the goals of restoration and refurnishing with an eye to the greatest possible authenticity, but they also added a deep concern for education. Fiske Kimball, an architectural historian, worked with Edwin Morris Betts, a professor of biology at the University of Virginia, to make certain that both the house and the grounds were restored to their original glory.

Jefferson had left not only garden plans, but also planting instructions. The trouble was that nobody knew which had been implemented and which were left on the drawing board. The Garden Club of Virginia's restoration plans were as far as the blueprint stage when Dr. Betts discovered a plan from 1807 safely filed away at the Historical Society of Pennsylvania. It bore a note in Jefferson's hand: "Planted and sowed flower beds as above April 15, 16, 18, and 20." The Garden Club scrapped its blueprints and substituted the 1807 plan.

As work on the flower gardens proceeded, evidence was uncovered that the roundabout walk on Monticello's west lawn, the fish pond, and even some surviving golden willows were noted on the plan. Once the ellipse had been laid out, it was obvious that it corresponded exactly to notes in Jefferson's "Garden Book."

In 1927, Mrs. William R. Massie of Albemarle County, the president of the Garden Club of Virginia, led an effort to save deteriorating trees, some that were actual survivors from Jefferson's own plantings. Two years later, Mrs. Massie was one of those who organized the Garden Club of Virginia's Historic Garden Week in Virginia, which by 2002 had become one of the ten top tourist attractions in the commonwealth and had grossed more than $10 million. But it wasn't until May 1938 that the foundation asked the Garden Club of Virginia to make Monticello its eighth historic garden restoration.

Some years after this major Garden Club restoration at Monticello, the foundation turned its attention to the landscape at large. Since 1975, an architectural historian, a landscape architect, an archeologist, and a horticulturist have worked on an exacting re-creation of the grounds, including research on the *Ferme Ornée*, Jefferson's idea of an ornamental farm.

Today the work goes on. Archeological excavations continue to confirm Jefferson's documents. Restorations or re-creations include the kitchen garden, the garden pavilion, the orchard, the vineyard, and the grove. Apart from Jefferson's gardens, the Center for Historic Plants allows Monticello visitors to purchase period plants, many of them rare early varieties and a number of them species grown by Jefferson.

ANNUALS
AND
PERENNIALS

THE COMMON HOLLYHOCKS

Alcea rosea

Hollyhocks have been garden stars for centuries, and almost every painted rendition of a typical English cottage garden features their tall spires of blooms. At one time, children made little dolls out of the blossoms and sometimes floated them on water.

Jefferson's *Garden Book* noted that pinks and hollyhocks were in bloom on June 10, 1767, and that their bloom continued until late July. In the calendar of bloom for flowers, 1782, hollyhocks were again noted as blooming. The plants that are found blooming today in the vegetable garden are possibly descendants of those long-ago blossoms.

Though Phillip Miller, author of *The Gardener's Dictionary*, thought hollyhocks too ungainly for small gardens and recommended the flowers only for larger "wilderness borders or Avenues," England's William Robinson called them "one of the noblest of hardy plants," saying that there were "many positions in almost all gardens where it would add to the general effect." He added, "Cottage beekeepers would do well to grow a few hollyhocks, for bees are fond of their flowers."

Hollyhock is the common name for a number of biennial or perennial herbs. The name is a combination of *holy* and *hock*, an old Anglo-Saxon word for mallow. Nursery and seed catalogs often mix *Alcea* and *Althea* in plant descriptions, making things confusing. The problem can only be sorted out by a reference to scientific names. The genus *Alcea* and the similar-sounding *Althea* both are mallows and members of the family Malvaceae, but *Alcea* includes the true holly-hock, whereas *Althea* is often used as a common name for the rose-of-Sharon *(Hibiscus syriacus)* and the marsh-mallow or white mallow *(Alcea officinalis)*. This latter plant is well known in herbal remedy tomes, and indeed, the generic name of *Althea* is from the Greek *althainein,* mean-ing to heal, because at one time this group of plants was very popular in both folk and serious medicine.

According to Mrs. M. Grieve *(A Modern Herbal,* New York: Dover Publications, 1971), the hollyhock was once eaten as a potherb, although, she says, "it is not particularly palatable," and the flowers were used for their emollient, demulcent, and diuretic properties for treating chest complaints. She adds: "The [petals] are also used for colouring purposes [and] should be gathered in July and early August, and dried in trays, in thin layers, in a current of warm air immediately after pick-ing." Somehow I can see this activity carried out at Monticello.

The most commonly known species is *Alcea rosea,* the hollyhocks that most people grow up against garden walls, if they are lucky enough to have them. Hollyhocks are natives of China. They grow tall and erect, usually between 5 and 9 feet in height. The single stems and the undersides of the heart-shaped, wrinkled leaves are hairy. Most bloom with single, five-petaled blossoms in late summer, but newer cultivars have double, ruffled, begonialike flowers.

The individual flowers are bell-shaped, three and a half inches or more in width, with separate smooth or lightly fringed petals of white or vivid colors such as yellow, salmon, rose, red, violet, purple, or the deepest maroon. The cultivar 'Nigra' has dark brown blossoms and is called the chocolate hollyhock.

As to other cultivars, most good seedhouses carry 'Chater's Dou-ble', which has double, peonylike flowers in a wide range of colors, including a spectacular yellow. They were developed by a great-uncle of my choir companion Bill Chater, of Asheville, North Carolina.

One winter, the Likels of Jeffersonville, New York, gave me an envelope of seeds collected from a hollyhock they saw blooming along the Street of Curetes, a thoroughfare that runs through the ruined

Turkish city of Ephesus. This was one of the world's richest and most fertile cities from the beginning of the Ionian Age through the end of the Roman era. I set the plants out the following spring and promptly forgot about them. By June of the next year, the plants were six feet high, and in early July, the flowers opened: a lovely shell pink with a white center. Such flowers must have been beautiful surrounded by aging marble and seaside sand.

The hollyhock was a favorite of classical painters as well as Chinese and Japanese artists. The great Flemish presurrealist painter Hieronymus (Jerome) Bosch knew of their garden presence in 1551. Hollyhocks are usually featured in every rendition of the cottage garden, including the paintings "In a Warwickshire Byway, Little Milton," by Henry John Sylvester Stannard, and "Lavington, Sussex," by James Matthews, as well as a great painting by Gustave Courbet entitled "The Trellis," where a charming peasant girl confronts a mass of unusual flowers including a great stand of double white hollyhocks.

According to Pizzetti and Cocker in *Flowers: A Guide for Your Garden*, the German poet Goethe "lived in a house set among the hills near Weimar, and from his garden he had a view over the fields to the placid course of the River Ilm. Along the drive leading up to the house, Goethe planted a double row of hollyhocks, which were his pride and joy."

Alcea rosea probably began its career in Asia Minor. Though classified as a perennial, it's usually used as a summer annual or, depending on when you plant the seed, a biennial. In cold climates, it will not winter over without sufficient mulching. In most of the Southeast, it will live through the cold. But plants rarely survive if planted in heavy clay soils without any added humus, because the roots resent standing water, especially when chilled.

The first year after germination, perennial and biennial forms develop a rosette of ground-hugging leaves, with one to several flower stalks developing the following year or years. Hollyhocks readily self-sow and may become a nuisance if seedlings are not culled from the garden.

Hollyhocks prefer a rich soil with lots of organic matter and a warm, sunny location. The plants dislike any amount of shade, so they require full sun. Overwatering creates problems with diseases and will result in a shortened plant life.

Propagation is usually by seeds, which should be sown an eighth of an inch deep. Use individual peat pots, as hollyhocks do not transplant easily. Seed can be started in a greenhouse eight weeks prior to the last spring frost. A temperature of seventy-two degrees Fahrenheit results in germination within five to ten days. Set plants into the garden when frost danger is past.

Hollyhocks are effective as background plants and are especially beautiful against a building, fence, or wall where plants are protected from wind. They are also useful in mass plantings to provide screening. In windy sites, staking may be required. Their only problem is hollyhock rust *(Puccinia malvacearum)*, an infection that results in tiny bumps appearing on the leaf undersides. On the leaf surface, the spots are larger, bright yellow or orange with reddish centers. The spots run together, causing death of large leaf areas. Remove infected leaves when first noticed. This fungus survives on old plant debris, so it is important to destroy old plant parts at the end of the growing season. Experienced gardeners suggest looking for rust-resistant cultivars and never planting in the same place more than two years. Leaf miners will sometimes dig their winding tunnels through the leaves, but with the great flowers hanging above, it's a minor problem.

THE AMARANTHUS FAMILY

Amaranthus spp.

The genus *Amaranthus* represents a tropical band of annual plants numbering about fifty species. Some are cultivated for ornament, a few are grown for their edible seeds, and others, like tumbleweed *(A. albus)*, are downright weeds. (Chiltern Seeds of England wrote the following of tumbleweeds: "How many plants are there, when dead, will roll themselves up in a ball, detach themselves from the soil, and—at the first suitable wind—bid you a fond farewell.")

Another relative is a North American weed called pigweed or green amaranth *(Amaranthus retroflexus)*, an unattractive, invasive plant that can reach a height of ten feet. Stems bear simple, alternate leaves and, at the top, tiny flowers on terminal spikes up to three feet long, boasting bristlelike bracts. These plants are found on waste ground, along roadside ditches, and often take over abandoned farmland.

The genus name is derived from the Greek word *amaranth*, for unfading, since many plants retain their color well into fall. Because of their flamboyant color, most of the amaranths look best when displayed with other colorful plants. They also do very well in pots. All of these plants are tropical and hate the cold, so never expose seed to chilly, damp soil. Sow seed in a warm greenhouse or using bottom heat, then grow the seedlings in small pots until they are large enough to plant out in early summer. The roots do not like to be disturbed, so start seeds in individual peat pots.

Although in ancient times the asphodel (*Asphodelus* spp.) was considered the flower of death, the amaranth, the flower of immortality in the symbolism of the Greeks, was used with exuberance at funerals. In countries observing the Roman Catholic faith, the amaranth is one of the flowers chosen to decorate churches on Ascension Day, showing the association with life everlasting. The Swedes feature the flower in the Order of the Amaranth, a fraternal, social, and charitable organization of the Masons.

The American Indians gathered some varieties for foodstuffs, using the leaves as greens, tender shoots as spring vegetables, and seeds made into a meal for bread.

For the most part, these plants have been cultivated in European and American gardens since the sixteenth century. Of the amaranths, Jefferson was familiar with prince's-feather, Joseph's-coat, and probably love-lies-bleeding.

THE PRINCE'S-FEATHER
Amaranthus hybridus var. *erthrostachys*

Jefferson first planted seeds of prince's-feather on April 4, 1767, at Shadwell, his childhood home, noting that it was similar to a cockscomb. Prince's-feather was used in America as early as 1709, when John Lawson published his book *A New Voyage to Carolina* and described the plant as being very large and beautiful. At that time, the scientific name of prince's-feather was *Amaranthus hybridus hypochondriacus;* it has since been changed to *A. hybridus* var. *erthrostachys.* Hypochondriacus referred to a general melancholy of the body and senses, and supposedly an elixir made from the leaves would effect a cure.

A native of India and tropical America, prince's-feather is the common cultivated form grown in gardens. Plants are usually tall, between four and five feet. The leaves are thin, alternate, and pointed, without marginal teeth. Erect spikes of inconspicuous flowers are surrounded by very colorful bracts. They were first sent to England in 1684.

THE JOSEPH'S-COAT
Amaranthus tricolor

Joseph's-coat was certainly planted at Monticello, as Jefferson sent seed back from Paris in 1786. Known today as *Amaranthus tricolor,* the plant is called *A. gangeticus* var. *melancholicus* in older books. (I suspect the species refers to the time-honored history of this plant's medicinal uses in the treatment of choleric disorders.)

This particular amaranthus was a pop-plant, not only in Jefferson's time, but also when the Victorian Age reigned in England. A formal bedding plan was a public failure unless somewhere near the center of the arrangement, Joseph's-coat reined supreme.

Typically, the base of the leaf is crimson-scarlet, gradually changing to bright yellow, ending in green at the leaf's tip. But over the centuries, new color combinations have emerged. Today look for 'Illumination', with bronze, scarlet, yellow, orange, and green bands of color, and a new entry on the scene with the improbable cultivar name of 'Tricolor Splendens Perfecta', featuring blends of deep red, yellow, and bright green and reaching a height of about three feet.

THE LOVE-LIES-BLEEDING
Amaranthus caudatus

Love-lies-bleeding is an example of the creativity of some common plant names, especially those coined back in the seventeenth century. Other popular names are kiss-me-over-the-garden-gate and tassel-flower, all referring to the long, drooping flower clusters, usually a deep red, which sprawl about like a salute to surrealism. Because of the bloody red color of the tassels, the French called it "the nun's scourge," because to the Gallic mind it seemed to suggest flagellations endured by penitents. Another French name is *queue de renard,* or fox-tail.

Known as *Amaranthus caudatus,* the plants originally came from India and the tropics, arriving in England about 1596. There is a green form usually sold as *A.* var. *viridis.*

This description of the plant was penned by Alice Morse Earle in *Old Time Gardens:* "This last-named flower I always disliked, a shapeless, gawky creature, described in florists' catalogs and like publications as 'an effective plant easily attaining to a splendid form bearing many plume-tufts of rich lustrous crimson.' It is the 'immortal amarant' chosen by Milton to crown the celestial beings in *Paradise Lost.* Poor angels! They have had many trying vagaries of attire assigned to them."

While striking in the border (I feel much better about the flower than Miss Earle did), this plant is also useful as a cut flower, and it does wonderfully in a pot for terrace or deck gardens (remember to fertilize it every few weeks). If dried slowly with even warmth, the color of the spikes will hold until well into winter, and by then it's time to throw them out and think again of spring.

THE BELLADONNA LILY

Amaryllis belladonna

The belladonna lily *(Amaryllis belladonna)* is also called the Cape Belladonna, Barbados lily, lirio, the true amaryllis, and naked lady, this last name because the lovely trumpet-shaped, lilylike, rosy-pink fragrant flowers appear on two-foot stalks after the leaves have died down. It is known in Cuba as Tararaco Doble. Bulbs left the shores of Cape Province, South America, about 1450, finally arriving on North American shores in the late 1700s. This single-genus species, introduced into cultivation in 1712, should not be confused with those popular winter-flowering Christmas gift plants that are shipped as bare bulbs and commonly known as amaryllis, which really belong to the genus *Hippeastrum.*

Bernard M'Mahon sent three bulbs of the belladonna lily to Jefferson in 1812, recommending that they be planted in the greenhouse in "pots of good rich mellow earth." He noted that the blossoms were both beautiful and fragrant, with their usual season of flowering in the fall.

M'Mahon (for whom the Oregon-grape was named *Mahonia*) emigrated from Ireland in 1796, arriving in Philadelphia, where he started a career as a nurseryman and seedsman. In 1806, M'Mahon published his outstanding garden book, *The American Gardener's Calendar,* which dominated gardens for fifty-some years. It is said that the Lewis and Clark Expedition was planned around a dinner at his home. M'Mahon felt that Americans admired size and would buy a plant because of its "bigness" rather than any attempt at horticultural excellence.

M'Mahon sent a copy of his book to Jefferson, as the two men had carried on correspondence for several years before publication. Jefferson, who owned many European garden books, was delighted to have one that was distinctly American. Over the years, M'Mahon sent many seeds, roots, and tubers to Monticello.

The genus name is taken from the Greek feminine name Amaryllis, itself derived from the Greek verb *amaryssein,* to shine. In Virgil's *Bucolics,* a shepherd sings to the fair shepherdess Amaryllis, and by the time of the Renaissance, the name was also given to dances and madrigals. Belladonna refers to the flushed pink color of the blooms, said to be rivaled only by the complexion of a beautiful woman.

Amaryllis belladonna is poisonous, the alkaloid lycorine being the principal toxin. Ingestion of large quantities may produce nausea and persistent emesis with some diarrhea, but human poisonings are rare because of the number of bulbs that must be consumed to bring about these results. Certain South American Indian tribes were reported to have crushed the plants and dipped arrows into the extracted sap for a potent killing point, but given the actual poison content, one wonders if this was a case of mistaken identity. Another plant with a similar name, deadly nightshade (*Atropa belladonna,* in the family Solanacae, along with tomatoes and potatoes), contains a far more dangerous chemical content, including atropine and other belladonna alkaloids. Here ingestion is far more lethal.

The less dangerous belladonna lily sports long, leathery, straplike leaves, as most of the amaryllis do. The bulbs produce large, lilylike flowers that range in color from dark pink to a rose red, opening on top of an eighteen-inch stalk.

The belladonna lily was probably introduced to America from the tropic islands to the south, including Jamaica or the East Indies, although there are reports of plants flowering in London's Chelsea Physic Garden in the mid-1700s.

Plant the bulbs in late fall in a standard potting mix, using a pot two inches wider than the width of the bulb, with the top third of the bulb exposed. Put the pot in a cool, semidark place for four to six weeks, or until the emerging leaves are several inches high. Then take the plant into a sunroom or greenhouse. Feed the plants with weak solutions of liquid fertilizer every three to four weeks while they are in active growth. Allow a rest period of three or four months between flowerings, and let the leaves die back on their own.

If bulbs are to be planted outdoors, they need protection in colder climates. Natives of the Southern Hemisphere, their vegetative stages are the reverse of the North.

One summer evening, just as the sky was turning a beautiful shade of deep purple and the stars began to twinkle, I heard a whirring noise from the direction of a blooming belladonna lily on our back deck. Hovering there was a pink-spotted hawkmoth *(Agrius cingulatus)* with a four-inch wingspread. The hind wings were gray shading to pink at the base, and the abdomen had pink crossbars. The moth was busily engaged in sipping the sweet nectar of the magnificent flowers and, at the same time, threw quite a bit of pollen about.

According to the National Botanical Institute of South Africa, Rudolf Marloth, a famous amateur botanist, believed that the belladonna lily was being pollinated by a hawkmoth. He also noticed that large carpenter bees visited the flowers during the day. This last pollinator would not be surprising to anybody living in the Southeast. Carpenter bees are very active throughout the summer months, drilling perfectly round holes into unprotected wood with the zeal of a woodworker who loves his or her job with a passion. They resemble bumblebees but differ in having a shiny black abdomen rather than one that is furred and striped.

ANEMONES

THE PASQUE-FLOWER
Pulsatilla vulgaris

The pasque-flower is a beautiful anemone that generally blooms at *Pasch,* or Eastertide. In French it's called *passefleur,* in Dutch *paaschbloem,* and in German *Osterblume* or *Kuchenshcelle.* Pasque-flower was thought to be named by Gerard in his famous herbal, who took the name from the Hebrew word *pesah,* to "pass-over." *Pulsatilla* was the original six-teenth-century generic name, derived from a Latin word for shake or sway, referring to actions of the wind. It also is listed as a rare wild-flower in a favorite book covering plants found in England, Scotland, Wales, and Ireland, *The Pocket Guide to Wild Flowers,* by David McClin-tock and R. S. R. Fitter (London: Collins, 1956).

During the late 1960s, there was a move to change the scientific name of this plant from *Anenome* to *Pulsatilla vulgaris,* and the genus was divided into two groups. Today both *Pulsatilla* and *Anemone* are found in texts and nursery catalogs. Plants belong to the great buttercup family, Ranunculacea.

Jefferson's first mention of the pasque-flower *(Pulsatilla vulgaris)* appears in a *Garden Book* entry dated September 30, 1771. In a "Calendar of the Bloom of Flowers" dated 1782, Jefferson noted anemones in flower from early to late May. In 1811, he wrote of their blossoms gracing the southwest corner of the portico and chamber gardens. Supposedly he first received seeds of this marvelous plant from André Thoüin, the director of the Jardin du Roi (the King's Garden, eventually known as the Jardin des Plantes), whom he met when visiting Paris in 1785. The two men became lifelong correspondents, and over the next four decades, Thoüin sent packages of seed to Jefferson yearly. But the fact that Jefferson wrote of it in 1771 means that the original plants must have had another source, not surprising because many colonials brought seeds for this stunning plant upon emigrating from Europe and England.

In early spring, the flowers open, glorious lavender saucers with golden stamens clustered in the center, the blossoms surrounded by ferny leaves resembling deep green feathers. Gerard described them thus:

> The first of these Passe flowers hath many small leaves finely cut or jagged, like those of carrots; among which rise up naked stalkes, rough and hairie; whereupon do growe beautifull flowers bell fashion, of a bright delaid [a corruption of the French word *delaine*, referring to a fine muslin of great thinness] purple; in the bottom whereof groweth a tuft of yellow thrums [stamens] and in the middle of the thrums thrusteth foorth a small purple pointell: when the whole flower is past there succeedeth an head or knoppe, compact of many graie hairie lockes, and in the solid parts of the knops lieth the seede flat and hoarie, every seede having his own small haire hanging at it.

Another association with Easter is the bygone custom of dying eggs with the sap of this plant. The juice of the purple sepals gives a green stain to paper and linen but is not permanent. The roots are thick and black, the flowers about an inch and a half across, borne singly on five- to eight-inch stalks. The sepals (really not petals) are usually a deep purple-violet color, very silky beneath. Seeds are small and brown, with hairy plumes called achenes, much like those found on wild clematis or Virgin's bower *(Clematis virginiana)*. The hairs result in quick wind dispersal, and the seeds travel great distances before landing. The second edition of *The Bernard E. Harkness Seedlist Handbook* describes twelve cultivars, with colors ranging from white ('Alba') to a dwarf red ('Red Cloak') to a pale shell pink ('Mrs. Van der Elst').

In England, these anemones grow in colonies across the chalk and limestone rifts of the Cotswolds, hence their desire for sweet soil, although they will survive with a more acid content. The problems faced by gardeners revolve around drainage. These plants dislike dank, wet soil, but those grown with plenty of gravel and shards added to the soil will amaze by their healthy growth. Varieties of pulsatilla cultivated in this country like a well-drained, light, but deep soil and will flourish in a peat or leaf soil, with the addition of lime rubble. Seeds sown when freshly ripe (usually in July) germinate with ease.

At the time Jefferson grew anemones at Monticello, they were highly regarded for supposed medicinal qualities. The drug pulsatilla is derived from this plant. It's recommended for certain diseases of the eye but is considered dangerous, especially when administered by untrained caregivers. The entire plant has a sharp acid taste, but it is freely eaten by goats, though cattle avoid it. The leaves, if bruised and applied to the skin, raise blisters. The FDA includes this anemone in its Poisonous Plant Database, a list of vascular plants associated with toxic effects. The AMA considers the entire plant to be poisonous, with a toxin called proto-anemonin. In homeopathy, it is considered very efficacious, a specific for measles and a good remedy for nettle rash. Some folks also used anemone preparations for neuralgic toothaches and earaches.

THE WINDFLOWER

Anemone coronaria

Another anemone that was popular in colonial gardens was the windflower, or double anemone *(Anemone coronaria)*, a many-petaled form of the original windflower of antiquity. Jefferson ordered tubers of this plant from Bernard M'Mahon in 1807, who had imported them from France, where it was known as the Mediterranean anemone.

The original flower's scientific name is from the Greek word for wind, *anemos*. Some believe this was because the flowers were thought to open only when the wind blew; other sources say that the term refers to the environment of this plant—windswept fields and breezy barrens.

In Christian symbolism, the anemone is associated with the crucifixion, and the original "lily of the field" is today thought to be the windflower. In the Holy Land, the anemone is called the blood-drops-of-Christ (a name also given to the wall-flower), for it is said that the sacred blood fell upon the anemones that were blooming forth on Calvary at the time of the crucifixion, and they turned from white to red and remained so from that time on. The triple leaf of the anemone is said to symbolize the three aspects of God, hence it's also known as the herb trinity.

Native to the Mediterranean and Asia Minor, where it was also known as the poppy anemone, this double is easily recognized by the fibrous roots that resemble flat, black claws and branch in every direction. Finely cut leaves all come directly from the rhizomes; they are long-stalked and palmate, with neatly divided lobes. The long stem is lightly pubescent. The cup-shaped flower has between six and eight rounded petals that vary in color from deep blood red to vivid pink, to violet-blue, to pure white. The petals surround many stamens, which in turn surround a pointed dome of fused pistils. A few inches below the flower is a collar of two or three deeply cut leaflets.

Over centuries of observation, new cultivars were spotted. Today the flowers are divided into three types: the single-flowered Caen strain, the semidoubles found in the St. Brigid strain, and the double forms. Jefferson's choice was one of the doubles.

The rhizomes are usually set out in the fall. They prefer full sun and well-drained soil. The roots should be covered with at least three inches of soil.

THE SNAPDRAGONS
OF SUMMER

Antirrhinum majus

Thomas Jefferson was born at Shadwell, the home of his father, Peter Jefferson, where the Jeffersons raised six children. Shadwell was located about three miles east of Charlottesville, Virginia, in Albemarle County. It burned to the ground in 1770. Today there's a marker indicating the probable site of the birth house. The Thomas Jefferson Memorial Foundation is currently conducting archeological excavations to determine Shadwell's exact location.

In 1767, Jefferson found snapdragons in bloom at Shadwell and thought they might be good flowers for naturalizing in the landscape. The flowers he saw were probably the original snapdragon, *Antirrhinum majus*, which is actually a herbaceous perennial but usually grown as a garden annual.

From their original home in southern Spain, the cultivated species spread throughout the entire Roman Empire, and they were usually a staple of European gardens. Nowadays remnants of these original populations, which all belong to the species *Antirrhinum majus*, are found blooming in Roman ruins and ancient cemeteries throughout southern Europe. Snapdragons were brought from the Old World to our shores and have graced American gardens for centuries.

The genus *Antirrhinum* was assigned to the snapdragons by Carl von Linné—whom we usually call Linnaeus—in the year 1753. But Theophrastus was the first to use the word. *Antirrhinum* is taken from the Greek word *antirrinon*, or noselike. The Greeks also called the flowers *kynokephelon*, or dog-headed, while the Romans used the term *leonis ora*, or lion mouth. The French used the term *muflier*, for snout or muzzle. The Italians called them *bocca di leone*, while the Germans preferred *Löwenmaul*, both words a salute to a lion's mouth.

This resemblance is still noticed today, as young children who confront a stalk of snapdragons soon find that by pinching the sides of a blossom, the lips open wide, like the mouth of a small beast.

Seeds were sold in America back in 1760, and snapdragons soon became favorites of colonial gardeners. They were beloved flowers of many garden writers, too. "Plant a clump of the clear yellow," wrote Alice Morse Earle in *Old Time Gardens*, "and one of pure white snapdragons, and see how beautiful they are in the garden, and how fresh they keep when cut. We had a satisfying bunch of them on the dinner table today, in a milk-white glazed Chinese jar; yellow snapdragons, with borrowed leaves of Virgin's bower *(Adlumia)* and a haze of Gypsophila over all."

From a medicinal point of view, snapdragons have been valued from days of old. Like their close cousin the toadflax, snapdragons were considered a protection against witchcraft. An ancient herbal told of a woman who wished to bring back youth and beauty to her face and believed that all she needed was an infusion of water and snapdragon seeds. Also, if a woman wanted to be more seductive, she need only put snapdragon leaves in her shoes.

Ippolito Pizzetti and Henry Cocker, in their excellent book *Flowers: A Guide for Your Garden*, reported that Dioscorides suggested that pounding the seeds in lily oil would produce an excellent facial lotion, and that if worn on the arm, the flowers served as an amulet to ward off illness. "In the Renaissance," they wrote, "it was said that 'by wearing a snapdragon on his sleeve, a subject is made welcome and is greeted graciously by his prince or suzerain.' This supposed power to make one magnetically attractive goes back to Theophrastus, who said that wearing snapdragons endowed a man with grace, honor and glory in the eyes of both his peers and his equals."

Snapdragons have bitter and stimulant properties, and the leaves have often been used to treat ulcers. The numerous seeds will yield an oil when compressed, but it is said to be less valuable than olive oil, or we would all be using snapdragon oil on our salads.

The flower has also lent its name to an English diversion. In the game known as snapdragon, players pluck raisins from a dish of burning brandy.

An old English garden book in my library, *In a Gloucestershire Garden*, by Henry N. Ellacombe, quotes Cardinal Newman's account of his departure from Oxford in 1846: "I took leave of my first college, Trinity, which was so dear to me [where] there used to be much snapdragon growing on the walls opposite my freshman's rooms there, and I had for years taken it as the emblem of my own perpetual residence, even unto death, in my University."

The blossoms of the snapdragon are faintly fragrant and come in a vast array of attractive colors, ranging from pure white to yellow, orange, scarlet, amber, coral, and a dark, velvety crimson with a silvery white throat. The color of a snapdragon's stems and leaves is an indication of possible flower color, in that pale or light green leaves signify that the flowers will be a clear or pale white, whereas dark green or reddish stems and foliage point to darker-hued flowers. Buds on the flower stalk open gradually from the bottom to the top.

Plants come in various heights, with dwarf varieties growing about ten inches tall and the taller choices up to three feet in height. Chiltern Seeds now offers seeds for the original wild form, described as an erect, bushy plant with narrow leaves and spikes of usually pink or purple, but sometimes pale yellow, fragrant flowers.

Pollination of snapdragons is done by a variety of different insects, but the usual pollinator is one of my favorite garden denizens, the bumblebee. Bumbles are necessary, as they have the heft to open the flower's lid; honeybees are just too small to do the job. Then, too, some seemingly clever bumbles actually go down to the side of the floral tube where it meets the calyx and chew their way into the nectar's source— without pollinating the flowers. At one time, gardeners were less than enthusiastic about snapdragons because the flowers would drop off when pollinated, but over the years, breeders have overcome that defect.

Snapdragons make excellent cut flowers and are perfect when massed in beds or the shorter varieties planted along the edge of a border. They flourish in well-fertilized soil and full sun. They resent overly acid soil; if necessary, add some lime to the mix. They love good drainage, so thick, hard clay must be loosened up with added drainage material in order to grow glorious snapdragons.

Sow seeds indoors eight weeks before the last frost. Transplant seedlings outdoors as soon as the soil can be worked, as they tolerate frost. In Zones 8 to 10, seedlings started in a sheltered seedbed may be moved outdoors any time in the fall for winter and spring flowering. According to the variety, plants should stand from six to twelve inches apart. Seedlings purchased from a garden center will usually bloom earlier than those started at home. Because the one disease problem associated with snapdragons is rust, choose rust-resistant varieties whenever possible.

For shorter but more abundant flower spikes, pinch off the stem tips when young plants are from two to four inches tall. As flowers mature, cut them for bouquets, because the cutting will force the plants to produce additional stems for bloom later in the season. Always deadhead to prolong bloom. As to location, while snapdragons delight in full sun, they will adapt to some shade (especially in the South), but flowering will diminish.

According to a study published by the West Virginia Extension Service, snapdragons are rarely damaged by deer. However, the Ohio State University Extension reports that the common rabbit, or eastern cottontail (*Sylvilagus floridanus*), can do considerable damage to flowers, vegetables, trees, and shrubs at any time of the year, and high on their list of desirable treats are snapdragons.

Snapdragons are easily grown under greenhouse conditions for the cut flower business. Seeds planted in July will provide blooming plants from December to March, and when planted in January, plants will bloom in May and June. If you are living in warmer climes, the temperature at night should be between forty-five and fifty degrees F and go up at least ten degrees by day.

THE WILD COLUMBINE

Aquilegia canadensis

Columbines had a long and interesting history in America, dating back to the American Indians' use of the plant in their medicines. Jefferson's son-in-law, Thomas Mann Randolph, saw the American columbine blooming on the Monticello grounds in 1791, and Bernard M'Mahon included the columbines in his book *The American Gardener's Calendar*.

The first historical mention of columbines in print was by Theophrastus (371–287 B.C.), who wrote of them in his *Eighth Book of Plants*, where they were called *Diosanthus*. By 1 A.D., columbines were partnered with plants called the *Dioscorides*.

Since the Middle Ages, European columbines *(Aquilegia vulgaris)* were so popular in the gardens of Europe and England that these flowers often found their way into great works of art. They can be seen in the Portinari Altarpiece, a large panel depicting the Adoration of the Shepherds (now in the Uffizi), by Hugo van der Goes (c. 1430–82), which caused a sensation when it was first exhibited in Florence in 1477. There, in the central panel beneath the infant Jesus, is a majolica vase containing a stalk of orange lilies, some blue and white German irises, some pinks, and a spray of blue columbine. The columbine was said to represent the seven gifts of the Holy Ghost.

Seeds of the American columbine *(Aquilegia canadensis)* were taken from Canada to France by early Jesuits, and the plant was pictured in *Cornut's Canadensium Plantarum* of 1635, so sometime between 1 A.D. and the 1600s, the term *Aquilegia* came into use.

Few spring flowers can lighten the heart like columbines can. The lovely flowers of the American species gleam with colors of bright ruby red and golden yellow, the downturned blossoms nodding on wiry stems and surrounded with lobed leaflets of woods green.

Wrote Emerson, his thoughts perfectly expressing the charm of this flower:

—A woodland walk,
A quest of river-grapes, a mocking thrush,
A wild rose or rock-loving columbine,
Salve my worst wounds.

The genus name *Aquilegia* is from the Latin *aquila*, for eagle, or *aquilegium*, for water gatherer. In the first interpretation, reference is given to the resemblance between the curved form of the petals and an eagle's claws. (But for years I've wondered if the comparison to an eagle comes not from the flower, but from the brown, ripened seed-pods, which to me look more like talons than anything the living flower possesses.) In the second case, the reference concerns dewdrops as they are caught, then tumble down on the petal edges and the leaves. The species *canadensis* refers to the plant's first discovery in Canada.

The common name comes from the Latin word *columbinus*, or dove, referring to either the birdlike claws, the beaklike spurs of the flowers, or the fanciful notion that each flower resembles a circle of doves at a medieval birdbath. But those who know medieval theater claim the plant is named after Columbine, the heroine of the *Commedia dell'Arte*, a symbol of the misadventures of love. The American columbine has also been known as eastern wild columbine (there is also a western species), honeysuckle, Our Lady's gloves, meetinghouses, and rock-bells.

It's probable that Jefferson also grew the European columbine *(Aquilegia vulgaris)*. The flowers of this columbine have shorter spurs and usually bloom in blue, violet, white, or pink. They've been natural-ized in some areas. And it's possible he also grew the alpine columbine

(A. alpina), because all three species were listed by Bernard M'Mahon in his *Calendar.*

Given good drainage—wild columbines are usually found in stony soil or clinging to rocky clefts—these plants adapt to most situations. The compound leaves are attractive in their own right and are often somewhat evergreen in warmer climates. If leaves get tracings on their surface, resembling unintelligible handwriting by an elf, it is the work of leaf miners, tiny insects that tunnel their way about inside the leaf and do not bother the health of the plant in any way.

As the long, nectar-bearing spurs indicate, the flower is adapted to long-tongued nectar feeders, notably hawkmoths and hummingbirds. The association between wild columbine and the eastern North American ruby-throated hummingbird, which is attracted to red flowers, is well known. Wherever there is a colony of columbines, the hummingbird is likely to be seen regularly as, in the words of one person, it "flashes like thought" among the flowers, draining all the inverted cornucopias. The yellow inside the petal may serve as a guide to the nectar. The constriction in the funnel-shaped spur just below the secreting bulbous tip undoubtedly prevents small bees from getting at the nectar.

Nectar-feeding visitors and bees visiting for the pollen are the agents of cross-pollination. The flower is adapted to prevent self-pollination. The stamens mature first, starting from the outside ring and moving toward the center, shedding all their pollen before the styles emerge at the mouth of the flower and spread their feathery stigmas to receive pollen. Even if the male and female phases overlap briefly, pollen cannot fall upward from the longer stamens onto the shorter styles in the hanging flowers.

Although many columbines are short-lived compared with most other garden perennials, the flowers self-sow and hybridize with ease, so there's never a lack of new plants, often with new color combinations. Older plants develop a tuberlike root system that does not transplant with ease, but younger plants quickly recover. Remove flowers before seed is set to prolong blooming.

Native Americans made treatment infusions from different parts of the plant for a variety of ailments, ranging from heart trouble to fever and even a wash for poison ivy. Pulverized seeds were used in minute quantities for headaches, fevers, and, in a marvelous salute to a devil-may-care attitude, for a love potion or rubbed in the hair to control lice. Roots were chewed or made into a weak tea for problems with diarrhea. The root contains aquilegunine, berberine, magnoflorine, and other alkaloids. Today's doctors caution of possible poisonings, so be warned.

Some claim that Native American men mixed the seeds with their smoking tobacco to give it a more pleasant aroma and, by so doing, thought it might work as a love charm. Mention has been made of their using such tobacco smoke to calm political dissent, and elders might have used columbine-infused smoke to sooth arguments at council meetings. If it worked, it should now be mandated for congressional use.

One final note on the columbine: For years there was a movement in America to make the columbine the national flower because of the resemblance of its common name to Columbus and Columbia, not to mention the scientific name's possible allusion to our national bird, including the eagle's talons. In addition, the plants are native to nearly all the states in America. But the movement failed, and today our national flower is the rose, a flower not easy to grow or to raise from seed, and—except for some wondrous wild species—not truly American.

THE BLACKBERRY LILY

Belamcanda chinensis

In 1788, Sir Peton Skipwith married Jean, the sister of his first wife, Anne, who had died in childbirth in 1779. Jean, Lady Skipwith, kept lists of the plants she grew. The blackberry lily *(Belamcanda chinensis)* is included in her list simply titled "Plants." The Skipwith collection of "bits and pieces" is found in the archives of the College of William and Mary at Williamsburg. Ann Leighton writes in *American Gardens in the Eighteenth Century* about these lists of plants, all falling between the years 1785 and 1805, found

> on the backs of old bills, a freshly copied list or two, some bills for seeds and planting, a list of wildflowers and another locating the same, a notice of an extensive modern auction, a photograph of a marble bust, two plans for geometrically designed garden beds, a note as to where vegetable seeds have been sown, another identifying fruit trees now bearing, a list of the consecutive fruit crops for one season and some notes on how to raise trees from cuttings.

Because Washington, Jefferson, and Lady Skipwith all used the Prince Nurseries on Long Island for plant material, these lists are a summation of the knowledge of interested gardeners in the eighteenth and nineteenth centuries.

In 1807, Jefferson received seeds of the blackberry lily from Bernard M'Mahon, planting them out in an oval flowerbed. According to Betts

and Perkins of the Garden Club of Virginia, the flowers are now growing wild on the estate.

Blackberry lilies are not lilies at all, but members of the iris family.
For some reason, folks throw around the term *lily* with little notice of
accuracy. The term is used so loosely that it's a good thing we have scientific names for identification. The genus *Belamcanda* is a name from
India for the species first brought into England back in 1823. At that
time, blackberry lilies were known as *Ixia chinensis* because of their similarity to the corn lilies of Cape Province in South Africa. Another common name is the leopard flower, referring to the spots on the petals.

The blackberry part of the common name refers to the pear-
shaped, green seedpods that, upon ripening in the fall, open to reveal
clusters of hard, shiny, black seeds, lined up in the pod like kernels of
corn. The whole affair does resemble a rather large blackberry. The
seedheads can be cut and dried, and they make great additions to
dried flower arrangements.

The plants have stoloniferous, clump-forming roots that produce
tall, slim, swordlike leaves much like gladiolus. The blossoms begin to
appear in high summer. When the blossoms mature and start to age,
the petals wrap and twist around each other like twisted rope, resembling a bizarre interpretation of a particular type of frozen custard
"with a curl on top."

Plants can be used in large clumps in the border or do very well in
large pots. Provide a good, well-drained garden soil (they often rot in
soggy soil), with full sun in the North and light shade in the South.
The plants generally reach a height of about three feet. Propagation is
by seed or by division of the rootstocks in the spring. They are hardy
in USDA Zones 5 to 10.

The seeds can be sown eight to twelve weeks before the last frost,
then set outdoors when the soil is getting warm. Although they are
bulbous perennials, they will bloom the first year, and many gardeners
recommend replanting every year or treating them like annuals.

The Chinese have long employed the blackberry lily as a medicinal
plant. Leaves and roots are used to treat coughs, sore throats, and
bronchitis, but the roots are potentially toxic and should be used only
under medical supervision.

THE POT MARIGOLD

Calendula officinalis

Jefferson planted "Marygolds" in 1767, but he was referring to the pot marigold, or calendula *(Calendula officinalis)*, not the popular sun-loving annuals belonging to the species *Tagetes*.

With a long season of bloom, calendulas have been favored annuals for centuries, grown successfully in small pots, large containers, herb collections, and gardens. The cheery flowers should be familiar to almost anyone who has ever gardened because of the combination of pale green leaves topped by golden orange flowers.

And they *are* long-blooming. On my desk, in a small vase, I have a pot marigold blossom that I picked today, December 14, from a plant set out in the garden last June; imagine an annual in bloom for seven months, still producing magnificent flowers.

Originally natives of the Mediterranean regions and Southern Europe, calendulas salute sunny climes. Common names include golds, ruddes, *Solsequium* (sun-follower), *Solis Sponsa* (bride of the sun), Oculus Christi (eye-of-Christ), Mary Gowles (from the Virgin Mary and the medieval word for gold), and in Italy, *fiore d'orni mese*. Unlike many flowers of history, it was not originally named after the Virgin Mary. Rather, marigold is a misreading of the old Anglo-Saxon word *merso-meargealla*, another name for the marsh marigold *(Caltha palustris)*. It was not until the seventeenth century that the religious association became the vogue.

The genus *Calendula* is taken from the Latin *kalendae,* referring to the first day of the month, because the flowers were in bloom on the first day of every month, year-round. Another explanation refers to the blossoms opening around nine o'clock in the morning and closing toward sunset, thus acting as a kind of calendar or clock. The first explanation sounds reasonable, while the second, I think, is stretching it just a bit.

Linnaeus noted the ritual opening of the flowers but had them closing about three o'clock in the afternoon. And Shakespeare wrote of them in *The Winter's Tale:*

> The Mary-budde that goes to bed wi' th' sun,
> And with him rises weeping.

Until recent times, these flowers were not usually grown for their charm or beauty, but were cultivated almost exclusively for medicinal purposes. Macer wrote in his *Herbal* that just by looking at marigolds, one would benefit from evil humours leaving the head and, in so doing, strengthen the eyesight.

> Golde [marigold] is bitter in savour
> Fayr and zelw [yellow] is his flowur
> Ye golde flour is good to sene
> It makyth ye syth bryth and clene
> Wyscely to lokyn on his flowres
> Drawyth owt of ye heed wikked hirores [humours].
> Loke wyscely on golde erly at morwe [morning]
> Yat day fro feures it schall ye borwe:
> Ye odour of ye golde is good to smelle.

According to Mrs. M. Grieve, some physicians noted that marigold medications must be taken only when the moon is in the sign of the Virgin and not when Jupiter is in the ascendant, for then the herb loses its virtue. And the gatherer, who must be out of deadly sin, must say three Pater Nosters and three Aves. Following these instructions will also allow the person who wears a flower to have a vision of anyone who has ever robbed him.

Mrs. Grieve also wrote that only the deep orange flowers are of medicinal value, the parts used being the flowers and the leaves. Leaves should be gathered only in fine weather, in the morning after the sun has evaporated the dew. The ray flowers should be quickly dried in the shade, spread out on sheets of paper (petals not touching), gently surrounded by warm air currents.

Among the many medicinal uses for calendulas, their best features include aiding the healing of open wounds and treating of internal and external ulcers. A tincture (tinctures are alcoholic extractions of the chosen herb) is helpful in healing cold sores. An infusion is good for the digestion and is helpful in relieving the discomforts of colitis. The petals and leaves have antiseptic properties and improve blood flow to affected areas. As an antifungal agent, it can be used to cure athlete's foot, and I can personally attest to this great quality. And if that's not enough to recommend this plant, an infusion of the petals can be used as a rinse to lighten and brighten the hair.

Beauty crèmes containing calendulas are good for acne. A friend of mine (who wishes to remain anonymous, as her complexion is flawless) gave me the following recipe for a great skin cleanser using marigolds:

> Warm 4 tablespoons of olive or almond oil in the top part of a double boiler. Then stir in 2 tablespoons of dried pot marigold flowers. Continue to heat gently for thirty minutes. Remove from heat, allow the mixture to cool, and stir in a few drops of violet, orange blossom, or rose water.

Another garden friend submitted the following recipe for marigold wine:

Marigold Wine

2 quarts pot marigolds (use *Calendula officinalis* only)
1 gallon boiling water
1 Campden tablet, crushed (Campden tablets are a measured amount of
     sodium or potassium metabisulphite used for sanitation purposes)
thinly pared peel and juice of 3 tangerines or other soft citrus fruit
thinly pared peel and juice of 1 lemon
5 1/2 cups sugar
1 1/4 cups white raisins, finely chopped
wine yeast
yeast nutrient

Wash the flowers and put into a large container. Add the boiling water, and stir in the Campden tablet. Leave for 24 hours. Then draw off 1 cup of the liquid, add citrus peel, and heat to just on the point of boiling. Add the sugar, stirring until dissolved. Cool to body temperature, then pour back into the original container. Add raisins, citrus juice, yeast, and nutrient. Cover and leave 5 days to ferment, stirring twice each day. Then strain through a double thickness of muslin. Pour into a fermenting jar fitted with a fermentation lock, and leave to continue fermenting. Rack the wine as it begins to clear. When completely clear, store in a cool, dark, dry place for six months to mature.

Calendula petals are used fresh or dried to give color to soups and custards. Because of their yellow coloring, they are often used as an inexpensive substitute for saffron. Flower heads can also be used to make a salad vinegar. The leaves, although bitter, are sometimes used to flavor soups, broths, and salads.

Finally, there are the magical uses of pot marigolds. By stringing garlands of the flowers over doorjambs, evil is prevented from entering your house (although what happens during the winter is anybody's guess). Keep a blossom in a vase by your bedside, and you will gain protection while asleep and, possibly, good dreams will come true. If added to your bath water, you'll win the respect and admiration of everyone you meet. And if a maiden touches the petals with her bare feet, she will suddenly understand the language of birds.

Pot marigolds love mild to cool weather, adapting to full sun or, especially in the South, light shade. They prefer a moderately fertile soil. Sow the seeds outdoors in early spring or in mild climates in the fall. Or start seeds indoors, beginning about eight weeks before the last spring frost. Set out seedlings about a foot apart. To keep calendulas blooming, especially those set out in spring, cut them back by one-third and fertilize in summer. They will continue to flower in a sunny window, but with reduced sunlight, they will get rather leggy. Pot marigolds make great cut flowers, continuing to bloom in water for days on end. And plants are grown in the vegetable garden to help with insect control.

Almost every fresh garden year sees the introduction of new cultivars. 'Radio', which dates back to the 1930s, has petals of a very deep orange; 'Golden Princess' has double golden-yellow flowers and prominent black centers; and 'Art Shades' features blooms of cream, peach, and apricot shades.

The only problem pot marigolds have is a proclivity for fungal disorders when days are damp and air circulation poor. Aphids find them attractive but are easily dislodged with a stream of water from the garden hose.

THE FANCIFUL COCKSCOMB

Celosia cristata

Depending on your point of view, cockscomb *(Celosia cristata)* either matches its common namesake or resembles something out of a 1950s science fiction film like *Brain from Planet Aros.* A popular plant in colonial America, cockscomb was grown at Mount Vernon by George Washington and at Monticello by Thomas Jefferson, who noted in his journals in 1767 that it was a "handsome plant" but quite a "curiosity."

Popular throughout America, cockscomb has peppered our gardens with color since the 1700s. These plants were especially favored in the early 1900s, when they were regularly exhibited in pots at small fairs, with the smallest plants sporting the largest crests taking the prize.

Celosia is taken from the Greek word *kelos,* meaning burned, referring to the plant's brilliant red and orange flamelike colors. In China plants are known as *chi kuan,* or cock's comb. Other common names include floramor, flower gentle, woolflower, and purple amaranth. The name cockscomb was given to the plant because in some forms it certainly does resemble a rooster's comb. *Cristata* is from the Latin word for a cock's comb.

Native to the Asiatic tropics, three forms were introduced into England in 1570 as "Amer. Coxcomb": 'Childsii', with ball-like knobs at the branch ends; 'Plumosa', with flowers that resemble feathers; and

'Spicata', with flowers blooming in slender spikes. Later that century, it became quite the rage in Britain to grow it indoors or in a greenhouse, where it escaped the ravages of early and late frosts, and the flowers held up without the destructive force of English damp and rain. Because of this, Elizabethans often called it floramor or flower gentle. By 1760, "Indian Branching cockscombs" were listed for sale in Boston, and Thomas Jefferson sowed seeds of cockscomb at Monticello on April 2, 1767.

Cockscombs are normal-looking plants with unusual and exotic-looking flowers that bloom from June to frost. The flower heads of the 'Childsii' are fanlike clumps that truly resemble chunks of coral taken from a restless sea. Though striking, they are often difficult to mesh with other, more normal flowers. They're probably best used as specimens in pots or as accent plants, by themselves or massed at the front of the border.

Cockscomb's broad flower clusters are three to six inches wide, with colors ranging from crimson to orange to pink. These plants grow up to thirty inches high, with medium green leaves, and a few forms are variegated. Cockscomb makes a striking cut flower, and it holds color well when dried.

Plume celosia has a vertical display of feathery-looking upright flowers that come in red, yellow, orange, pink, or purple. Sometimes likened to a flame, plants grow up to three feet high. When massed together as a bedding plant, plume celosia makes a bright display.

Celosias do not transplant well; sow outdoors in place as soon as the soil warms, or start seeds indoors about six to eight weeks before the last frost, using peat pots to avoid disturbing the roots when transplanting. Light is needed for germination, so barely cover seeds and keep them moist. Make sure temperatures are above sixty degrees F at night, as these are delicate tropicals. Celosias are quite tolerant of heat and drought, so provide full sun whenever possible. To dry, cut flowers at their peak and hang upside down, providing plenty of ventilation.

THE CHARMING WALLFLOWER

Cheiranthus cheiri

Wallflowers *(Cheiranthus cheiri)* are favorites in England and sometimes France, and in spring, window boxes all over London and Paris spill over their edges with these charming flowers and their sweet fragrance. Wallflower charm led to their popularity, especially during the Middle Ages, when minstrels and troubadours always sported such flowers in their buttonholes as amulets for luck and good fortune. It isn't quite clear whether these were wallflowers of the genus *Cheiranthus* or stocks of the genus *Matthiola,* because both had been grown for centuries, both are members of the family Cruciferae, and both are fragrant. This association with good fortune belies their history of being connected with death, as they were said to have the tendency to fade when the head of a household passed away. Mrs. M. Grieve wrote that "in olden times this flower was carried in the hand at classic festivals, hence it was called Cherisaunce by virtue of its cordial qualities."

A number of similar plants are also called wallflowers, including the orange-flowered Siberian, or western, wallflower *(Erysimum asperum),* which occurs both wild and in cultivation in North America. In his *Gardener's Dictionary,* Phillip Miller mentions sixteen varieties under the name *Cheiranthus,* but includes in the group the dame's violet, the stock called gilliflower. Jefferson's old friend, Bernard M'Mahon, offered wallflowers, suggesting that the plants be grown in pots so that if the weather became dreadful, flowers could be brought into the greenhouse for protection. In 1807, Jefferson bought wallflower seeds.

The common use of the word *wallflower* to suggest a person, especially a woman, who sat alone, usually against a wall, while others had a good time refers to the ability of the plants to grow on the broken mortar in stone and brick walls.

In 1735, Linnaeus bestowed the name *Cheiranthus* on the plant, with references saying that the name was derived from the Greek *cheir,* hand, and *anthos,* flower, because people held the flowers in their hands to inhale the special fragrance. Other authorities claim the name came from the Arabian word *kheyry* (or *cheiri*), for flowers that were red and intensely fragrant.

According to Pizzetti and Cocker in *Flowers: A Guide to Your Garden,* the active chemical principles of the plant have rarely been studied, but the leaves and seeds contain a glucoside with a cardiac action, and the seeds contain another type of glucoside.

Many country people, especially those with a limited education, once believed that the color or shape of a plant or plant part pointed to its use in curing a disease. This was known as the Doctrine of Signatures. Thus the lungwort (*Pulmonaria* spp.), with its white or silverspotted leaf somewhat resembling lung tissue, was thought to cure diseases of the lung. And a yellow flower was believed to cure jaundice, a disease that results in yellowed skin.

Wallflowers are mentioned in a book entitled *New, Old and Forgotten Remedies,* arranged and edited by Edward Pollock Anshutz. In its pages is an 1897 contribution to the *Hahnemannian Monthly* by one Dr. Robert T. Cooper of London, who reported the story of a twenty-year-old clerk who had become deaf in his left ear and whose symptoms were worsening. The doctor used a tincture of wallflowers (made by pounding the plant to a pulp and macerating it in two parts by weight of alcohol) to treat the ear canal, and eventually the man's hearing was restored.

Wallflowers like cool weather and prefer the climate of England or our own Pacific Northwest. The usual summers experienced in Virginia and North Carolina, especially out of the mountains, don't lead to the best flowering. But they do well where winters are mild and should be enjoyed as spring annuals, with cuttings taken for the fall season.

Sow seed outside, one-fourth inch deep, in June or July. Seed can be sown outdoors up to two months before first frost. Seed germinates within a week when grown indoors at temperatures between fifty-five and sixty-five degrees F. Space seedlings nine inches apart. Take cuttings after the plants have bloomed.

THE PRINCE'S PINE
AND THE
SPOTTED WINTERGREEN

Chimaphila spp.

There are two charming eastern wildflowers in the *Chimaphila* genus of plants. The first is the species *umbellata*, known as pipsissewa or prince's pine, or sometimes pyrola, rheumatism weed, bitter wintergreen, ground holly, king's-cure, love-in-winter, noble pine, or pine tulip. The second is the species *maculata*, known by some in Jefferson's time as dragon's-tongue or the spotted wintergreen, sometimes called pipsissewa, spotted piperidge, or ratsbane. In a 1779 letter to the plant trader Peter Collinson, the botanist John Bartram called it the pyrola with variegated leaves. Records show that the spotted wintergreen was transplanted from the woodlands onto an estate as a native plant of value.

The scientific name *Chimaphila* is from *cheima*, winter, and *phileo*, to love, referring to the beautiful dark, glossy leaves of deep winter that peep up through the snow with textured glamour. They belong to the wintergreen family.

The common pipsissewa (*C. umbellata*), or prince's pine, is a small herb a foot or less in height, with a long, running, partly underground stem and somewhat leathery, shining, dark green, evergreen leaves.

The leaves are one to two inches long, rather crowded toward the top of the stem. From June to August, its handsome, waxy white or pinkish fragrant flowers are borne in nodding clusters from the top of the erect stem. Although most people overlook them, the flowers are deliciously scented.

The spotted pipsissewa (*C. maculata*), or spotted wintergreen, is a small subshrub with creeping stems moving along the forest floor. Nodding, very fragrant, waxy white or sometimes pinkish flowers bloom in small clusters at the top of the stem. It is readily distinguished from the common pipsissewa by its whorled evergreen leaves, which are olive green marked with white or light green along the midrib and veins. In winter, the leaves take on a dark, purplish color. The plant's height varies between three and nine inches, and it succeeds brilliantly in dry, but woodsy, acid soil. Flowering is from June to August, and many is the time in late July that I see the blooms and striped leaves poking through the Japanese-style moss garden next door. The fruits are dry, red capsules, turning brown and remaining on the plants until well into winter.

These plants need a light, moist, but well-drained, absolutely lime-free soil and shade from direct sunlight. They are usually the only wildflowers to survive in that moss garden because the soil is so acidic. In fact, these plants can be bellwethers as to your garden's pH.

Like many wild orchids, these species are difficult to propagate and grow in cultivation, because the plants develop mycorrhizal associations in the wild, and any soil that becomes their home must have the same organisms present. It's a good idea to use some soil collected from around an established plant when sowing seed or planting out into a new position. These plants have fibrous roots that spread out from the crown, and they will die or fail to grow if the roots are disturbed.

This plant is considered rare in Canada and New England, and a few states now protect the plant by law.

From 1820 up to 1916, pipsissewa was listed in the U.S. Pharmacopeia. Native Americans used the plant for a number of ailments, and a leaf tea treated rheumatism and was also a diuretic.

In 1814, Frederick Pursh wrote: "This plant is in high esteem for its medicinal qualities among the natives; they call it Sip-si-sewa. I have myself been witness of a successful cure made by a decoction of this plant, in a very severe case of hysteria. It is a plant eminently deserving the attentions of physicians." Pursh was a famous botanist, born in Tobolsk, Siberia, in 1774. He came to America in 1799 and spent twelve years in botanical explorations around the United States. Until the publication of Torrey and Gray's *A Flora of North America*, Pursh's book *Flora Americae Septentrionalis; or, A Systematic Arrangement and Description of the Plants of North America* was considered the most important on the botany of North America. He died in Canada in 1820.

THE LARKSPUR
AND THE
TALL DELPHINIUM

Consolida orientalis, Delphinium exaltatum

On June 4, 1767, the larkspurs *(Consolida orientalis)* bloomed at Shad-well, Jefferson's boyhood home, along with the lychnis and the pop-pies. By July 18, they were still in bloom. Jefferson again mentioned their blooming in September 1771. In April 1810, he planted them in the roundabout flower border at Monticello.

This particular larkspur is a hardy annual that reseeds itself with ease. Described as the poor man's delphinium, larkspurs were often found in cottage gardens of England, where, with their airy growth and charming flowers, they mixed with hollyhocks, poppies, and daisies. The blue, pink, and occasionally white flowers usually appear during the early summer months. The plants will grow to four or five feet in a sunny or partially shaded site.

While the perennial species are called delphiniums, the annual forms have always been called larkspurs, the name referring to the spur on the rear of the flower and its resemblance to a bird's foot. The scientific name *Delphinium* is from the ancient Greek word for the larkspur. Today, thanks to one of the many and sundry scientific name changes, the flowers that Jefferson grew now belong to the genus *Consolida*. This is a Latin word that once referred to the plant called comfrey, then the larkspurs and the daisies, because they all at one time were thought to have medicinal uses. Larkspurs have no healing qualities; in fact, a number of the native larkspurs of western America are second only to locoweeds *(Astragalus)* as livestock poisons, especially of cattle.

As for being the poor man's delphinium, when compared with the strikingly tall and heavy-blossomed delphiniums found in many English and Scottish gardens, they may be equated with the word poor in terms of cost, but certainly not in charm. And thanks to the continuing threats of American summer storms, especially in the Southeast, not to mention the skyrocketing temperatures, delphiniums have a history of fading early on, while larkspurs bloom for several months.

Today the most common variety is the 'Giant Imperial', widely available in mixed color packets featuring white, pink, lavender, and purple.

When sowing seeds, there's one way north of the Mason-Dixon line and one way to the south. Up north, larkspur seeds can be sown in early spring for summer bloom because they do best in cool weather. The seeds also need cool, moist conditions in order to germinate.

Down south, the best process to guarantee beautiful larkspurs is to purchase seeds in the spring, store them in a cool place for the summer, and during the last part of August, put the seeds into a shallow plastic container, adding just enough water to moisten them but not enough to allow them to float. Since larkspurs resent being moved about, choose the best place for next year's display, remembering that they prefer moderate fertility and slightly alkaline soil. By the middle of September, the seeds will begin to swell, and a tiny taproot appears. That means it's time to plant them outdoors. Put the seeds into a half quart of sand or light potting soil, gently stir, then sprinkle lightly over your prepared beds. Sift a fine cover of soil over the seeds. Keep the beds moist. By March, the plants should be a foot tall, and by May, they should be gearing up for bloom. Unfortunately, summer heat defeats the plants, and by July they will be only a memory. Florists often buy home-grown larkspurs for bouquets and for dried flowers.

The tall delphinium *(Delphinium exaltatum)* is native to eastern North America, from Pennsylvania and Ohio south through the Appalachians into northern Alabama, with a few isolated populations in the Ozarks of south-central Missouri. In 1811, Jefferson planted it in the roundabout flower border.

The plants are from four to six feet tall, with a two-foot spread. The blossoms are a glorious gentian blue. Leaves are palmately divided into three to five lobes. As is the case with many of the buttercup family members, all parts of this plant are poisonous.

These delphiniums are best grown in a fertile, medium wet, well-drained soil. Add lime to acid soils, as they are most commonly found in the wild where soils are calcareous. They prefer full sun, although in the South, these flowers appreciate some afternoon shade. While they evidence a dislike for the hot and humid conditions of the Deep South, they generally do better than any of the popular English-style delphinium hybrids. Because of their height, they need protection from strong winds. Fertilize regularly, and deadhead for additional bloom.

THE LILY-OF-THE-VALLEY

Convallaria majalis

Gardeners and plant growers have been active in America for centuries. In the late 1500s, plant swapping and seed exchanges became popular as gainful vocations and delightful avocations. In the horticultural world of the 1700s, Peter Collinson stood high on the list of active plant traders, men who sent plants and seeds back and forth across the Atlantic with a passion. Collinson was a Quaker linen draper, or dealer in dry goods, with a shop in London. He was a great lover of gardens and gardening and continually badgered his business contacts, especially those in America, to send him seeds and plants. He set up a kind of trading relationship with the great Quaker botanist John Bartram. By 1735, the relationship between Collinson and Bartram became a business, especially when Bartram sent one hundred species of plants (mostly tree seeds) to Collinson, who distributed them to various patrons at five guineas a packet.

According to Alice M. Coats in her fascinating book *The Plant Hunters*, "All this [trading] involved Collinson in considerable trouble and expense . . . but was only a small part of the traffic that flowed back and forth across the Atlantic, in spite of many hazards [including] rats, damp and decay, wrecks, war and piracy, and the resulting losses."

But the business of trading seeds and plants was ever expanding, and among Collinson's customers was John Custis of Virginia. In *American Gardens in the Eighteenth Century*, Ann Leighton described Custis as a "prominent and peppery planter, land-mad, encumbered by debts inherited by his wife and her sister, and a great gardener." (He died intestate in 1757.)

Between 1734 and 1746, Custis and Collinson kept up a devout exchange of letters and a happy exchange of seeds, bulbs, plants, and information. Among others, Collinson sent double-blossomed peaches and double Dutch tulips to Custis, and in return, Custis sent dogwoods, laurels, and chinquapin nuts to Collinson. In 1738, Custis received a package from London containing lily-of-the-valley pips.

Thomas Jefferson learned of the plant and thought it would be perfect for naturalizing. Records show that he ordered lily-of-the-valley from Bernard M'Mahon, but obviously he probably had the plant long before that.

In addition to the popular name of song and story, other local names of the lily-of-the-valley include dangle bells, fairies' bells, innocents, ladder to heaven, lady's tears, May blossoms, and white bells. To the French, the flowers are called "the tears of the Holy Mary."

The heritage of the lily-of-the-valley can be very confusing. Some botanists claim there is only one species, *Convallaria majalis*, a native of the British Isles, Northern Europe, and North America. But reference books list two more species: *C. montana*, an American native, and *C. keiskei*, a native of Japan. Today, however, most horticulturists agree that they are all one species with minor physical variations, hence var. *montana* and var. *keiskei*.

In certain parts of England, as in America, the plants are very common, but in many other spots, they are quite unknown. They are rare in Scotland, but naturalized in Ireland.

The genus name refers to the Latin *convallis*, a valley, denoting the plant's natural habitat. The species name *majalis* means "that which belongs to May." Plants have wide, oval-oblong leaves of a pleasant light green, always borne in pairs, with one leaf often larger than the other. Like the flower stalk, they all arise directly from the rootstock just below ground level.

Despite the *valley* part of the name, I've found it growing beautifully in open woods and dry soil. In rich and shady woods, the plants will cover the forest floor with a rich carpet of green. Masses of these charmers are found in abandoned cemeteries, as families often planted both lily-of-the-valley and myrtle as low-care but usually beautiful groundcovers.

The flower stems are slightly curved and bear a one-sided raceme of small, bell-shaped, white flowers with a singular, very sweet fragrance. The flower contains no dripping nectars, but a sweet, juicy sap is stored in a tissue around the base of the ovary. This proves a great attraction to bees, which visit the flower to collect its pollen and play an important part in flower fertilization.

The rootstock forms a small, scaly rhizome or tuber, often called a pip in older books. The word *pip* refers to the flowering crown or the individual rootstocks of the plant and is derived from the English word *peep.* While dictionaries cite the connection as unknown, it is perhaps because in early spring, the green shoots would peep out of the ferns and other woodsy dwellers, welcoming spring in a big way. In the wild state, the fruit rarely comes to maturity, and propagation is mainly effected by the quickly creeping underground stems.

Flowering is usually limited to May and June, but the leaves persist all season and in the fall become a beautiful shade of tan. Fruits appear in late summer as small, orange-scarlet balls. The berries are poisonous.

During the Middle Ages in Europe, the perfume distilled from these holy flowers was considered so precious that only gold and silver vessels were fit to hold it.

In an allegory that arose out of a legend in Sussex, England, St. Leonard met the frightful dragon, Sin. The saint battled against the dragon for three days but never gave up. On the fourth morning, he had the satisfaction of watching the dragon creep back into the woods, trailing its slimy tail behind it. And wherever the dragon's claws or tusks had struck the saint and his blood spilled upon the earth, up sprang a lily-of-the-valley.

As to legends, there are more. One night, the Queen of the Fairies decided to hold a party for her friends and asked a group of gnomes to gather nectar. The gnomes trooped out into the woodland, but after collecting only a few drops of nectar, they hung their little porcelain cups on blades of grass and began to dance. Then suddenly it was evening, and gnomes were forbidden to be out after sunset. They ran to get their porcelain cups, but found that the cups had grown fast and could only be removed by killing the plants, something gnomes just couldn't do. The Queen of the Fairies saw their plight and just laughed and laughed. Then she raised her magic wand and pronounced the magic words "Convallaria majalis," and each of the cups became a flower bell of the lily-of-the-valley.

Lily of the Valley was Balzac's favorite among all of his writings. The novel told the story of Felix and his fiancée, Henrietta, whose correspondence on the subject of love revealed her to be far more experienced than Felix had thought.

In 1881, Charles W. Fry wrote a hymn entitled "The Lily-of-the-Valley" for the Salvation Army, with music by William S. Hays:

> I have found a friend in Jesus, He's everything to me,
> He's the fairest of ten thousand to my soul;
> The Lily of the Valley, in Him alone I see
> All I need to cleanse and make me fully whole.
> In sorrow He's my comfort, in trouble He's my stay;
> He tells me every care on Him to roll.
>
> *Refrain*
> He's the Lily-of-the-Valley, the Bright and Morning Star,
> He's the fairest of ten thousand to my soul.

Finally, to bring things radically up-to-date, there's an all-girl folk-rock-funk-punk group in Germany known as Lily-of-the-Valley from Wiesbaden.

The lily-of-the-valley has long been used for its medicinal virtues, and that use stretches back to ancient times, for Apuleius, writing in his *Herbal* of the third century (not to be confused with Apuleius, the author of *The Golden Ass*), declared it was found by Apollo and given to the world by Æsculapius, the leech.

When collected in flower, the entire plant is dried and used for medicines. The inflorescence is said to be the most important active part of the herb. The flowers are dried on the stalk, the whole stalk being cut before the lowermost flowers are faded. While drying, the white flowers assume a brownish yellow tinge, and the fragrant odor usually disappears, being replaced by a somewhat heady scent; the taste of the flowers is bitter.

When flowers are mixed in oil of sweet almonds or olive oil, they impart to it their sweet smell, but to become really fragrant, the infusion has to be repeated a dozen times with the same oil, using fresh flowers for each infusion.

The chief principles of the plant are two glucosides. The first is convallamarin, a white crystalline powder, soluble in either water or alcohol, that acts upon the heart like digitalis. The second is convallarin, soluble in alcohol and slightly soluble in water, a compound with a purgative action. Russian peasants long used the lily-of-the-valley for certain forms of dropsy.

Old writers tell of a decoction made of bruised roots, boiled in wine, that was good for pestilential fevers, while bread made of barley meal mixed with the juice was an excellent cure for dropsy.

Lily-of-the-valley are easy plants to cultivate, preferring well-drained, rich, sandy loam, in moist situations. The earth should be worked to a fifteen-inch depth, adding compost or manure if available. Plant crowns about six inches apart, and leave at least nine inches between the rows. Keep the crowns well below the surface, and above all, plant firmly.

There are two attractive cultivars: 'Fortin's Giant', with longer flower stems and larger flowers, and 'Rosea', with light pink flowers.

Lily-of-the-valley plants are not to be confused with the Canada mayflower, or Canadian lily-of-the-valley *(Maianthemum canadense)*. This wildflower sports two heart-shaped leaves appearing in very early spring. They clasp a stem that bears tiny, white flowers followed by little berries, white with spots, later turning red.

THE CROCUSES OF MONTICELLO

Crocus spp.

In 1807, Bernard M'Mahon sent saffron crocus *(Crocus sativus)* to Monticello. Jefferson was fascinated with this particular plant, which not only blooms in the fall, but also was a plant of great value to commerce, being grown as the source of saffron, an important condiment, medicine, and dye. Then, in 1812, M'Mahon supplied Monticello with a very popular spring crocus known as the cloth of gold crocus *(Crocus angustifolius)*. Finally, M'Mahon provided the gardens with the popular Dutch crocus, noting that the variety he sent was "of very early bloom; flowers white inside [and] beautifully striped outside."

According to Greek legend, the crocuses were named for a beautiful youth of the Grecian plains, known far and wide as Crocus. As so often happens, the lad was smitten with a shepherdess of the hills, named Smilax (the differences between the mountain folks and those who live down below began long, long ago). Smilax did not return his love, but she did bestow her name on the genus *Smilax*, a large group of mostly vining plants belonging to the lily family, many with thorny stems. As for Crocus, after he pined away and died, so the story goes, the gods changed him into the flower that bears his name.

More likely, the spring crocus was named by the great botanist Theophrastus, who used the Greek word *kroke*, or thread, to describe the flower's stigma.

As to the original crocus and its appearance on earth, a reference is made to an elixir of life prepared by Media to resuscitate the aged Aeson, the father of Jason of Golden Fleece fame. Media prepared a potion made of herbs, seeds, and flowers with acrid juice, hoarfrost, the head of a screech owl, the entrails of a wolf, and many other things "without a name," then boiled these items, stirring them up with a dry olive branch. Behold! The branch turned green, and wherever the liquor boiled over and bubbled on the ground, grass grew and crocuses sprouted, announcing the coming of spring.

Crocuses are continually called bulbs but in reality are corms. A corm is a solid, thickened, underground stem that is rich in starch for nutrition and, unlike the onion and the lily, doesn't grow in layers. The roots grow off the lower side of the corm, poking through four or five wrappings of a white, paperlike material.

Crocus blossoms appear in many colors, usually white, yellow, orange, or purple, the last often striped or feather-veined. Although many pearl-like seeds may develop in the oblong ovary located deep within the stem, it is chiefly by corms that the crocus multiplies. On top of the mother corm of the present year, smaller corms will develop on the top, each capable of growing a plant for the following year. But after a few years, the corms push up through the top of the ground, so crocuses must be replanted every few years.

That first crocus grown in Jefferson's garden, the saffron crocus *(Crocus sativus)*, along with dates, flax, and papyrus, is one of the oldest of cultivated flowers on earth and thought to be the *Karkom* of the Song of Solomon. (The name of a mountain in Israel originally known as Jebel Ideid, Arabic for Mountain of Celebration or Mountain of the Multitude, was changed to Har Karkom, meaning Mount Saffron, because at certain times of the day, the mountain assumes the color of that spice.)

As for the original name of the saffron crocus, legend says that a child called Krolis was accidentally killed by a quoit (a flattened, ring-shaped piece of iron) flung from the hand of Hermes. For amends, Krolis was dipped into celestial dew and changed into the flower.

A native of the eastern Mediterranean, this plant produces narrow gray-green leaves long before the flowers appear in October. The petals are a deep purple-red, veined in the throat with darker streaks of purple and a large scarlet stigma. The blossoms open flat and never close, even at night, as many crocuses do. The corms must be baked in hot summer sun and suffer with too much rain. The soil need not be great stuff, but it must be well drained, as the corms will rot if waterlogged.

The ancients often used this flower to adorn their marriage beds because, according to the Greek poet Homer, the crocus was one of the flowers used to decorate the couch of Zeus and Hera. At the time of Nero, crocuses were considered to be a great cordial, a tonic for the heart, and a potent love potion. At that time, Romans, obviously having more money than tact, would strew the blossoms throughout their banquet halls, and the flowers also tumbled on the waters of fountains and small garden streams out near terraces. But caution was often advised, because the true autumn crocus *(Colchicum autumnale)* is a potent poison.

The fashionable ladies of Rome used a concoction made from the plant as a hair dye, thus the Roman Church eventually forbade its use. And later in the Middle Ages, Henry VIII ruled against the use of the saffron crocus as a linen dye, favored by the Irish, whose women used it with the belief that a cloth so dyed did not need as much washing as a white material, because the stain had a sanitary value.

In Cashmere, saffron was strictly controlled by the ruling classes, but an English traveler in the days of Edward III stole one corm and, concealing it in a hollow staff, took it back to England to his home in Walden, where it produced such a harvest of flowers that the place has been called Saffron Walden ever since.

The Indians thought the world of saffron, using it in cooking. Legend also has it that upon suffering a defeat in war, the rajahs put on saffron-dyed robes of state and, gathering their unhappy wives around them, were burned to death.

In the process of drying, the stigmas produce a glycoside called picrocrocine, which then forms safranal, with a characteristic smell, and the carotenoid pigment crocine. Saffron stimulates the appetite and, in normal use, is a spice or condiment, especially favored for food coloring. Too much saffron can be toxic and fatal, however, causing violent hemorrhaging.

The cloth of gold crocus (*Crocus angustifolius* or *C. susianus*) is a native of the Crimea, receiving its popular name from the golden anthers, surrounded by small petals of the deepest orange and striped on the outside with dashes of purple or brown. The flower is described by Clusius in his *Rariorum Plantarum Historia*, wherein he told of receiving the corms back in 1587, and by Parkinson, who talked about it in his *Paradisus* of 1629. The plants are considered dwarfs and flower earlier than most other species and varieties of crocuses.

When it comes to growing crocuses, it must be remembered that these are plants generally of Mediterranean origin. There summers are warm and dry, and the corms usually get a thorough baking during the summer months. So for success, crocuses must have well-drained soil and rarely succeed in waterlogged soil. If you have heavy clay soil, it's a good idea to plant them in raised beds.

LADY'S SLIPPER ORCHIDS

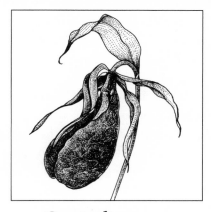

Cypripedium spp.

THE PINK LADY'S SLIPPER
Cypripedium acaule

According to *Thomas Jefferson's Flower Garden at Monticello,* in 1809 the English naturalist John Bradbury, who had been sent to America to collect plants for the Liverpool Botanic Gardens, visited Monticello and commented upon some of the unusual native plants, including three pink lady's slipper orchids *(Cypripedium acaule).* Jefferson included these "mockaseen," or moccasin, flowers in his list of cultivated plants.

Their scientific name of *Cypripedium* is from the Greek *Kypris,* a name for Aphrodite (the Roman Venus), and *pedion,* an anklet, instep, or reference to the foot. So *Cypripedium* translates as Aphrodite's shoe or Venus's slipper. The specific name, *acaule,* derives from the Latin prefix *a,* meaning without or lacking, and *caul* from the Latin *caulis,* for the stem of a plant; hence *acaule* translates as stemless, a reference to the lack of a stem in this species. In this case, the flower's stalk is not considered a plant stem.

Lady's slippers are both exotic and beautiful. Mark Catesby (1682–1749) arrived in America in 1712 and was the country's first professional full-time collector, botanist, and gardener, as well as a fine illustrator. In *The Natural History of Carolina, Florida and the Bahama Islands,* he said of the lady's slipper: "This plant produces the most elegant flower of all the [orchid] tribe and is in great esteem with the North American Indians for decking their hair, etc. They call it the Moccasin Flower which also signifies in their language a shoe or slipper."

The fragrant (smell them if you find them), solitary, large, and showy slippers hang from the end of an eight-inch to foot-high stem (properly a scape), surrounded by two-inch-long, greenish purple, lance-shaped sepals and petals, the petals being longer and narrower than the sepals. Two pleated, elliptical leaves arise from the base of the scape, about eight inches long.

Writing in *Nature's Garden,* Neltje Blanchan remarked: "Because most people cannot forbear picking this exquisite flower that seems too beautiful to be found outside a millionaire's hothouse, it is becoming rarer every year, until the finding of one in the deep forest, where it must now hide, has become the event of a day's walk. Once it was the commonest of orchids."

Where I once lived in the Catskill Mountains, and today in the Appalachians, the lady's slipper also was very common and now is rarer and rarer. That doesn't prevent unscrupulous collectors from digging them up in spring bloom and selling them along the roadside, where they are bought by uninformed people for their gardens—and sooner or later die. The plant is also sometimes gathered from the wild by old-timers for medicinal uses, as the root of lady's slipper has been employed as a remedy for toothache, nervousness, and muscle spasms. But the greatest enemy is loss of habitat from uncontrolled and unconcerned development.

Lady's slippers take many years from seed to flowering plant, and they only survive in very specific locations. At our home in Sullivan County, New York, we lived at the edge of thirty-three acres, the middle section being a gently sloped second-growth forest of white pines and aged hemlocks. There, in fairly dry and very acid soil, grew a colony of these glorious plants. In the spring, their lilylike leaves would poke through a mantle of pine needles, close to the tree roots; they rarely saw direct sunlight except for the rays that filtered through the branches above. Below the colony of orchids grew a thicket of common blueberry (*Vaccinium* spp.). Not far to the left were painted trilliums (*Trillium undulatum*), bunchberries (*Cornus canadensis*), and fringed polygala (*Polygala paucifolia*). I hope they're all still there.

The pink lady's slipper, like all other orchids, starts life as a very tiny seed, a seed only slightly larger than a dust mite. Unlike corn or walnuts or milkweed pods, orchid seeds are little more than a few cells constituting an undifferentiated embryo. In order to survive, they must germinate in the right habitat and, to make matters more difficult, in the presence of a symbiotic fungus. Upon meeting the initial root sent out by the seed, the fungus intends to invade that root and eventually use the seed contents as food. But the orchid absorbs the fungus within its tissues to help in taking up nutrients from its environment. Unless an orchid removed from its home environment is replaced in a spot with the same fungus, it eventually will die.

Looking at the blossom head-on, you will see that the pink pouch has a fissure that runs down the center. Bumblebees are the pollinators, and that fissure isn't wide enough to allow a bee to enter directly, so the insect must apply some force to push though and enter the large banquet chamber, where nectar is secreted among fine white hairs in the upper part. Blanchan described it vividly:

> Presently he has feasted enough, and presently you can hear him buzzing about inside, trying to find a way out of the trap. Toward the two little gleams of light through apertures at the end of a passage beyond the nectary hairs, he at length finds his way. Narrower and narrower grows the passage until it would seem as if he could never struggle through; nor can he until his back has brushed along the sticky, overhanging stigma, which is furnished with minute, rigid, sharply pointed papillae, all directed forward, and placed there for the express purpose of combing out the pollen he has brought from another flower on his back or head. The imported pollen having been safely removed, he still has to struggle on toward freedom through one of the narrow openings, where an anther almost blocks his way.
>
> As he works outward, this anther, drawn downward on its hinge, plasters his back with yellow granular pollen as a parting flight, and away he flies to another lady's slipper to have it combed out by the sticky stigma as described above. The smallest bees can squeeze through the passage without paying toll.

Sometimes a bumblebee gets impatient with walking around the slipper's walls and simply chews his way to liberty. You can usually find some mutilated sacs as evidence of an unfair escape.

THE YELLOW LADY'S SLIPPER
Cypripedium calceolus

The beautiful yellow lady's slipper was reported blooming at Monticello in the spring of 1791. Although thought to be less common than the pink, this has less to do with disposition and more with habitat, for the pink slippers like only acidic surroundings, whereas the yellows prefer a sweet or limy outlook.

A solitary, large, showy flower sits atop a leafy stem up to two feet high. The flower has three long, narrow sepals, two of them united, greenish or yellowish and striped with purple or dull red, and two brown petals that are also narrow but twist about.

The yellow lady's slipper is known scientifically as *Cypripedium calceolus*, the species name Latin for little shoe, in reference to the slipper-like shape of the labellum, or floral lip. Today we recognize three separate varieties. The first variety is *pubescens*, Latin for downy or hairy, in reference to the hairy nature of the plant. The second is *parviflorum*, from the Latin *parvis*, meaning smaller, distinguished primarily by a smaller labellum and darker sepals, which are never as light-colored as those of variety *pubescens*. The third variety is the most common, known as *calceolus*.

While woods walkers might have a bit of difficulty in recognizing the variety, there is no problem with the species. Though it might not be as splashy as the showy pink lady's slipper, it's a most beautiful flower in its own right.

Like the pink lady's slipper, the yellows are also pollinated by bees, and in much the same process as found in the pink, an invading bee must trade previous pollens in order to escape back to the real world.

THE HAY-SCENTED FERN

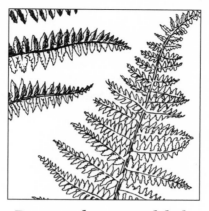

Dennstaedtia punctilobula

On October 28, 1785, Jefferson wrote to James Madison from Fontainebleau:

> After descending the hill again I saw a man cutting fern. I went to him under the pretence of asking the shortest road to the town, and afterwards asked for what use he was cutting fern. He told me that this part of the country furnished a great deal of fruit to Paris. That when packed in straw it acquired an ill taste, but that dry fern preserved it perfectly without communicating any taste at all. I treasured this observation for the preservation of my apples on my return to my own country. They have no apples here to compare with our own Newtown pippin.

I have no way of knowing what species of fern that Frenchman was shearing, but I suspect it was something fairly common, quick to regenerate, and with a good odor.

The hay-scented fern *(Dennstaedtia punctilobula)*, or as it's sometimes called, the boulder fern, grows wild on Jefferson's land. The creeping rhizomes, and they will creep, produce delicate and fragrant leaves usually about sixteen inches tall, yellow-green, lance-shaped and widest at the bottom, cut into about twenty pairs of leaflets.

Jefferson probably knew the hay-scented fern as the genus *Dicksonia*, named in honor of James Dickson (1738–1822), a British nurseryman and botanist. But thanks to the continuing round robin of scientific name changes, the genus name is now *Dennstaedtia*, in honor of August Wilhelm Dennstedt, a German botanist of the early nineteenth century.

Growing equally well in shade or full sun in the Northeast, the second popular name of boulder fern refers to its ability to prosper not only along the edges of country woodlands, but also in places of almost pure rock, slightly covered with soil.

In her 1899 book *How to Know the Ferns*, Frances Theodora Parsons wrote that this fern often grew "along the roadsides [forming] great masses of feathery foliage, tempting the weary pedestrian or bicycler to fling himself upon a couch sufficiently soft and luxurious in appearance to satisfy a Sybarite." She went on to describe doing just that on a memorably hot August afternoon when, during a trip over an unused mountain road, her party succumbed to weariness. Gathering armloads of fern fronds for a night's rest, Parsons had to admit, "I must frankly own that I never slept on so hard a bed."

Waning sunlight and cooler nights apparently prime the hay-scented fern for the coming demise of its upper parts, for as early as late September in the mountains around Asheville, North Carolina, the fronds begin their color decline from light green to pale green to light tan and often to pure white as the season marches on to winter.

Thoreau called the odor of the hay-scented fern the "sweet fragrance of decay," but I think he was overdoing it a bit, because that particular smell is quite nauseous. Instead, these ferns really do smell like new-mown hay.

The reason for the fragrance is the chemical coumerin, contained within glandular hairs that sprout from the leaflets. Coumerin is a white crystalline substance with a vanillalike odor. It is found in many plants, including a number of grasses. Not only does it evoke memories of sunshine on hayfields, but it also resembles the smell of sweet clover; American sweet grass (*Hierochloe odorata*), which Native Americans used both as a flavoring and for weaving into baskets and mats; and zubrowka, a drink made by adding to a quart of Russian vodka three or four blades of Russian buffalo grass (*H. australis*), which soon impart their sweet odor to this clear liquor.

THE GAS PLANT

Dictamnus alba

Ann Leighton, in *American Gardens in the Eighteenth Century,* counted the gas plant *(Dictamnus albus)* as being most frequently cultivated in the 1700s. In 1807, Thomas Main, a Washington nurseryman who in the same year wrote a little book with the very long title *Directions for the Transplantation and Management of Young Thorn or Other Hedge Plants, Preparative to Their Being Set in Hedges,* sent a plant of this unusual species to Jefferson.

This is the only species in the genus *Dictamnus,* unusual perennials originally found from Southern Europe to northern China. Other common names include dittany and fraxinella. The plant is about three feet tall and produces tall stems topped with unusual-looking, fringed, rosy purple flowers with five petals, blooming in late spring to early summer. According to many reports, the crushed leaves smell of a mix of anise, sweet clover, and lavender, but I find the odor decidedly citrus.

The genus name *Dictamnus* refers to it as a plant that grew on Mount Dikte, on the Greek island of Crete. The first name used for the gas plant was tragium, a variation on *tragos,* the Greek word for goat, because the plant's seedpods supposedly smelled like a goat. An origanum, now called *Origanum dictamnus,* caused additional confusion. So to avoid confusion, by the seventeenth century, herbalists used the name fraxinella for the plant, a word that means small ash.

There is a problem when it comes to categorizing the gas plant's particular gift. Most books divide perennials by flower or leaf characteristics, and there is sometimes even a category for those that bloom at night, but there is none for night-burning flowers, an attribute of the gas plant according to two urban myths. One is that if, on a warm summer's night, a lighted match is held to a crushed leaf, the volatile oil in the leaf will burn with a blue flame, much like the flame produced by burning brandy. The other myth holds that if a match is applied to the entire plant, it will be enveloped in a bluish flame for a second or two, without hurting the plant.

Alice Morse Earle told the tale of an old Swedish lady—she just happened to be the daughter of Linnaeus—who, one sultry night in the summer of 1762, went on a nocturnal stroll in her garden and saw strange flashes of light sparkling out of the nasturtium flowers. Linnaeus's daughter did some more checking and finally reported that flames were flickering about her fraxinella. In 1762, the great poet and philosopher Goethe reported similar flashes of light circling around oriental poppies. These were not exaggerations of flying saucer believers, but reports from educated people of the day.

On a number of sultry evenings when the gas plant was in bloom, I went out to the border with a box of kitchen matches. I lit match after match, but to no avail. Leaves and flowers just shriveled with the heat of the flame. And without a flamethrower, there was no way to ignite the entire plant.

I must admit that the entertainment value of the entire enactment is worth the effort. Mike, the neighbor across the street, was curious as to what I was doing, and soon the whole neighborhood was involved with the experiment. And on some warm summer evening, it just might light.

Another suggestion refers to lighting the flower heads, which will burn with a rather weak orange flame and at the same time release the smell of lemon into the night air. It does work, but I find it best to wait for the seedpods to develop.

Then I received a letter from the English garden guru Graham Stuart Thomas, who told me the best way to put on a show is to squeeze the ripening seedpods, light a match, and you will get a surprising, yet genteel, burst of flame.

The flammable compounds found in the gas plant are termed monoterpenes, chemicals with a very low flash point. These volatile oils are secreted by tiny hairs, called trichomes, that grow on the seedpods and the leaves. These chemicals guarantee that gas plants are among the few perennials ignored by insects and even voles.

In addition to the monoterpenes, gas plants also produce a number of toxic alkaloids that easily cause allergic reactions in susceptible people. Like the giant hogweed (*Heracleum mantegazzianum*), these alkaloids are phototropic and cause phyto-photodermatitis, skin irritations caused only when the plant saps are exposed to sunlight or ultraviolet light.

As to garden advice, the words of Philip Miller written in 1760 are still the best advice when growing this plant:

> The roots of this plant continue for many years; but the stalks decay in the autumn, and new ones are produced every spring. The older the roots are, the greater number of stalks will be sent forth from each, provided they are not disturbed; to have this plant in perfection, plant the roots when young, in the places where they are designed to remain; for they do not bear transplanting well.

THE VENUS FLYTRAP

Dionaea muscipula

A gardener like Jefferson must have been fascinated by a plant known as Venus flytrap. After all, any man who could cut a circular hole in a floor so that a room with less-than-adequate height could accommodate a vertically chained eight-day clock must have been delighted with a plant that not only moved its leaves but speared insects as well. While there are many references to Jefferson ordering seed, we have no records of his successes or failures with this plant.

While not a giant among plants (nor especially fond of the undressed maidens that sci-fi interpretations love to feature as potential victims), this is a great plant for introduction to the wonders of nature. Another common name is meadow clam, and in German it's known as *Venusfliegenfalle.*

Originally found only in sixteen counties of southeastern North Carolina and three in South Carolina, today it's protected by law from poachers. And thanks to the process of cloning, what was once an endangered species is now housed in little plastic greenhouses and sold throughout the world as a novelty item.

As reported by Francis Ernest Lloyd in *The Carnivorous Plants,* the plant was probably first noticed around 1759 by Arthur Dobbs, the governor of North Carolina, one of the founders of the Royal Dublin

Society, an amateur botanist (most curious men of that time were), and the man who first wrote about this horticultural curiosity:

> The great wonder of the vegetable kingdom is a very curious unknown species of sensitive; it is a dwarf plant [with] leaves like a narrow segment of a sphere, consisting of two parts, like the cap of a spring purse, the concave part outward, each of which falls back with indented edges (like an iron spring fox trap); upon anything touching the leaves, or falling between them, they instantly close like a spring trap. . . . It bears a white flower; to this surprising plant I have given the name of Flytrap Sensitive.

Purists always inject at this point the probability that Native Americans were the first to know this plant, but if they did, they were certainly quiet about it—and it is rather small and insignificant.

Governor Dobbs sent a letter by sea to the London linen draper and garden lover Peter Collinson that included a reference to the "catch fly sensitive." Collinson immediately wrote back requesting more information and asked his friend John Bartram, who lived in Philadelphia, to check out the plant. Bartram tried in 1760, but now couldn't find one specimen.

Then in 1762, Bartram's son William met Dobbs at Cape Fear and found some plants and seed to send back to Collinson. But the ship was attacked by Spanish pirates, and living plants never made it to London.

In 1768, William Young, a rival of John Bartram, carried living plants across the Atlantic, claiming responsibility for the flytrap's introduction into England, where it caused quite a stir. But most collectors credit Dobbs, then Bartram, with the discovery of what Bartram called his tippitiwitchet.

Tippitiwitchet! Some research into that name reveals it used as a lovable cat, Tabetha Twitchet, in Beatrix Potter's *The Roly-Pudding*, but that was in 1908, and long after the first botanical forays into North Carolina. Some neologists think that the word refers to the similarity between the two halves of the trap, especially when flushed with red, and the rump or buttocks of horses or a slang word for a woman's privates.

That said, the flytrap is a one-genus species known as *Dionaea muscipula*, with Dionaea being one of the names of the Greek goddess

Aphrodite, while the species name translates to fly-catching or, more properly, mouse-catching.

The traps are green in poorer light and turn a deep crimson as exposure to sunlight increases (although some authorities attribute the leaf's color differences to changes in the pH). The surface of each trap has three stiff hairs, which respond to touch by closing the traps. The time needed to snap shut can be several seconds or less than one-half second, depending on the age of the traps and the ambient temperature; the greater the heat, the faster the traps will close.

The signal hairs must be touched twice within about twenty seconds or they will not close, probably to prove to the leaf that it has a live catch and not just a wind-blown or fallen bit of useless or dead material. And they do not generally open when pelted with raindrops, although I suspect that in hurricane season, with horizontal winds, it could happen.

They will usually reopen within a day if fooled by a broom straw, matchstick, or other object used to demonstrate the plant's unusual abilities. If the plant does catch a meal, it's digested in four to twenty days, depending on the victim's size. After a few meals, or possibly due to increasing age, the traps turn black. If snipped off, new traps will grow.

In late spring, the plants produce small, whitish flowers with wavy-edged petals that are very dainty and attractive.

As to the evolutionary question regarding the small size of the traps, nature is usually parsimonious. So the size of the trap needed to ensnare extra-large insects (or small mammals) would require so much growth (and so much eventual waste), not to mention the ability of larger insects to possibly struggle out of a trap, that it just isn't practical. Gnats and small flies are fine.

Mature plants will grow up to twelve traps at the same time. They may be moved outdoors during the summer to a sunny and moist spot, to be brought inside when temperatures begin to drop below fifty-five degrees F, on a seasonal basis. If the environment gets too cold or extremely dry, the bulbs enter a dormant stage of about two months' time. This is the normal yearly cycle. When buying bulbs, be aware that they are graded by age, not size. A good growing medium is half sphagnum moss and half clean builder's sand. In the wintertime, keep plants in a cool place while they go into dormancy, to burst forth again in the spring.

Like the majority of insectivores, the Venus flytrap likes lots of sunshine and high humidity. Though the roots resent sitting directly in water, they do prefer constantly moist surroundings. Provide them with clean water, and avoid chlorinated waters at all costs. Do not fertilize flytraps, and do not, for whatever reason, feed them hamburger or raw meat.

In nature, flytraps grow in grasslands, some swamps, sandy bogs, and scattered marshlands, protected from above by short-stalked grasses and sedges. The soil is usually acidic, ranging from pH 3 to 5. The soil is usually very low in organic matter. While plants will develop flowers and seedpods under those conditions, they produce more seed when able to digest animal prey and the nitrogen thus provided. Cultivars are available from specialty growers, including plants with overall colors that range from a reddish purple to a bright yellow-orange. There are also differences in the shape of the traps.

The International Carnivorous Plant Society is found at www. carnivorousplants.org.

THE EXOTIC FRITILLARIAS

Fritillaria spp.

The gardener John Custis (described as a difficult man in the chapter on lily-of-the-valley) wrote to Peter Collinson in 1739, "I had this spring a lemon-colored crown imperiall you were kind to send me . . . looked on as a great rarity. I have two roots of the orange-colored."

The crown imperial lily *(Fritillaria imperialis)* was a coveted plant in America long before it came Jefferson's way, through the efforts of Bernard M'Mahon, in 1815.

Alice Morse Earle wrote in *Old Time Gardens:* "A strong personal trait of the Fritillaries (for I may so speak of flowers I love) is their air of mystery. They mean something I cannot fathom; they look it, but cannot tell it. Fritillaries were a flower of significance even in Elizabethan days. They were made into little buttonhole posies, and, as Parkinson says, 'worn abroad by curious lovers of these delights.'"

In 1911, Charles M. Skinner wrote in *Myths and Legends of Flowers, Trees, Fruits, and Plants,* about the crown imperial:

> The golden cups of . . . the fritillary [resemble] a crown when viewed in mass, and the commanding aspect of the plant lends color to its claim of empire over the lesser creatures of the garden. This Persian lily was a queen whose beauty, instead of contenting her husband, the king, made him jealous, and in a moment of anger and suspicion he drove her from his palace. She, conscious of her innocence, wept so

constantly at this injustice, as she wandered about the fields, that her very substance shrunk to the measure of a plant, and at last, in mercy, the Divine One rooted her feet where she had paused and changed her to the crown imperial, still bearing in its blossoms somewhat of the dignity and command she had worn in her human guise.

To add legend to legend, Alfred Carl Hottes wrote in *Garden Facts and Fancies* the following about the crown imperial:

As the Savior one day was walking in the Garden of Gethsemane each flower bowed its head in reverence. Only one, a sort of Lily, stood erect. The other flowers whispered, "Bow your head, Lily, bow your head," but this flower only answered, "I am the Crown-imperial. I am a royal flower and I bow to no one." And this proud white Lily reared its head ever higher, growing an inch each hour until it towered above all the other flowers of the garden.

Finally, the Savior came by and gazed at her gently. The Lily flushed deeply and bent her head while a tear-drop appeared in the center of each of her petals.

Since that day the Crown-imperial, has been blood-red, with pendant flowers surmounted by a crown of leaves, but if you will look, you will find a dewdrop poised in the center of each petal. This is a tear that never dried.

According to Roy Genders, writing in his classic *Bulbs: A Complete Handbook*, fritillaries, or frits, as most gardeners call them, were introduced into Europe by Charles de l'Ecluse (Clusius) in 1576, reaching England soon after. Clusius was a friend of Sir Francis Drake, who sent him plants collected in America, and "the crown imperial lily may have been sent to Drake in exchange, for in 1580 he had returned, in the *Golden Hind*, from the circumnavigation of the world."

The frits are a bulbous genus of around one hundred species distributed throughout Asia Minor, Siberia, Europe, and North America. One species, the beautiful snakes head fritillary *(Fritillaria meleagris)*, is native to Britain.

The flowers exhibit strange colors in shades of brown, green, yellow, pink, purple, blue, maroon, orange-scarlet, and almost (but not quite) black. There are dwarf plants only a few inches high and those reaching heights of up to four feet, but most species grow about eighteen inches high.

Tufts of bright green, lance-shaped leaves that protect the pendant flowers from rain crown the flower heads. At the base of each petal is a drop of nectar that forms in a tiny cavity, a drop of honey that Gerard called a "pearl of the Orient."

Fritillaria comes from the Latin *fritillus,* a dice box (a popular game for eons), and refers to the checkerboard pattern of the petals found in the snake's-head lily, where the markings are used by insects as a nectar guide. There are a number of cultivars of the crown imperial: 'Aurea' is bright red-orange, 'Lutea' is bright yellow, and 'Rubra' is deep red.

Most books describe the bulbs, and some flowers, as having a fetid odor. Since that association was probably made when most Europeans bathed only when necessary, it seems harsh criticism to a smell that is best described as being foxy, exactly like the smell of a boxwood hedge on a rainy or misty afternoon. If it bothers you, just keep your nose away from the blossoms.

A bulb with the frit history has uses as a medicinal, although it's basically dangerous, as it's a cardiac poison. Fresh plants contain the toxic alkaloid imperialine. The cells in frit bulbs also contain exceptional amounts of DNA, having the highest quantities known in any plant species. Human beings have just five-millionths of a gram of DNA in each cell; *Fritillaria assyriaca,* from the mountains of Iraq and Iran, has some twenty-five times more, but nobody knows why.

Frits are survivors. Adapted to habitats where plants must crowd growth, flowering, and seed production into a short time before a long, hot summer, frits can take a lot of punishment. Many are found growing on mountainsides or arid upland plains.

Frits survive best in a rich, deep loam, especially if the bulbs remain undisturbed for years. Think about planting it at the edge of a wild area or on the fringe of shrubbery. Bulbs should be purchased in the autumn and planted out immediately upon receipt. The soil must be well drained, as heavy clay soil does not grow great bulbs. Sometimes, as is the case in part of my garden, a stem appears year after year without blooms. If so, plant new bulbs in another spot.

Frits are under threat in the wild because of habitat loss and bulb collectors. Luckily, not only do the flowers reproduce by seed, but mature plants form little bulbs called bulbils around the base of the parent bulb.

Recently I read of another fascinating fact about frits. It seems that in the 1980s, a zoology student at Kew Botanical Gardens discovered that birds are attracted by the bell-shaped flowers' dripping nectar, and the English blue tit is now known as the pollinator for the flower, the only such plant in the United Kingdom.

THE SNOWDROPS
OF EARLY SPRING

Galanthus nivalis

According to *Thomas Jefferson's Flower Garden at Monticello*, in 1808 Ellen
Randolph wrote in a letter to her grandfather, "The third of April
snow drops bloomed, you have none but I will give you mine if you
want them, and have them set out in your garden when we go to
Monticello."

Now in that area of Virginia that Jefferson called home, snowdrops
usually bloomed in February, and it's also probable that Jefferson
already had these winter blooms, because they had been grown in
English gardens since at least the 1600s. Gerard, in his *Herbal*, wrote
of the "Timely flowring Bulbus violet," and in 1659, Sir Thomas
Hanmer talked in his *Garden Book* of bulbous violets, of which *Galanthus nivalis* is the early white, "whose pretty pure white bellflowers are
tipt with a fine greene, and hang downe their heads."

Snowdrops, or *Galanthus*—the genus name from the Greek for milk-
flower—often bloom a bit earlier than the crocuses but carry over and
produce fresh blossoms for weeks. *Nivalis* is for snowy or white. The
common name of snowdrop was probably borrowed from the German
Schneetropfen, though the usual German name is *Schneeglöckchen*, or snow-
bell. Because they bloomed in February, at least in England, they were

also known as Candlemas bells, as Candlemas, the Feast of Purifica-
tion, is on February 2. In several English counties, they were also known
as Death's flower and were thought unlucky to bring into the house.

The bulbs give rise to two narrow leaves, usually about four inches
long, followed by inch-long waxy, white flowers, their outer segments
being white and the inner segments tipped with green.

According to Alice Morse Earle in *Old Time Gardens*, snowdrops
bear the mark of one of the few tints of green that we like in white
flowers. Its "heart-shaped seal of green," sung by the poet Rossetti,
has been noted by other poets; Tennyson wrote:

> Pure as lines of green that streak the white
> Of the first Snowdrop's inner leaves.

Like aconites, they need a shady spot with a good, woodsy, well-
drained soil.

You will need a number of these bulbs to make a decent floral display, at least 180 per square yard. Since they are not very expensive,
here's one place not to stint. Plant new bulbs in the fall, but when
your time-honored plants become crowded, dig them up and divide
them in the late winter or early spring. This procedure does not harm
snowdrops at all. Since their roots form in August, however, digging
them up at that time can be fatal.

I first learned about moving snowdrops in one of Beverly Nichols's
English garden books, in this case *Merry Hall*. The time was mid-Feb-
ruary, and Nichols said, "I got a spade and transplanted the snowdrops to the copper beach and in case you didn't know it, snowdrops
lift best when they are in full flower, providing that you dig them up
in a solid chunk of soil."

One weekend last winter, we had a garden visitor who said she
assembled wonderful centerpieces for the table by digging up clumps
of snowdrops, surrounding the plants with an assortment of dried
mosses and ferns, then plunking everything into a charming old basket—and the dinner guests were delighted. In the days when zinc lin-
ers were easy to make, such baskets were often found at many dinner
tables. With today's plastic bottles, bags, and such, it's easy to water-
proof such a basket.

Many of the more progressive bulb companies carry a number of snowdrop cultivars, including 'Flore Pleno', which has more and larger flowers, and 'S. Arnott', a new snowdrop on the scene that reaches a height of ten inches. *Galanthus nivalis* is not harvested in the wild, but the other species often are. Be sure you know your supplier when you buy other snowdrop species. The rules say that bulbs harvested in the wild—by Dutch growers—will bear the legend "Bulbs from Wild Source," and as of 1992, labels will always state the place of origin. Let's hope.

When naturalized along a woodland path or out at the edge of the garden proper, nothing is more cheering in the spring than the sight of hundreds of snowdrops in full bloom.

There is an old story about a European queen who came upon a single snowdrop while walking in the woods and was so moved by the sight that she ordered a guard to stand over the plant so that nobody would trample the flower. Years later, someone noticed that a guard was still standing on the spot, since the queen's order was never rescinded, and the guard was replaced daily. Whenever I hear stories like that, it always reminds me of county and state governments; in fact, it sounds like the Pentagon could have been involved.

As to the flower that Ellen Randolph sent to her grandfather, it was probably the spring snowflake (*Leucojum vernum*), originally from Central Europe and sent to England in 1505. The genus is the name used by the Greek Hippocrates for the original flower, and *vernum* means spring. In New England, the flower was called the high snowdrop. It has at the end of each snowy petal a tiny perfect dot of green.

Snowflakes will tolerate sun but prefer light shade. They also insist on well-drained soil and are always found growing in sandy places along the Southeast shore. The fragrant flowers are found only on mature plants. Plant the bulbs about six inches apart and three inches deep in early fall. The plant grows a foot tall. Propagate by division when the foliage matures, but only when the plants really need it. These bulbs are great for naturalizing and random planting in the grass under tall trees or at the edge of a wild garden. *Leucojum aestivum* is known as the summer snowflake, and *L. autumnale* as the autumn snowflake, blooming at summer's end.

THE GLADIOLUS

Gladiolus spp.

The gladiolus of today, those stiff sprays of crowded flowers, their rigid staffs stuck into containers often made of twisted wicker or polished brass, are a far cry from the flowers that Jefferson first encountered in 1812. For that year, Bernard M'Mahon sent to Monticello corms of the purple-flowering native plant of the Mediterranean regions known as *Gladiolus communis*.

The genus name is derived from the Latin word *gladius*, meaning sword, referring to the sword-shaped leaves of that genus. The species means common.

Back in 1596, these members of the iris family were first introduced into England and were considered quite a find, especially because of their bright purple flower color, although there were detractors.

Then, in the 1620s, the corn flag of Constantinople, or *Gladiolus byzantinus*, appeared with its bright red flowers blooming in August, prompting John Parkinson (the author of this great line: "Whoever wants to compare Art with Nature and our parks with Eden, indiscreetly measures the stride of the elephant by the stride of the mite and the flight of the eagle by that of the gnat") in 1629 to write in his famous volume *Paradisi in Sole Terrestris:* "If it be suffered any long time in a Garden, it will rather choak and pester it, than be an ornament unto it."

In the mid-1700s, gladiolus from South Africa were introduced. In 1841, hybridizing began in France when Pierre Louis Victor Lemoine (1823–1911) began to improve the early species, only to be bested by an American, Arthur Kunderd, who in 1907 introduced the first glad with ruffled petals.

Usually, gladiolus are not planted until spring because their corms are not at all winter-hardy, but G. *byzantinus* is hardier than most, and I have also noted that with milder winters in Asheville, many glad corms live over the winter. This species, however, is an exception because its natural habitat differs from that of most of the other gladiolus species.

The species glads are great in rock gardens and as cut flowers. About the only requirements are full sun and well-drained soil. You can also raise them from seed. If you live below USDA Zone 7, gather the corms after the first frost has hit the leaves, cut them back to corm level, dust off the dirt, store over the winter in a dry, frost-free spot, and use the corms again next year.

Writing back in 1968, Pizzetti and Cocker stated in *Flowers: A Guide to Your Garden* that gladiolus had achieved such great economic importance that in Germany up to ten thousand acres were in cultivation, and in Holland more than one hundred thousand acres were devoted to these blooms.

In England in 1856, a clergyman found *Gladiolus illyricus* in the New Forest, where it grew and bloomed in the midst of the bracken, "which overtops it before it comes into flower." The flowers are crimson-purple on three-foot stalks.

The evening-blooming *Gladiolus tristis*, found growing wild in South Africa, usually along ditches and the borders of swampy areas, has creamy yellow blossoms that are intensely fragrant at night with a spicy-sweet perfume. They rise above very unusual leaves that have a most peculiar structure—they look like a pinwheel when cut in half. The frost-tender corms are small, and six or more will do quite well in a six-inch pot.

HEMP AND HOPS

Cannabis sativa and *Humulus japonicus*

Jefferson grew both hops and hemp in his garden. The first mention of hops was in 1794, when it was included with a number of vegetables featuring French sorrel and nasturtiums. In February 1812, he wrote, "Manure and make up hop-hills." As for hemp, he actually built and perfected a hemp-breaking machine and was one of the first American farmers to import a new Scottish threshing machine. He grew both hemp and flax for spinning and weaving, and noted in *The Farm Book* that with hemp, you "plough the ground for it early in the fall & very deep, if possible plough it again in Feb. before you sow it, which should be in March. A hand can tend 3. acres of hemp a year." He followed with preparation of the seed, including the advice that "as soon as male plants have shed their farina [pollen], cut them up that the whole nourishment may go the female plants."

"To stretch hemp" is a slang phrase for hanging, but Charles M. Skinner, in *Myths and Legends of Flowers, Trees, Fruits, and Plants,* sums it up beautifully:

> The plant that furnishes the means for death might be thought to be of evil omen; but since more rope is used for goodly purposes than for shutting off the wind of rougues, the weed has a kindly aspect, especially for maids who wish to see their future husbands before they

are led to the altar. . . . The damsels must run around a church at night, scattering hemp seed as they go, and repeating, "sow hemp seed. Hemp seed I sow. He loves me best, come after me and mow."

Sicilians use hempen threads as a lure for lovers, for there would seem in this to be a suggestion of the tying of hearts together.

The hemp family is small, consisting of only two genera: *Cannabis* and *Humulus.* The two are very much alike, yet worlds apart. *Cannabis,* or hemp, is frowned upon by our society, while still worshiped in many parts of the world; *Humulus,* or hops, is revered by most of the frowners as an important contribution to one of the world's great entertainment beverages and is worshiped the world over.

Cannabis sativa is the classical Latin name for the classic plant commonly known as hemp; *sativa* means cultivated. For generations, hemp has been grown for the exceptionally strong fibers in the stems. In addition, the fruit, a small achene, yields the drying aid hempseed oil, as well as bird feed. Dried flowering and fruiting tops of the female plants are used to produce marijuana (a Spanish corruption of Mary-Jane) or cannabis, hashish or charas, bhang, and ganja. Bhang is made in India, is brownish green in color, and has little taste but a heavy odor. It is used chiefly for chewing or smoking, with or without tobacco added, or as a drink when infused with water. Ganja is a powerful form of hashish made entirely from the pistillate tops of hemp, smoked like tobacco. Although the leaves are smoked illegally, there is a legitimate use of marijuana in the treatment of glaucoma, and the chemical components of the plant relieve much of the nausea connected with chemotherapy.

Originally from Central Asia, *Cannabis* has naturalized in many countries, including the United States. It is dioecious, with separate male and female plants, the males dying after shedding pollen and the females living on until killed by frost.

At one time, *Cannabis* found its way into every classic ornamental border. In his 1883 book *The English Flower Garden,* William Robinson said:

A well-grown annual of the Nettle Order, *C. sativa* is largely cultivated for its fibre. In our country it is 4 to 10 feet high, but in Italy sometimes 20 feet high. In plants growing singly, the stem is much branched, but in masses it is generally simple. It is useful where tender sub-tropical plants cannot be easily grown, well-grown plants looking graceful, and are useful at the backs of borders; and a few look well as a separate group. One of the few plants that thrive in small London gardens.

In the 1909 edition of *The American Garden,* by Neltje Blanchan, hemp was listed as *Cannabis sativa* var. *gigantea.* The entry reads: "Greenish flowers. August; 10 feet. A rough-looking plant for bold foliage effects or screen. Best to sow where wanted, but may be started in heat and transplanted. Rich moderately moist soil."

But the following entry for hemp appeared in the 1936 *Practical Encyclopedia of Gardening,* by Norman Taylor: "It has little or no garden value and the cultivation of female plants is forbidden in many countries because from their dried flowers is derived the narcotic hashish."

Jefferson wrote of the plant: "The best hemp and the best tobacco grow on the same kind of soil. The former article is of the first necessity to the wealth and protection of the country. The latter, never useful."

As to hops, according to the *Flora of Japan,* published by the Smithsonian Institution, there are two kinds: Japanese hops *(Humulus japonicus),* an annual vine, and common hops *(H. lupulus),* a perennial. The first is a valuable ornamental plant, often growing thirty feet in a good year. The second is the commercial source of hops and deemed not as attractive. *Humulus* is from the Latin word *humus,* or ground, the place to which these plants will tumble, if they lack support.

Admittedly, Japanese hops can be a rambling terror, and if kudzu is a Toyota truck, then this plant is a two-door Mazda, not only wild enough to cover an unwanted trash pile, but able to climb the garage in a single bound.

The leaves are rough to the touch, deeply divided into five to seven lobes, and the stems are serrate—a nice word meaning covered with sawlike teeth—allowing them to cling to shirt sleeves and garden gloves. The flowers are very small, green, full of pollen, and not particularly attractive, but they are usually hidden by the leaves anyway.

Perennial hops is *Humulus lupulus.* The species is from the Latin *lupus,* or wolf, because as Pliny said, it strangles others by its climbing embrace, as a wolf does a sheep. The English name hop is derived from the Anglo-Saxon *hoppan,* to climb.

H. lupulus is a native of Europe and has naturalized in moist soil, especially along riverbanks and waste places, and it ranges from Nova Scotia to Manitoba, Montana, and California, and south to North Carolina, West Virginia, Kentucky, much of New York, and some in northern New Jersey. The fruits are used in brewing beer. Yellow glands that secrete the bitter lupulin are found in many parts of the plants, but chiefly on the fruit.

A fast grower, a vine has been known to clock thirty feet in one season. Plants are dioecious; the greenish yellow male flowers are in panicles on one plant, while the female flowers, which produce the fruits called hops, grow in axillary spikes. There is an attractive form with yellow foliage called 'Aureus'.

The Romans raised hops, using the young shoots as a luxury food. In 1566, Rembert Dodoens, a Belgian botanist, called hops a kitchen herb and wrote in his herbal, *Cruxdeboeck,* "Before its tender shoots produce leaves, they are eaten in salads, and are a good and whole- some treat."

But for beer, hops have been around since antiquity. In central Europe, cultivation dates from the middle of the eighth century. They were introduced into England from Flanders in 1524, but were not used in making brew until 1530, during the reign of Henry VIII.

C. Pierpont Johnson, in *The Useful Plants of Great Britain,* a title of masterful understatement, wrote, "Before the use of hops, the beverage always went by the name of ale . . . brewed either from malt alone, or from a mixture of the latter with honey, and flavored, not with hops, but with heath-tops, germander, and various other bitter and aromatic herbs." Long after hops entered England, brew flavored the old-fash- ioned way was called ale. The German or Dutch word *Bier* was used only when hops were employed to produce the characteristic taste.

On September 3, 1814, Jefferson wrote: "Began to malt wheat. A bushel will make 8. or 10. gallons of strong beer such as will keep for years, taking 3/4 lb of hops for every bushel of wheat."

The hops and leaves were once also used when dried as a pillow stuffing to treat insomnia. In 1919, hops were still found in London's Covent Garden, tied in small bundles for table use. The shoots were chopped very fine and dressed with butter or cream. And Julian A. Steyermark, in the 1963 *Spring Flora of Missouri*, wrote of the use of hops in breadmaking prior to commercial yeast.

Horticulturists do not agree on the use of hops in the garden. Taylor said: "The hop of commerce is widely grown for brewing. Its culture, however, is an agricultural operation and scarcely a hort. subject for *The Garden Dictionary*." But according to Robinson: "*H. lupulus*, a well-known vigorous twining perennial is admirable for bowers, especially when vegetation that disappears in winter is desired; and will soon run wild in almost any soil, among shrubs or hedgerows. A slender plant climbing up an Apple or other fruit tree, near the mixed border, looks well."

Neltje Blanchan's entry reads: "Hop, perennial *(Humulus Lupulus)*. Common hop, growing 15 to 20 feet. Effective when in fruit. Bold, palmate foliage, dark green. Herbaceous top, dying down annually."

At the Herb Garden of the Brooklyn Botanic Garden, tall tripods made of bamboo stakes and intertwined with hop vines make an attractive summer display.

HYACINTHS

On March 30, 1766, Jefferson noted in his *Garden Book* that the purple hyacinth was beginning to bloom. He watched these bulbs blooming again on March 23, 1767, and added that the feathered hyacinth bloomed on April 25. Then again in April 1782, both the hyacinth and the feathered form were noted on his "Calendar of Bloom Flowers." In 1807, Jefferson planted an oval bed with four different colors of double hyacinths, their distribution probably based on a plan drawn by Bernard M'Mahon for his book. Between 1807 and 1812, M'Mahon made four shipments of hyacinth bulbs, noting, "They are of the first rate kinds, and nearly of as many varieties as roots."

Lady Skipworth listed four kinds of hyacinths: double blue and blush-colored; grape hyacinths; and feathered hyacinths. And Ann Leighton noted in *American Gardens in the Eighteenth Century* that Jefferson's *Hyacinthus comosus* bloomed in 1791, but the scientific name is properly *Muscari comosus* var. *monstrosum*, the tassled hyacinth.

In Jefferson's time, the hyacinth was not what it is for today's gardeners. The bulbs were grown in production fields for their flowers, without any special selections produced by the nurseries. In fact, M'Mahon's list of hyacinth bulbs includes such common names as the bending hyacinth, the musk grape hyacinth, and European harebells, which were called by the scientific name of *Hyacinthus non scriptus* (today known as *Endymion nonscriptus,* and having nothing to do with the oriental genus).

THE ORIENTAL HYACINTH
Hyacinthus orientalis

Over the years, the scientific names have been culled, and today *Hyacinthus* is a one-species genus, the species being *orientalis.* The genus is from the ancient Greek name extolled by the classic poets from Homer and Virgil to Pliny. Descriptions of the flower of old honor the petals as being a violet-red, said to spring from the blood of the dead Hyacinthus.

Hyacinthus was a handsome youth passionately beloved by Apollo. The lad accompanied the god everywhere he went. One sunny afternoon, they played a game of quoits, and Apollo sent the heavy metal iron ring high and far. Hyacinthus ran forward to catch it but missed it, and upon striking the earth, the quoit bounced up and struck the lad's forehead. No matter what powers Apollo called upon, Hyacinthus died on the spot. (Godly rumor said that Zephyrus, the West Wind, also loved the boy and blew the quoit off course.) Linnaeus confirmed the scientific name in 1737.

The first bulbs to reach England arrived from Persia in 1560 and were immediately popular. Parkinson, writing in his *Paradisus,* described a number of varieties, and one hundred years later, the Dutch were said to have raised over two thousand varieties, one being called 'The King of Great Britain' and fetching £100 for each bulb.

As the bulbs became easier to buy and prices fell, soon everybody was growing them in pots and hyacinth glasses (for they force easily in water), the floral scent probably helping alleviate the musty smell of closed-up apartments.

Shelley wrote in his poem "The Sensitive Plant":

And the hyacinth purple and white and blue,
Which flung from its bells a sweet peal anew,
Of music so delicate, soft and intense,
It was felt like an odour within the sense . . .

Cultivating the hyacinth is very simple. The bulbs need a good, rich soil, reasonably well drained. Once planted, they can remain in the same spot for years.

THE GRAPE HYACINTH
Muscari botryoides

Grape hyacinths are natives of Europe and have been favorites in gardens for centuries. They are perfect mixed with other spring-flowering bulbs, in rock gardens, or grown in pots. The most popular garden species is *Muscari botryoides*, with the genus referring to the Latin *moschus*, or musk, alluding to the heavy scent produced by some species. Their common name is taken from the clusters of unopened buds, piled up like little grapes. *Botryoides* is from the Greek for little grapes.

The English artist and critic John Ruskin said of the grape hyacinth, "[It was] as if a cluster of grapes and a hive of honey had been distilled and pressed together in one small boss of celled and beaded blue."

A white-flowered cultivar known as 'Alba', which Parkinson called pearls of Spain, was very popular in Elizabethan gardens.

THE FEATHERED HYACINTH
Muscari comosus

Jefferson's *Hyacinthus comosus* is known today as *Muscari comosus* (syn. *plumosum*), a plant that is either liked or hated. Parkinson called it "the great purple faire haired Iacinth, or Purse tassel," and in point of fact, it looks more like a tassel than a flower. According to Louise Beebe Wilder, America's great garden writer of the 1930s and 1940s, the late Reverend Joseph Jacob, who made an exhaustive study of the various grape hyacinths, classed it among his "lunatic flowers," as the upper flowers are sterile, and the drooping lower fertile flowers bloom in a curious green color.

The variety known as *Muscari comosus* var. *monstrosum*, or feathered hyacinth, is, according to Wilder, "a curious-looking individual, for all its flowers are turned to slender filaments (vegetable hairs, some one called them) of a soft purplish or dove color. If the weather is kind, the effect of his floral feather is very pretty; otherwise it is well to keep the eyes busy elsewhere, for the soaked and bedraggled plume presents a sorry spectacle. One feels it would rather not be looked at."

She adds that it doubtless appealed to the Victorian taste.

THE JEFFERSON'S TWINLEAF

Jeffersonia diphylla

On May 18, 1792, American botanist Benjamin Smith Barton read a paper before the American Philosophical Society, which met that day in Philadelphia. Included in the activities planned for the meeting were the changing of the name of a native Virginia wildflower from *Podophyllum diphyllum* to *Jeffersonia diphylla.*

I was reminded the other day that no botanist or collector would name a new plant *Bushii* or *Goreacii* or even *Cheneyei;* there already is a *Clintonia,* but it was named back in the 1700s for Gov. De Witt Clinton of New York, who was an accomplished botanist.

Originally, Linnaeus christened the twinleaf as *Podophyllum diphyllum,* making it a sister species of the May-apple, basing his classification on herbarium plants collected in Virginia. Forty years later, Benjamin Smith Barton saw the twinleaf growing in the garden of his fellow Pennsylvania botanist and gardener William Bartram. Noticing the distinctive qualities of the plant, he renamed it *Jeffersonia diphylla,* the species name for the two-parted leaf that superficially appears to be two leaves. At that time, Jefferson was already a famous statesman of Virginia and was currently George Washington's secretary of state, soon to be the nation's third president.

Lest you think these men were but financiers who dabbled in horticulture for society's sake, or owned hardware stores and attended meetings to push gardening supplies, or were politicians seeking power, let
me introduce you to Barton and Bartram, typical educated men of
America in their day.

Son of a clergyman, Benjamin Smith Barton (1766–1815) was
born in Lancaster, Pennsylvania. His mother was sister to the distinguished astronomer David Rittenhouse. In 1785, Barton accompanied a party headed by his uncle, who had been commissioned to
survey and mark the western boundary between Pennsylvania and
Maryland. Meeting with Indians while so engaged, Barton began a
lifelong study of their customs, history, and diseases. In 1786, he
went to Edinburgh to study medicine, spent two years there, and then
completed his medical training at Gottingen. Upon his return to
Philadelphia, he was appointed, at the age of twenty-three, to the first
professorship of natural history and botany in the United States, at
the University of Pennsylvania, a chair he held for twenty-four years.

According to one authority, "he did more than any one of his con-
temporaries in diffusing a taste for the natural sciences among the
young men who then resorted to that school." He authored *Elements of
Botany; or, Outlines of the Natural History of Vegetables,* published in 1803,
the first textbook of botany written in the United States. And because
of his early death he never did edit the scientific portions of Jefferson's great project, the Lewis and Clark Expedition.

John Bartram (1699–1777) is known as the father of American
botany. Born on May 23, 1699, in Darby, Pennsylvania, he was self-
educated but through constant reading became an intellect of his
day. Married twice, he had nine children, including son William
(1739–1823) who became a famous ornithologist.

In 1728, Bartram senior founded the first botanical garden in
America, in Kingsessing, Pennsylvania, on the Schuylkill River. There
he housed native and exotic plant species and delved into the lore of
medicinal plants.

Along the way, he became a great native plant collector as he wandered the mountains and valleys of the fledgling United States, at a
time when travel was not only difficult, but often hazardous to one's

health. He visited Maryland, Virginia, New York, and the Carolinas, including the Blue Ridge Mountains, where he wended his way on trails not over ten miles from where I write these words.

In 1765, he was appointed botanist to King George, with an annual salary of £50, and with his son William in tow, he began a journey up the St. John's River, going farther than any European had ever gone before. All along the way, he collected and sent plants back to Philadelphia while William took care of the record keeping, a job that John never really cottoned to.

At the American Philosophical Society meeting in 1792, after ample food was served, Barton stood before the gathering and said, "As I have not found it described by any authors, except Linnaeus and Clayton, neither of whom had seen the flowers and it is, certainly, a new family genus, I take the liberty of making it known to the botanist by the name *Jeffersonia*, in honour of Thomas Jefferson, Esq., Secretary of State to the United States." Barton went on to say that Jefferson was being honored not for his political character or literary reputation, but because "in the various departments of . . . botany and in zoology, the information of this gentleman is equaled by that of few persons in the United States." Not having the benefit of a contemporary wormhole in space or a time machine, especially as envisioned by H. G. Wells, I can only imagine that smoke-filled room, with its well-worn, hand-hewn tables, heavily marked with endless intertwined circles from countless tankers hitting the wood, not only for emphasis, but for celebration as well. Unfortunately, Jefferson was not present; he had been unable to attend the meeting because of official political duties.

Jeffersonia is at home in the rich and fertile woods of eastern Pennsylvania, New York, and Ontario, west to Wisconsin and Iowa, then south to Virginia and Tennessee. In Virginia, it grows at an altitude of twenty-five hundred feet. Other common names include ground-squirrel pea, helmet-pod, Dutchman's pipe, yellow-root, and rheumatism-root. There are two species; the other is *Jeffersonia dubia*, which grows in Southeast Asia, including Manchuria, and has light lavender flowers.

Palmately veined and palmately lobed leaves arise from a tangled root and in very early spring twine around eight-inch stems topped with small, white flowers with eight petals, looking a great deal like neighboring bloodroot *(Sanguinaria canadensis)*. Upon maturity, the ripening ovary forms a capsule that closely resembles a helmet or the kind of capped pipe that burgermeisters once smoked in Rembrandt paintings. When ripe, the lid of the seedpod lifts up, and the seed is scattered like salt from a shaker.

The leaves eventually reach a length of six inches, just about the time that the seed capsule is ripe, and they are parted lengthwise into two wings, hence the common name of twinleaf. A well-grown plant gets larger as time goes by. When mature, it is an obvious stellar addition to any garden.

Jeffersonia belongs to the barberry family, Berberidaceae, which represents some 15 genera and about 650 species, widespread across the north temperate zone. Of these, 8 genera and 33 species are indigenous to the continental United States and Canada. Many are well-known plants, including that beautiful wildflower the blue cohosh *(Caulophyllum thalictroides)*, the May-apple *(Podophyllum peltatum)*, and the Oregon-grape *(Mahonia spp.)*.

Native Americans used a root tea for cramps, spasms, nervous excitability, diarrhea, dropsy, and urinary infections. It also served as a diuretic for kidney stones, a gargle for sore throats, and externally, as a wash to treat rheumatism, ulcers, inflammation, and cancerous and other sores. But the medical profession of today warns that any preparation should be used with extreme caution, as the chemical constituents are probably toxic.

Plants are easily grown from seed and will often self-sow around the garden. Twinleaf also transplants well and is a garden natural, when provided with good light but summer shade, plenty of humus in the soil, and moisture when rains are sparse. The American Rock Garden Society usually has twinleaf seeds in its seed exchange.

For best germination, seeds should be fresh. Collect them as the capsules ripen, before ants can carry off the seeds to their nests. Allow at least three years from seed to flower. It can also be grown in pots in a cool greenhouse.

In the wild, *Jeffersonia* is surprisingly adaptable to various soil conditions. Some gardeners advise growing the plants in calcareous soil;

others prefer a humus-rich acidic soil. Mulch well, especially in areas with wide temperature fluctuations in winter.

To me, the twinleaf is worth a year's wait for a sighting of the blooms. According to T. S. Eliot in "The Love Song of J. Alfred Prufrock," one way to note the passing of time is measuring out the years with coffee spoons. Frankly, I'd rather use the twinleaf as a benchmark—it makes the measurement far more worthwhile.

PEA FLOWERS

Lathyrus spp.

THE SWEET PEA
Lathyrus odoratus

Jefferson obtained sweet pea seeds *(Lathyrus odoratus)* from André Thouin of Paris and in 1811 set the plants in his oval beds. These English favorites were so popular with eighteenth-century gardeners that Bernard M'Mahon listed five varieties in his calendar. Among the other common names were lady peas and painted lady peas.

In part of the continuing love-hate relationship between the Americans and the English, sweet pea seeds were listed by the early seedswomen of Boston, who carried them back in 1760.

The scientific name is *Lathyrus,* from the ancient Greek name for the pea used by Theophrastus. It's a genus of about one hundred species of often tendril-climbing herbs, usually natives of temperate regions, with a few coming from tropical mountain ranges.

The first leaves of a pea seedling have no tendrils, but the next alternately compound leaves consist of seven leaflets. The stems are winged, with a pair of large, grasping stipules of clasping threads at the base of each leaf.

The sweet pea blossom has such a garden history that each part of the flower has a name. The great upper petal of the blossom is called the banner, and when it stands upright, the flower is open. Beneath the banner you find the wings, two petals which hang like a peaked roof above the bottom structure known as the keel. Within the keel are found the pistil and the stamens. If you touch the point of the keel with a fingertip, a pollen brush appears and will dust your finger, or a bee whose weight opens the keel; the pollen is then deposited on another stigma.

After fertilization, the petals fall, and a young pod appears. As the pod ripens, its moisture is lost, and the pod becomes dry and hard. From a combination of dew-damping at night and the sun's heat by day, the pod finally warps, and each side coils into a spiral, flinging seed in many directions and over a distance of many feet.

Sweet peas have been English favorites since they were introduced to English gardens in 1699 by one Father Francisco Cupani, who sent seeds from southern Italy and Sicily to his friend Doctor Uvedale, a surgeon who lived near London, close to the present Uvedale Road, named in the doctor's memory. The doctor was an enthusiastic amateur gardener who collected many rare and exotic plants. These peas disappeared from sight for about twenty years, until at the London flower market a new plant surfaced, having the characteristics of a low climber and bearing powerfully scented red and purple flowers.

Sanitation in London of that time was marginal at best, and these flowers were quite popular. Even Good Queen Anne, when walking through her own court, carried the pocket melon *(Cucumis melo)*, inhaling its fragrance now and then, so as to be revived from the palace odors of the day.

By 1730, sweet peas were available commercially, and the first variety appeared. It was called 'Painted Lady' and was pink and white. In the 1850s, the flowers were also well known in what is today the Czech Republic, as a monk, Father Gregor Mendel, used them for his experiments in plant genetics (unhappily, because of monastery politics, his discoveries were not recognized until 1900).

To quote Alice Morse Earle, from her *Old Time Gardens:*

We have all seen the print, if not the portrait, of Queen Elizabeth garbed in a white satin robe magnificently embroidered with open pea-pods and butterflies. A "City of London Madam" had a delightful head ornament of open pea-pods filled with peas of pearls; this was worn over a hood of gold-embroidered muslin, and with dyed red hair, must have been a most modish affair.

They have been a much-loved flower of the people both in England and America, and they were at home in cottage borders and fine gardens; were placed in vases, and carried in nosegays and posies. . . . They had beauty of color and a universally loved perfume. A bicentenary exhibition of sweet peas was given in London in July, 1900; now there is formed a Sweet Pea Society.

Keats, who wrote in his letters that his love of flowers was wholly for those of the "common garden sort," penned these words about the sweet pea:

Here are sweet peas on tiptoe for a flight,
With wings of delicated flush o'er delicate white,
And taper fingers catching at all things,
To bind them all about with tiny rings.

Unfortunately for lovers of floral odor, the last two hundred-some years have not been for the best, as the majority of modern sweet peas have sacrificed much of their aroma for bumptious size and color. H. L. V. Fletcher wrote of this in "The-Great-Lament-of-the-Sweet-Peas-Which-Lost-Their-Perfume," pointing out that by the year 1800, big and beautifully colored blossoms were quite common, but the bigger the flowers, the weaker the scent. The same thing happened to roses: The bigger and blousier the blossom, the poorer the scent. Nature is parsimonious: Blossoms get gaudier, so pollinators need less odor to find the flower. Nature hates waste, so the flowers lose fragrance. Eventually bees, bugs, and butterflies are led to flowers by the same fierce attractions that lead many of our citizens to the gaudier malls and fashion outlets.

Then Charles Unwin, of the English seedhouse that bears his name, received some sweet pea seeds from an English village almost lost at the edge of time. The seeds produced flowers that were small and not very attractive, but their fragrance was sheer delight, leading

Unwin to say, "Until that moment I never fully realized why sweet peas were so named."

In 1904, again in England, Silas Cole, the gardener to Count Spencer, exhibited a new form of sweet pea flower with larger blossoms and wonderfully ruffled edges. It was the beginning of an entirely new variety called 'Countess Spencer'. Plant breeders then crossed the ruffled with the others, and today the varieties are amazing. Buy your seed from only the best sources, where the words that surround the fantastic floral pictures are less hyperbole and more truthful, especially when it comes to scent.

Few gardeners realize that before 1913, no sweet peas were available in the winter. A few years earlier, some tall and rangy plants were found to come into bloom shortly before Christmas, and these led to the now popular winter-flowering sweet peas.

Thanks to plant genetics, the present-day sweet pea not only climbs up to eight feet high, but also crawls, so strings and staking for a vining support are not always necessary. Besides being excellent cut flowers, the dwarf and trailing types of sweet peas can be used as flowering screens in a bed or border.

Sweet peas need deep, moist, cool, and well-prepared soil, and the gardener should start as soon as the ground can be worked. Sow the seeds directly outdoors, or start them indoors in a cool place about six weeks before the last frost, using individual three-inch peat pots. Soak the seeds overnight in warm water. Space them according to the variety used. Sweet peas prefer cool surroundings, so gardeners in the warmer parts of the country should look for heat-resistant varieties.

THE EVERLASTING PEA
Lathyrus latifolius

The everlasting pea *(Lathyrus latifolius)* has naturalized over much of the United States and parts of Canada. It was among the hardy perennial flowers mentioned by Jefferson in 1771, and he planted it in his oval bed in 1807. Unlike the sweet pea *(Lathyrus odoratus)*, the everlasting pea is not fussy as to soil or climate. It grows along roadsides throughout the Southeast, happily consumed by fat and sassy ground-hogs, continuing to flower until cut back by frost and cold.

A native of Southern Europe, this is a vigorous climber and scram-bler, often reaching lengths of nine feet in just one growing season. It has broadly winged stems and petioles, dark green oval or elliptic leaves consisting of a single pair of lanceolate leaflets up to three inches long, and a branched terminal tendril for clasping. The flowers are three-quarters to one inch long, usually purplish pink, though there are variations from plant to plant, with as many as ten blossoms on long-stalked axillary racemes.

Because this is a tough (especially when compared with the typical sweet pea) and very attractive plant, it should come as no surprise that a few cultivars are available. These include 'Pink Pearl', with flowers of a lovely pearly shade of pink in very conspicuous clusters, each con-taining up to six flowers; 'White Pearl', with flowers of a beautiful pearly white; and 'Red Pearl', with flowers of lovely carmine red.

In my garden, I have a Russian olive in the center of the perennial border, a shrub that is clipped back with passion every spring and kept at a height of seven feet. At its base are planted the everlasting pea 'White Pearl'. By midsummer, the vines clamber up the olive, and the top is covered with the beautiful blossoms.

THE TREE MALLOW

Lavatera olbia

In 1807, Jefferson planted seeds of the tree mallow, which he called the shrub marshmallow, in the nursery at the southeastern end of the vegetable garden. Dr. Antoine Gouan (1733–1821), of Montpelier, France, sent seeds from France. Gouan was the first botanist to introduce binary nomenclature into France, the first to publish a flora almost totally Linnaean in its approach to classification, and most likely had a great deal in common with Jefferson. He was also known for his collections of algae taken from the waters around Marseilles.

The nickname of marshmallow for a flower that bears no resemblance to the confection seems somewhat strange, until a little research provides the answer. Today a marshmallow is made of cornstarch, syrup, gelatin, and lots of sugar, but back in the eighteenth century and earlier, the sap found in the roots of hollyhocks or rose mallows, specifically *Althea officinalis*, was something else again. The roots contain a mild mucilage, described by Girard as a "thick, tough, white within [containing] a clammie and slimie juice." Some European sweetmeat makers used the roots for a confectionary paste thought to be valuable for coughs and sore throats. Marsh, of course refers to a favored habitat of damp meadows, by the sides of ditches, and in salt marshes.

But Jefferson's shrub was properly called the tree mallow *(Lavatera olbia)*. It's one of a genus of summer-flowering plants, once widely cultivated in European and American gardens, but today having (sadly) considerably less cachet. They originally came from around the Mediterranean, with a few species found in the Canary Islands and the Channel Islands off Southern California and Baja California. Growing plants with histories, ones that originate in far-off lands, always lends a sense of adventure to gardening, and if you could find the plant that Jefferson grew, there would be a garden link not only with Monticello, but with the warm sands and seas of Sardinia.

The genus was named in honor of the Lavater Brothers of Zurich, sixteenth-century Swiss naturalists and physicians. The species is named for the city of Olbia, the ancient Roman port on the eastern shore of Sardinia.

Tree mallows made their way to English gardens in 1570, imported from southern France. They're a branched shrub, up to seven feet tall, with three-lobed leaves and flowers with rounded petals, usually a reddish purple.

Today they've been largely replaced by another tree mallow, *Lavatera arborea*, a native of Southern Europe. If started early in the spring, this treelike biennial will bloom the first year. It has soft, velvet-to-the-touch leaves and is quite capable of bearing a profusion of purple-pink flowers, petals veined with purple, all summer long—if happily sited in full sun and well-drained soil. A variety called var. *variegata* bears white variegated leaves. Roots of these mallows resent disturbance, so start seeds in early spring where the plants are to grow, or use large peat pots for germination.

There is an annual member of the tree mallows known as *Lavatera trimestris*, a wonderful, heat-tolerant plant that can reach a height of three feet by summer's end. By midsummer, the twiglike branches are covered with hollyhocklike trumpets until cut down by frost.

THE GARDEN LILIES

Lilium spp.

Lilies represent about eight species of bulbous plants, natives of the temperate regions of the Northern Hemisphere. They have been gardened for thousands of years. *Lilium* is an old Latin name akin to the Greek *Leirion* and used by Theophrastus for the Madonna lily.

When it comes to American lilies, in 1734 Collinson wrote to Bartram: "Please to remember all your sorts of lilies as they happen in thy way. Your Spotted Martagons will be very acceptable." Martagons referred to the style of turban worn by Sultan Muhammed I and was applied to lilies with recurved petals rather than bell-shaped blossoms.

In Paris in 1786, Jefferson wrote home to his gardener requesting that a number of seeds be sent over, including the so-called lily of Canada, or the Canada martagon *(Lilium canadense)*. This lily is found in deciduous woodlands of eastern North America and grew wild not far from Monticello. In fact, it's at home from Nova Scotia south to Georgia, growing between four and five feet in height. Flowers are borne on long stems or pedicels, four or five on each stem, and orange-yellow in color, spotted with purple-brown. Petals recurve outward without being reflexed. The bulbs prefer an acid soil.

The Madonna lilies *(Lilium candidum)* have been in gardens since the Minoan culture was at its height, fifteen hundred years before the birth of Christ. Not only did they grace walled gardens, but they also flourished in pots and as cut flowers.

After that stellar career in the days of old, however, the lily supposedly fell from grace in the Garden of Gethsemane, when Christ walked through the night before his death, for every other flower except what was thought to be a lily, but turned out to be a fritillaria, bowed its head.

Whatever the flower was, the beautiful white petals of the Madonna lily soon restored the lily's reputation for purity, and these flowers became symbols of the Virgin. The Greeks and Romans used these white lilies to crown the bride and groom, combining the blossoms with sheaths of wheat, supposedly leading to a clean and fertile life.

On the night she went to Holofernes, Judith was said to have worn a Madonna lily to keep away the evil she intended to inflict upon him. And in Spain of 1048, an image of the Virgin was seen to emerge from a lily while a nearby king lay in his death throes. When word of the lily reached his bed, he sprang from his bedclothes, completely restored to health. Thus the Knights of St. Mary of the Lily was formed, some three centuries before a similar organization was founded by one of the French kings.

While Jefferson grew the Madonna lily, it was so common by the 1700s that it merely gets a brief mention: A "Calendar of the Bloom of Flowers" from 1782, found in *The Garden and Farm Garden Books,* has a note on top saying, "They were planted this spring, and the season was very backward."

A "Fiery Lil." is noted as blooming in May, but this was probably *Lilium chalcedonicum.* In 1742, Peter Collinson in England sent this lily to John Custis in America. The specific name refers to Chalcedon, a city of Bithynia in Asia Minor where, in 451 A.D., the Catholic Church held its Fourth Ecumenical Council. Chalcedony, a mineral that exhibits a waxy glow, is also found there. This species is thought to be the actual "lily of the field" mentioned in the Bible. Gerard wrote in his *Herbal* that "it groweth wild in the fields many days journey beyond Constantinople." One of the most intensely colored lilies for gardens, each stem holds up to ten sweetly fragrant, bright mandarin red, pendulous blooms with thick, recurved, waxy petals. The attractive leaves are edged with silver. Today this lily is rarely found in gardens.

The American Turk's-cap lily *(Lilium superbum)* is a featured flower in *The Temple of Flora,* Dr. Robert Thornton's salute to incredible flowers, where it's called the superb lily (and incorrectly drawn with mountains in the background rather than wooded wetlands). In 1812, Jefferson ordered the bulbs from M'Mahon—a momentous year.

At one time, the Turk's-caps ruled in the East. Railroad passengers who traveled between New York and Boston could look out on low meadows and marshes in July and August and see clusters of deep yellow, orange, or flame-colored lilies, standing above the other plants and grasses. It even outnumbered the purple loosestrife *(Lythrum salicaria)*, itself a flower once spoken of in terms of beauty rather than with curses, before the spread of its blatant magenta spires had gotten out of hand.

Our native Turk's-cap is not to be confused with the English *Lilium martagon,* a plant with many blossoms but only reaching a height of six feet or so, modest by *superbum* standards. This great lily was one of the earliest of the so-called exotic lilies introduced into Europe and has been known to grow in continental gardens for over 250 years. It was described by Linnaeus and was illustrated by Pierre Joseph Redouté in his book *Lilies and Related Flowers.*

Plants will rarely have just a few flowers. Rather, they will usually bear up to thirty blossoms on stems often topping eight feet, and even forty blooms have been counted on one plant. The three petals and their adjoining sepals come in bright oranges, yellows, and reds, spotted with black, and are beautifully reflexed. Six stamens end with coats of dark brown pollen, and the single pistil is clearly exposed.

The pollinators are specialized bees, usually the leaf-cutters. They snip more or less circular pieces out of leaves and petals, then fit these pieces together with great skill to form tight, thimble-shaped cells in which to lay eggs in underground nesting sites.

These lilies are great at the edge of a woodland or in front of a rock wall. Damp bottomland is a perfect place to incorporate these plants so that the bulbs are close to water and thus, even in the hottest of summers, will never lack for moisture.

Madonna lilies prefer shallow planting, but most of the other species and cultivars have flowering stems that produce roots as they grow up to the surface, and depth must be allowed for this growth habit. This means setting the bulbs four to eight inches deep. Use good, well-drained, fertile soil, laced with compost, and add a teaspoon of bonemeal in the bottom of each hole.

Lilies grow beautifully in pots, giving them great advantages over many perennials. Unlike other bulbs, those of lilies are never dormant. Once blooming is over, the bulbs begin to grow new roots, a process that should not be interrupted. If you purchase bulbs, plant them immediately. The scales that surround each bulb have no protective covering and are easily broken, so handle with care is the rule when planting lilies.

THE BRILLIANT CARDINAL FLOWER

Lobelia cardinalis

Often Americans find out about their best and brightest from other parts of the world, never realizing that the star is on their own turf.

In 1807, Jefferson planted the cardinal flower *(Lobelia cardinalis)* in his garden with seed obtained from Bernard M'Mahon. At that time, it was considered one of the showiest plants for the English herbaceous border. Lafayette was so enchanted by the plant that he requested seeds from Washington.

Jefferson may not have realized this, but the plant grew not far from home. In his book, M'Mahon had urged American gardeners to go out and look for wildflowers, pointing out that from mid to late summer, their gardens were "almost destitute of bloom," while nearby meadows were awash with color.

Every summer, about the middle of July, when you begin to think it will never be cool again, there's nothing like a peaceful afternoon walk in the woods, especially if you can amble along a watered creek or stream. Though the air might be excessively warm even under a canopy of leaves, there always seems to be a faint breath of cool air drifting up from the tumbling waters.

The birds are silent. A few gnats bob up and down, and a wasp or two tests the mud at the stream's edge. Blue sky is just visible through the leaves of the canopied trees that bend over your head; the only sound is that of the ripples rushing between the rocks.

Suddenly, out of the corner of your eye, you are aware of a flash of brilliant color. Bright dots of a rich, deep red dance before you, the uppermost blossom at least three feet from the ground.

No other flower of the woods is as blatant as this. It is that one touch of red found in a Corot painting, the brilliance of a red balloon against a Carolina blue sky, or a single stoplight on an empty city street on a gray and rainy day. Even the bird that shares its name cannot hold a candle to its intense hue.

Seeds of the cardinal flowers were sent back to France after being found "neere the river of Canada, where the French plantation in America is seated," when Rembrandt was a teenager, for they were growing in English gardens before 1630, having been introduced to the Brits in 1626. One of the duties of any explorer was to send home rare and unusual plants, but the original discoverer of this particular flower has been lost to time.

Imagine that parade of wealth passing before the French court, where both royal family and churchly eyes looked upon furs of every description; Native American garments with beads shimmering on patches of deerhide; and there, at the rear of the presenters, a vase of newly blooming flowers grown quickly from seed in the Jardin Royal at Paris and viewed as as much of a symbol of wealth as gold.

The popular name for *Lobelia cardinalis* reflects the shade of red found in the hats worn by seventy ecclesiastical princes of the Roman Church. Years later, Linnaeus named the genus *Lobelia* in honor of Matthias de l'Obel, a Flemish botanist who became physician to James I of England. The cardinal flower has other common names, including red lobelia, Indian-pink, red-birds, and red-flags, but somehow they do not convey the brightness of the most common alias.

At one time, the cardinal flower was used by Native Americans as a root tea for the treatment of stomachaches, typhoid, and even social diseases, but today's journals note that the plant is potentially toxic.

It's a lucky thing for the world of beauty that this flower—forever freely picked by those who see it—sets abundant seed and germinates with ease, or it would have long since passed from the scene.

Even though its home in nature is along streambanks and wet places, the cardinal flower can be adapted to grow in the garden. Most dealers in wildflowers carry either seeds or plants grown in nurseries, as cardinal flowers are one of America's favorites. And sadly, for the choice has been made, it would have been a far wiser selection for a national flower than the rose.

Plant breeders have developed new forms, often with larger blooms. Some have flowers in lavender shades, and there is even a white form. A few of them are interesting, but perhaps the breeders should leave well enough alone.

Use plenty of peat moss when planting, and mulch well to keep the soil cool and moist. Make a slight depression where water can easily be added when rains are lacking.

Some years ago, while wandering through the Brooklyn Botanic Garden, I noticed a marvelous stand of cardinal flowers planted in front of a very large rock.

"There's a good reason for this flower's success," said one of the gardeners in attendance, "and that's water. This area is a bog area since I trenched it down about a foot or more and lined it with plastic sheeting. Then I added this rock." He pointed to the rock, about two feet high. It was no ordinary piece of rock. The crevices and channels that were part of its surface made it look like a mountain range in miniature.

The garden hosted a rock Penjing exhibit a few years earlier, in which rocks, single or in small groupings, were arranged in trays to depict miniature landscapes, often emphasizing the majesty of high mountains. The gardener asked if they could keep the unusual rock after the exhibit was over. He ran copper tubing underground from a source of water on the other side of the walkway, then up a cleft in the rock, filling in the cleft with cement to match the stone's color. The water trickled down to provide refreshment for moisture-loving plants, especially the cardinal flower.

Winter-kill usually happens when there is not enough moisture in the soil, so be sure your garden has plenty of water before winter knocks on the garden door. The best way to have flowers every year is to let a few plants go to seed; new plants will continually arise. Many gardeners separate and replant the clusters of new basal rosettes in the fall after bloom is over, but this can be a tricky proposition at best, especially in the mountain areas, where autumn frosts come early.

Another member of the *Lobelia* genus that was quite popular in Jefferson's time was the great blue lobelia *(Lobelia syphilitica)*. American and Canadian Indians had suggested the plant to Col. William Johnson, an early Indian negotiator and administrator, for its curative powers in treating syphilis or the French pox. Johnson had arrived from Ireland in 1738 to set up a trading business with the Indians and was considered, next to Benjamin Franklin, the most powerful American of his day.

Recipes said to take a handful of the roots, boil them in a quart of water, and drink the resulting liquid, beginning with half a pint at first, then increased to a full pint every day—if the patient could stand it—until cured. The other contemporary treatment involved the deadly poisonous chloride of mercury.

Johnson sent roots and seeds back to Europe, where Linnaeus began selling it to young Swedish socialites as a cure for the disease. In 1766, Sir John Hill (1717–75), author of the popular book *A British Herbal,* wrote a letter to John Bartram asking him to send four pounds of the blue cardinal to be used as a medicine.

Needless to say, the cure never worked.

HONESTY IN THE GARDEN

Lunaria annua

On April 9, 1767, Jefferson wrote that the lunaria were in bloom. On April 25, he noted that the lunaria were still in bloom but mentioned an indifferent flower. And Lady Skipworth and Bernard M'Mahon both talked about the plant.

As early as 1665, these flowers were growing plentifully in New England gardens, where they reminded colonial families of their English homes. It is now so common that both the white and the lavender-flowered forms grow along many roadsides and in gardens in the Southeast. Although many English gardeners grow honesty planted in masses as bedding flowers for early spring color, as well as their fragrance, generally lunarias are featured for their marvelous seedpods.

Lunaria is a plant that goes back many centuries. *Lunaria annua* is commonly known as honesty, penny-floure, money plant, silver-plate, satin-flower, and my favorite, the pricksong-flower. These names do not refer to the flower, but to the oval and shiny seedpods (or orbicular siliques), with their satiny, paper white septums. *Lunaria* comes from the Latin word for the moon. *Annua* means annual.

Most of the common names seem logical, but perhaps an explanation is in order for pricksong. On a sheet of English music from the Elizabethan period, the notes of music are called pricks, and the

134

whole sheet of notes is known as a pricksong. If you ever see such a sheet, you will immediately note the resemblance borne by the honesty seedpods.

According to Alice Morse Earl in *Old Time Gardens*, the use of honesty as a common name came into prominence at the close of the eighteenth century, when the Reverend William Hanbury advertised honesty seeds in a 1771 circular. I suspect because a man of the cloth was selling "money," it was considered an honest transaction. Others say that because you can see the seeds within their silky packet, it's a perfect example of honesty.

There are at least two species, both originally from Central and Southern Europe. *Lunaria annua* (syn. *Lunaria biennis*) is grown as an annual because if planted early, seedlings will quickly grow and flower the first year. But they are really biennials and sometimes will grow on for three years before perishing. *Lunaria redivia* is a perennial, with less effective seedpods. There is also a variegated form of both species.

Honesty reached maximum popularity in the 1800s, when the Victorians, both here and abroad, doted on such things as artificial and dried flowers, fruits, and stuffed squirrels in natural settings, and the lunaria's moonlike seedcases were actually hand-painted with tiny designs.

Well known to floral arrangers because of those delicate and shiny siliques, the flower was much used in charms and spells, as was just about everything even remotely connected to the moon.

When given a choice, honesty is a woodland plant, preferring partial shade or, in the South, full shade. Cut honesty seedpods and stems as soon as seeds start to turn brown. After drying, rub off the outer part of the pods to expose the papery silver disks. Hang bunches of honesty upside down in a dry, dark, open, airy place.

English seed companies, such as Chilterns, offer various cultivars, including 'Alba', which has white flowers, and 'Munstead Purple', grown by that grande dame of English gardens, Gertrude Jekyll. Flowers are described as being of great substance and quite distinct, being a bright rosy-purple, perfect for bedding out in spring.

But with the twenty-first century, new things are appearing on the lunaria scene. Springdale Crop Synergies, which has been growing this plant for many years, holds the record in the United Kingdom for the highest seed yields of any commercially grown crop, being the first U.K. company to bring this biennial into commercial production.

It all has to do with honesty seeds. An oil that's extracted from those seeds has been used on a small scale as an industrial lubricant. And their erucic acid component, like that of rape, a member of the mustard family, is important for several industrial uses. But because honesty is a biennial, it is uneconomical to grow as a source of erucic acid.

It's a third component that's of major interest, for the seeds' nervonic acid content has pharmaceutical uses. This fatty acid is found in several important groups of lipids in the human body, in particular, the very long chain fatty acids in central nervous system tissues. Eventually they might prove useful in treating demyelinating diseases such as adrenoleukodystrophy and multiple sclerosis.

All this from a plant that's been in gardens for centuries.

THE VIRGINIA BLUEBELL

Mertensia virginica

Back in April 1766, Jefferson wrote about "bluish colored, funnel-formed flowers in low-grounds in bloom." This was a reference to one of our most beautiful native wildflowers, the Virginia bluebell *(Mertensia virginica)*.

Arching stems up to three feet high bear clusters of pink buds that open to small, blue bells. They bloom with more exuberance in northern regions if they have nearly full sun during the early spring months. A place under late-leafing deciduous trees or trees that provide high, filtered shade is best. Smooth, pale green, oblong leaves reach up to two feet when plants are mature for the season.

Growing over much of the northern two-thirds of the country and down along the Appalachians, these native bluebells have a host of common names. Between 1734 and 1746, in correspondence with Peter Collinson of London, John Custis of Williamsburg referred to the Virginia bluebell as the "Mountain blew cowslip." Jefferson sometimes called them blue funnel flowers. They were also known as Virgina lungwort, probably for the leaves' resemblance to those of the regular lungwort *(Pulmonaria* spp.), and oysterleaf because of the oysterlike flavor of the leaves—although I've never tasted them to make sure. In the 1800s, New Englanders called them blue and pink ladies, in reference to a folk belief that the blossoms were hung on pins and used in fairy dances. Other names include Roanoke-bells and the Virginia-cowslip.

The plant was first described by John Banister (1654–92), a young clergyman sent to Virginia to be in charge of the spiritual health of the American colonies, a job best described as daunting. In 1678, Banister arrived at Charles Court County in Virginia, where he immediately became involved with collecting and drawing plants. Within two years, he sent a selection of those plants for publication in his *Catalogue of Plants Observed by Me in Virginia*, which saw print in 1688.

Banister was a botanist who specialized in freshwater snails, and who, upon writing about the backbone of a whale, was described by a colleague as a "Gentleman pretty curious in those things." Among his other publications were *Observations on the Natural Productions of Jamaica*, *The Insects of Virginia*, *Curiosities in Virginia*, *On Several Sorts of Snails*, and *A Description of the Snakeroot, Pistolochia or Serpentaria Virginiania*.

Banister died early. In 1692, while on an excursion above the falls of the James River, he was reported as having fallen from some high rocks and perished in the descent. But according to other eyewitnesses, he was accidentally shot by one of his companions.

His son John received a classical education in England. Upon his return, John was a well-known patriot. He was a member of the state assembly and the Continental Congress (March 1778 to September 1779). He died in 1787 near Hatchet's Run, Dinwiddie County, Virginia.

So why aren't Virginia bluebells called *Banisteria virginica?* Well, there are other bluebells in America, among them the leafy bluebell *(Mertensia oblonifolia)*, growing up to seven thousand feet in Montana and northern California; the mountain bluebell, or ciliate bluebell *(M. ciliata*, referring to a fringe of fine hairs that can be seen on the margins of back-lighted leaves), found at high altitudes from Oregon to New Mexico; and the Idaho bluebell *(M. campanulata)*, a meadow plant occurring only in central Idaho.

The German botanist Karl Heinrich Mertens (1796–1830) was collecting plants while on a Russian scientific expedition to Alaska in

1827. Upon discovering the various species of bluebells, he applied the name *Mertensia* to honor his father, Franz Karl Mertens (1764–1831), who was also a botanist.

The crucial factor when growing Virginia bluebells is adequate spring moisture. Add plenty of humus to the soil when planting, mulch well, and use the hose when springs are dry. The plants grow naturally in shaded spots and tolerate most soils, although a sandy, peaty soil is preferred. Once plants are established, they resent being disturbed.

Their habit of early withering away makes them a bit difficult to site in the garden, but their springtime show is so ethereal, it's worth the extra bit of trouble. They combine well with daffodils, bleeding-hearts (*Dicentra* spp.), tulips, and phlox (*Phlox subulata*). Plant something else in the area that will remain when the bluebells disappear. Ferns or hostas are great, or use a bunch of merrybells (*Uvularia grandiflora*) to make up for the loss of the bluebells. They are also ideally suited for planting under deciduous trees or along the banks of streams or ponds.

Mature bluebell tubers are best treated as bulbs and planted one to two inches deep in the fall, when they are usually offered by nurseries. Eventually, in the right spot, a single tuber makes a very large clump of flowers. Large roots can be divided during dormancy, but it's better to encourage self-sowing to increase the display.

Mertensia's location should be carefully marked to avoid damage from weeding or summer soil cultivation. Propagation is by seed or division, but seeds are more reliable. The best planting time is in October or from March to April.

MIMOSAS

THE SENSITIVE PLANT
Mimosa pudica

Over the past few centuries, hundreds of different vegetable, fruit, and flower seeds have disappeared, among them several species that provided entertainment or were some sort of curiosity.

During the time of the Civil War, gardeners often grew pseudoinsects—plants with parts resembling caterpillars, snails, and worms—used to liven up salads. The caterpillar plant *(Scorpiurus vermiculata)* is a hardy annual and a member of the legume family. The flowers are yellow, streaked with red, and not too attractive, but the seeds are produced in green pods that strikingly resemble their namesakes. In addition to the common caterpillar, there were three other species: the furrowed caterpillar, which had brown pods with gray-green furrows; the prickly caterpillar, with quarter-inch pods of brownish red with shades of green; and the villous or hairy caterpillar, larger than the prickly but marked with small points placed along longitudinal ridges. "No part of the plant is eatable," wrote Fearing Burr in *The Field and Garden Vegetables of America*, "but the pods, in their green state, are placed upon dishes of salads, where they so nearly resemble certain species of caterpillars as to completely deceive the uninitiated or inexperienced."

Snails (*Medicago orbicularis*) were an annual with seedpods that distinctly resembled some species of snails to a remarkable degree and were, according to Burr, "placed on dishes of salad for . . . pleasantly surprising the guests." Worms (*Astragalus hamosus*) were another annual plant with pods that in their green state resembled some descriptions of these animals.

In Jefferson's time, one plant grown as an entertainment or a vegetable curiosity was the sensitive plant (*Mimosa pudica*). On April 2, 1767, Jefferson planted seeds of the true sensitive plant at Shadwell. The last notation about the plant was on March 22, 1811, when Jefferson planted its seeds in the oval bed of the Northwest Piazza, along with mignonettes and delphiniums.

The plants have been around for a long time. In 1637, John Tradescant introduced the South American sensitive plant to English gardens. In 1773, William Bartram (son of John) explored the savannas about St. Mary's in South Carolina, where he found another species of mimosa that he called *M. sensitive*, a plant he described as having a larger flower and lacking prickles. Today it is known as *M. viva.*

The sensitive plant is also known as the humble plant, sleeping grass, and a host of names from tropical countries, including *vao fefe* in American Samoa, *rakau pikika* in the Cook Islands, and *pope ha'avare* in Tahiti. A native of Brazil, this short-lived evergreen subshrub is usually treated as an annual. The generic name is from the Latin *mimos,* for mimic, as the leaves in many species resemble animals with their sensitiveness. *Pudica* refers to the Latin for bashful or shy.

The plants have been popular for centuries as an entertainment, because when touched, the fernlike leaves with their hundreds of tiny, oval leaflets will close up just like a zipper in action, droop a bit, then within minutes open again to their original place. The stems are prickly, and small, fluffy, pink floral balls appear in the summer. The plant reaches a height of about three feet, and in many tropical areas, it's become a major pest.

The best explanation that I've ever found for the plant's activity was suggested by Pizzetti and Cocker in their book *Flowers: A Guide for Your Garden.* They pointed out that "the energy and complicated mechanism that would cause such a large plant to collapse completely in a manner of seconds is remarkable; especially so when the collapse is only temporary and reverses itself."

They also noted that the degree of sensitivity is highest when temperatures stay around eighty degrees F. At higher or lower temperatures, below about sixty degrees F or above one hundred degrees F, plants react more slowly—an action that possibly confirms the theory that mimosa's reaction to touch is actually a form of defense against grazing animals. And such animals would probably not feed at night, when temperatures drop, or during the hottest part of the day.

There have been a number of medicinal properties ascribed to the sensitive plant, including use as a form of birth control, to reduce fever, and to cure an attack of hysteria by tying this plant around the neck in order to rid the body of evil spirits and fevers they caused.

Grow these frost-tender plants from seed, providing full sun and a good, well-drained soil. When in active growth, water well.

THE MICHAUX'S SILK TREE
Albizia julibrissin

On April 13, 1809, Jefferson planted thirty-two seeds of a tree called *Mimosa julibritzin*, today known as *Albizia julibrissin*. It is not the sensitive plant, but the mimosa tree or silk tree, which has very similar leaflets except that they do not move. The genus honors the Italian naturalist Fillipo degli Albizzi; *julibrissin* is the Latinized form of an old Persian name.

André Michaux found the seeds in Paris, where they had originally arrived from China in the hands of that intrepid Frenchman Pierre d'Incarville, who also introduced the tree-of-heaven *(Ailanthus altissima)* into our country. Michaux started a small nursery at Ten Mile Station, north of Charleston, and by 1790 had planted those seeds that gave *Albizia* its beginnings in North America.

The silk tree is a glorious plant to some people and a noxious weed to others, since it does have the ability to seed about, and those seedlings, because of a tenacious taproot, are difficult to remove. But the waving leaves, made up of small leaflets, are tropical and attractive, and the flowers, packed with threadlike stamens, are very beautiful.

As a tree, it is hardier than many people realize. I know of trees in upstate New York that survive temperatures well below freezing. The powder-puff flowers are very fragrant during the day, but they also produce their sweet smell for the evening garden. They prefer a well-drained soil and flower best if planted in full sun.

THE MIRACLE OF PERU

Mirabilis jalapa

The miracle flower of Peru, the four o'clock, or as the French call it, *belle-de-nuit*, has been in gardens since sometime in the 1540s, when seeds were brought to Europe from the Peruvian Andes. *Mirabilis jalapa* caused such a stir in flower and garden circles that the first name for the genus was *Admirabilis*—at least until Linnaeus changed it to *Mirabilis*—from the Latin for wonderful.

The fact that single plants could bear flowers of different colors fired the imagination, especially since the miracle occurred without grafting other strains on the mother root (like the tomato/potato plant of today's supermarket weeklies). And the flowers punctually opened around four o'clock in the afternoon, except for areas with daylight saving time, where five became the rule. Finally, there was the perfume, a marvelous scent of sugar and lemony spice that varied from plant to plant.

The French were so excited by *Mirabilis* that the famous House of Worth actually designed ballgowns for women of fashion to wear at four-o'clock parties, where everyone would stand around sipping champagne and waiting for the miracle flowers to open, upon which they would all cry out: "Mon Dieu!"

THE MIRACLE OF PERU

Jefferson was said to have received his seeds from André Thoüin, but his first mention of *Mirabilis* appeared in "The Garden Book," where he reported their opening on July 18, 1767—just about the right time for bloom in that area of Virginia. And those seeds probably came from a local seed merchant, because the sale of these plants was common by the late 1600s. Ann Leighton, in *American Gardens in the Eighteenth Century*, mentions *Mirabilis* as being one of the most frequently cultivated plants in eighteenth-century American gardens.

The species name *jalapa* is frankly a mistake. Pharmacists believed that the purgative jalap (named for the Mexican town Jalapa) could be obtained from the tuberous roots of four o'clocks. But it turned out that that particular cathartic was too violent to use, and today the only benefit the tubers have is to manufacture a dye that makes Chinese seaweed noodles look more appetizing. Gregor Mendel used the plants in genetic experiments to prove that one grain of pollen was sufficient to produce a viable seed.

In the early 1900s, four o'clocks were noticed to have variegated leaves. In one strain, the leaves were mottled dark green and yellowish white, the color being caused by variations in the chlorophyll of individual plant cells; where two zones of color met, there was a band of cells that contained both colors. Experiments showed that seeds produced from flowers on green branches produced green plants regardless of the pollen used for fertilization. Flowers from variegated branches produced seedlings that were green, variegated, or white. Thus, plastids or cell bodies could be unaffected by chromosomal genes.

Four o'clocks are wonderful plants for the evening garden. They form little bushes often reaching a height of three feet and are covered with flowers. A number of colors are available, including red, yellow, white, or rose, and many blossoms will be striped or dashed with other colors.

In tropical America, four o'clocks are perennials and if left alone will soon form tuberous roots that weigh up to forty pounds. In our temperate gardens, the black tubers can reach the size of a baked potato. If dug in the fall and kept in a warm, dry place over the winter, they can be planted out the next spring as soon as the ground warms, just like a favorite bulb—although self-seedings from four o'clocks grow quickly. By the end of the second season, the tubers lose some of their resiliency and produce smaller plants.

In 1812, Bernard M'Mahon sent Jefferson seeds of our western native the sweet four o'clock (*Mirabilis longiflora*). Described as a leafy plant with stout, forking stems, and bearing long, slender leaves, this night bloomer has the most exalted white or pale pink trumpet flowers that bloom in the axils of the upper leaves. They look more like angels' trumpets than flowers.

There are a number of native American plants belonging to the four-o'clock family in addition to the original marvel of Peru. *Mirabilis multiflora* is a plant in many ways superior to others in the genus. The flowers open in late afternoon and on cloudy days, closing the next morning, but the color of the flowers is a brighter purple-rose than that found even in cultivars of *M. jalapa*, and they are larger, too. The plant itself is large, with branchings capable of making a circular mound four feet wide and up to twenty inches high. Because the flowers open in succession, the plants are often smothered in color, the blooms continuing throughout the summer.

Mirabilis nyctaginia, or in the older books, *Allionia nyctaginia*, has the common name umbrella wort because the developing seedpod resembles an umbrella with several warty seeds fastened at the center. The plants reach a two-foot height and are not as attractive as *M. longiflora* or *multiflora*, but are still worth having around for the small clusters of pink or purple flowers that open later in the evening and drop off the plants early the next morning. Both of these species are found from Montana to Wisconsin and south to Mexico. They will adapt to any well-drained garden soil in full sun.

THE GARDEN NASTURTIUM

Tropaeolum majus

Jefferson must have loved nasturtiums, as he planted them everywhere. He noted plantings in twenty-two entries of *The Garden and Farm Books*. The first such entry was made on March 26, 1774, when nasturtiums were planted in the meadow in thirty-five little hills. Nasturtiums were mentioned in the 1782 "Calendar of the Bloom of Flowers" as blooming from early June to late September. They continued to be planted, year after year, with the last entry being May 13, 1824, with the notation "—from Richmond. very late."

Jefferson called the plants "Indian cress," but they are also known as bitter cress or nasturtium, resulting in some confusion. The leaves, flowers, and stems of Indian cress contain mustard oils, providing them with a great peppery flavor, and the green seedpods can be pickled and used as a substitute for capers. When mature, the seeds can be roasted, then eaten. That peppery flavor is similar to the taste of watercress leaves, also used in salads, which have the scientific name of *Nasturtium officinale*, hence the confusion with the common names. Luckily both plants are edible. Their chemistry is also very similar, and the cabbage white butterfly often completes its life cycle on both watercress and garden nasturtiums.

The scientific name of the garden nasturtium is *Tropaeolum majus,* a designation provided by Linnaeus, a man who, as Pizzetti and Cocker suggested, "possessed a picturesque mind and an imagination not far removed from the baroque."

Upon seeing the leaves of the nasturtium, Linnaeus thought their unusual rounded shape resembled an old-fashioned Greek or Roman shield, and upon spying the generally red or orange flowers, he imagined they looked like army helmets pierced by lances and spattered with blood.

Nasturtiums are native to many areas of the South American Andes, from Bolivia to Colombia. Today they are common weeds in many of the warmer parts of the world.

Although truly perennial, nasturtiums are so frost-tender that the slightest touch of freeze will kill them. The five-petaled, very fragrant, funnel-shaped flowers, usually two inches wide and with a prominent spur, bloom in colors of deep red, mahogany, scarlet, orange, yellow, and today, after an absence of decades, white. Because the stems are elongated, the plants have a spreading habit. The vining forms grow up to eight feet in a season and are at home on a trellis, strings, or even chicken-wire forms. They are also excellent in pots or larger containers, where they can trail over the edge of a wall or along the ground.

Hummingbirds hover over nasturtium flowers and sip the nutritious nectar. While double-dipping, they transfer some pollen on their feathers, then deliver it to the next flower.

These plants are suitable for growing in all but the coldest climates, but they need full sun and adequate drainage. They thrive even in poor soil. In fact, exceptional soil produces a crop of great leaves and fewer flowers. Nasturtiums do not transplant well, so sow the seeds directly in the garden at eight- to twenty-inch intervals, depending on the variety. Frequent picking prolongs the flowering period, so cut flowers often, and they will persist until frost. Nasturtiums self-seed with exuberance.

As garden stars, nasturtiums do have one problem: They are magnets for aphids, especially the black varieties. In fact, some gardeners actually plant nasturtiums next to the vegetable patch, using these peppery plants as aphid decoys. Use an organic, like a pyrethrum spray, but be sure to wash the leaves if used for salads.

The Alaska Series are small, bushy plants under eighteen inches in height, with single flowers and white mottled leaves of great charm; the Jewel Series have double flowers; the Gleam Series are trailing plants, up to five feet in length, which bloom in a great variety of color. 'Peach Melba' is small, to about a foot tall, with pale yellow petals and orange centers. 'Milkmaid' was originally a pale yellow form, and extensive breeding work and selection have produced a stable seed-raised variety in a shade of pale cream to white. 'Empress of India' bears brilliant red blossoms over a unique blue-green foliage.

POPPIES

Jefferson planted many different types of poppies at Monticello. Some of them were unusual then, and thanks to the general public lack of garden inquisitiveness, the same are rare today.

Peter Collinson, the draper, sent the oriental poppy *(Papaver orientale)* to John Bartram in 1741, calling it the Armenian poppy. Supposedly Jefferson grew this plant, but so far I've found no documentation that he actually grew this plant at Monticello.

Because of their history in the world of drugs, those marvelous drifts of scarlet flowers in Flanders Field that conjure up memories of World War I also bring to mind the dark and demonic shadows of opium dens and unspeakable vice, horrors of the netherworld belonging to Fu Man Chu and Doc Savage.

The genus *Papaver* is from the ancient Latin name for poppies, said to refer to the sound made in chewing the seeds. It represents some fifty species of annual, biennial, or perennial plants ranging from the opium poppy *(P. somniferum)* to the delicate alpine of rock gardens, *P. burseri*.

Grown for millennia, poppies had great meanings back in the classic days of Greece and Rome, including references to deep sleep and death. It was sacred to the Greek god Morpheus, and some classic scholars insist that it's also the flower picked by Demeter's daughter,

Persephone, when she was kidnapped and taken to Hades, thus signifying the beginning of winter.

During the Middle Ages, because they were the source of opium,
poppies were usually regarded with distrust and aversion. English poet
Edmund Spenser (1552–99) called the flower "dead-sleeping," and
John Clair (1793–1864), who worked as a hedge setter, day laborer,
and was gardener at Burghley House from 1810 to 1811, wrote:

> Corn-poppies, that in crimson dwell,
> Called Head-aches from their sickly smell.

In fact, some folks thought that the dazzling red color could actually bring on headaches, if not stupor. Alice Morse Earle wrote in *Old
Time Gardens* that when she was a child in the mid-1800s, a visitor to
her mother's garden, upon seeing the children eating poppy seeds, was
terrified that "we would fall into a stupor."

Poppies missed most Christian symbolism, but they were very popular in the late nineteenth and early twentieth centuries, when the
symbolist poets and painters took the flowers, and their sinister impli-
cations, to both paper and canvas. Some of the most effective art
nouveau designs were based on poppy buds and flowers.

Mrs. C. W. Earle, writing in her fascinating and chatty book, *More
Pot-Pourri from a Surrey Garden*, offered the following advice on poppies
in the vase: "I do not think I mentioned before that all kinds of poppies travel beautifully if they are gathered in bud; and if, on arrival,
the hard husk is peeled off from the buds, they revive and flower and
last longer. Forcing open the buds exhausts the flowers, and then they
open, but to fade and die. The Shirley poppies are prepared this way
for the London Market."

THE OPIUM POPPY
Papaver somniferum

What Jefferson called the white poppy, with seeds planted along the
roundabout flower border in the spring of 1812, was the true opium
poppy. A plant considered a necessity in the practice of medicine in
Jefferson's day, it was found in many gardens.

I should note at this point that today, growing opium poppies is an illegal act in the United States. But the nursery industry, an industry never at a loss for words or a solution to a sales problem, quickly dubbed the opium poppy the peony-flowered poppy (var. *paeoniflorum*), never mentioning the true species name in any publications.

Opium is extracted from the poppy heads before they ripen, usually from plants grown in the Far East, many parts of Central Asia, and Afghanistan.

When the petals fall from the flowers, incisions are made in the wall of unripe capsules, and the exuded juice is partially dried, then formed into cakes, and wrapped in poppy leaves to further dry in the sun. The juice darkens with age, and pure opium is a reddish black, the color of coffee grounds.

The most important constituents of opium are alkaloids, including morphine, narcotine, and codeine. These drugs were known in remote history, and both the Greeks and the Romans collected them. Unexcelled as a hypnotic and sedative, it is thought that the practice of smoking opium began in Persia. A syrup obtained from the flower capsules is prescribed as an ingredient in cough medicines.

But poppy seeds are without any toxic alkaloids, and in addition to sprinkling them on poppy-seed buns, rolls, and pastries, and using them for bird feed, the seeds are also the source of a fine oil once used to adulterate olive oil but now known to be just as important a foodstuff in its own right. The petals are still used as a pigment source in the Far East.

THE CORN POPPY
Papaver rhoeas

"In Flanders' fields the poppies blow between the crosses, row on row," from the poem by John McCrae, refers to the annual field poppy of Flanders, the corn poppy.

Papaver rhoeas bears flowers often three inches across on two-foot stems, in colors of pink, scarlet, crimson, salmon, and white. In 1807, Jefferson planted the double-flowered cultivar of this species in an oval bed. It was probably the "lesser poppy" he observed in 1767 blooming at Shadwell.

The petals are unequal in size, with two large and two small, and the center of the bloom is black. When the buds first open, they look for all the world like samples of crushed silk, and when fully open, they have ruffled edges of great charm. When picking these poppies, singe the cut in the stem in boiling water or an open flame, and they will last as cut flowers for several days.

Another common, but inaccurate, name for these annuals is the Shirley poppy, named in honor of the Reverend W. Wilkes, secretary of the Royal Horticultural Society (and who also has an apple named after him), who found a form of these poppies at the edge of a field, a cultivar with white-edged petals and lacking any touch of black at the flower's center. Wilkes once said, "It is interesting to note that all the gardens of the world, whether they be rich or poor, are ornamented by the direct descendents of the single seed capsule cultivated in the vicarage garden at Shirley during the August of 1880."

THE PRICKLY POPPY
Argemone mexicana

Known by many names, the Mexican prickle-poppy is also called argemony (pronounced with four syllables), the thorn-apple (not to be confused with the daturas or Jimson weeds), goatweed, cardo santo, cardo amarillo, chicalote, and herbe a femme. Seeds were first cataloged back in 1592.

Jefferson wrote about planting seed for this curious plant at Shadwell, noting the first flower on June 18, 1767. A month later, he reported one more bloom, totaling four that year.

The scientific name is *Argemone mexicana*, the genus referring to the Greek word *argema*, meaning cataract of the eye, because at one time the juice of the plant was used to treat such disorders. The genus has about forty species of annual or perennial herbs and one shrub, native to North and South America and Hawaii. They belong to the great poppy family, or Papaveraceae.

Prickly poppies are found in old fields and pastures, waste ground, industrial sites, and gardens throughout the warmer parts of the country. Originally an American native, the plant is now a pantropic weed, spreading throughout the tropical and subtropical regions, and has been naturalized in Brazil, Hindustan, and Africa. Amazingly, seed of this plant has made its way to India, where it's called *sialkanta* or *phirangi dhatura*.

Argemony is an annual herb with simple, alternate leaves tipped with spines and a whitish wax that easily rubs off. The flowers have four to six bright yellow petals surrounding a disk with many stamens.

The round seeds are a blackish brown. When pressed, they yield pale yellow latex ooze that becomes argemone oil. It is a semidrying oil that contains, among other alkaloids, sanguinarine and dihydrosanguinarine, two very toxic substances. If ingested, symptoms are vomiting, diarrhea, loss of vision, fainting, and without immediate medical attention, coma, followed by death. The latex is also considered a narcotic.

And, believe it or not, in India, unscrupulous wholesalers used argemone oil as an adulterate in their mustard oil. After a round of food poisonings in which sixty-some people died, in September 1998, the Canadian government warned its citizens not to consume any foodstuff cooked or processed in oil from India, as it could be adulterated with argemone. Because human life often has a low value in India, there the deaths were passed off as just another tragedy. But in Canada, it led to a nationwide crackdown on food adulterators. Recently, however, in India, an argemone detection kit was developed, with a fluorescent chemical that will react to the presence of argemone oil in mustard oil.

Despite all this, these plants are not dangerous to grow in your garden. Hundreds of plants plus very scientific processing are needed to produce enough poison to be dangerous.

Sow the seeds directly into the ground where you want the plants to grow, as they, like all poppies, have a long taproot that does not take to transplanting. Soil fertility can be low, but good drainage is a must.

Seeds will germinate in the cool weather of fall or early spring, forming lovely rosettes of an intense silvery blue color. As spring passes into summer, two- to three-foot stems growing from the center of the plant bear large, bright yellow blossoms.

THE HORNED POPPY
Glaucium flavum

According to Ann Leighton in *American Gardens in the Eighteenth Century*, the horn poppy, or sea poppy, was one of the earliest and most successful escapes of plants originating in Europe, and it greeted seventeenth-century voyagers to our eastern shores. In 1807, Jefferson noted planting the seeds in an oval bed southeast of the house. Today this poppy is fairly well distributed in small patches up and down the Atlantic beaches, especially rocky slopes and cliff edges, where soils are sandy and poor. When we summered out on Long Island and walked the beaches around Amagansett, this was one of the lovelier wildflowers of the area.

As to how the plant arrived on our shores, seeds could have been transported on the bottoms of boots or shoes, clinging to unwashed clothing, or in the ballast of ships, which often consisted of raw dirt that was shoveled out of a ship's bottom and left on the beach.

The scientific name is *Glaucium flavum*. The generic name is derived from the Latin word for sea green, referring to the glaucous foliage, and *flavus* means yellow. The common name of horned poppies refers to the seedpods, which are sometimes up to a foot long.

As with many plants from the Old World, especially members of the poppy clan, there were medicinal uses associated with the sap or roots. The horned poppy is listed in *Hunayn's Book of the Ten Treatises on the Eye*, published some twelve hundred years ago, when Baghdad was the center of much medical learning, with Muslim, Jewish, and Christian scribes and scholars working together to solve society's ills, helped along by the recent introduction of paper. These seeds also provide a long-burning oil for lamps and were once used to make soap.

Known as a biennial because their life cycle takes two years, the plants can reach a height of two feet and bear large, single flowers with two pairs of petals that form a cross, blooming in the summer. The thick, blue-green leaves are pinnately lobed and form a rosette, above which rise the branching stems terminating in large, bright yellow flowers. The cultivar 'Aurantiaca' has attractive orange flowers.

If planted early in the season, plants will bloom the first year. Like all poppies, they resent movement, so plant the seeds in peat pots or sow them on-site. Don't give these poppies a rich soil. The site should be well-drained and in full sun. The plants are hardy to USDA Zone 8.

THE SOUTH AFRICAN GERANIUM

Pelargonium zonale

In the Philadelphia of 1784, Charles Wilson Peale (1741–1827) opened a museum dedicated to the wonders of art and nature. Both Peale and the museum are illustrated in a famous self-portrait showing the owner pulling aside a curtain to reveal a theater of nature. Therein a visitor would find displays of stuffed exotic animals, painted dioramas, and portraits of great Americans.

Peale was a fascinating man in all aspects of the word, not the least being his seventeen children, which included four men who became well-known artists: Raphaelle was a painter of trompe l'oeil and still lives, Titian worked with portraits, Rubens painted miniatures, and Rembrandt produced historical portraits, including a portrait of Thomas Jefferson.

In 1809, Jefferson wrote to Peale about his continual battle between a public and a private life: "I have often thought that if Heaven had given me choice of my position and calling, it should have been on a rich spot of earth, well watered, and near a good market for the productions of the garden. No occupation is so delightful to me as the culture of the earth, and no culture comparable to that of the garden."

Perhaps one of Rembrandt's most telling portraits was that of his young brother Rubens, dressed in a stylish suit jacket, wearing glasses that would be in vogue today, and holding a large and rangy (by today's standards) geranium in a terra-cotta pot. The year was 1801, and Rubens (the family botanist) was exceptionally proud of his plant—especially because Jefferson had it on his list of desired specimens back in 1786.

A likeness of that terra-cotta pot is sold at Monticello today, but it's the geranium that should hold our full attention. It's painted with such loving care, including the sparse blossoms (this plant was not up to today's blousy cultivars), and it assumes the same importance as the brother. After all, which was more important to an intellectual of the times: an expensive knickknack or a rare plant?

Jefferson grew the African geranium (*Pelargonium zonale*, not to be confused with the American wildflower) both at the White House and at Monticello. He referred to having a pot containing several sprigs of geranium, stuck round a plant supposed to be orange, in a letter to his granddaughter Anne in 1807. Margaret Bayard Smith, a Washington friend, wrote to Jefferson with a request for a cutting of a geranium that was growing in a window of the White House. She said that upon his retirement to Monticello, the plant would be "watered with the tears of regret." He gave her the plant, answering, "If plants have sensibility, it [the geranium] cannot but be proudly sensible of her fostering attentions."

The genus *Pelargonium* refers to *pelargos*, a stork, because of the similarity between the long seed vessel and the bird's beak. The species name *zonale* is derived from the zones of color on the leaves. The common name geranium stems from the Greek word *geranos*, or crane, again because the fruit resembles the beak of that bird.

In 1609, the first of the African geraniums to reach Europe was probably the horseshoe geranium, or zonal geranium (*Pelargonium zonale*), with plants included in a shipment sent to Holland from South Africa by the governor of the Cape Colony. These geraniums grew on rocky slopes and along the forest edge from the Southern Cape to Natal. They preferred the hot, dry climates of South Africa. In 1652, the Dutch East India Company opened a trading post at Table Bay that eventually became a colony, and from that spot, hundreds of geraniums made their way to Europe. The plant was brought to England in 1710 by sailors who returned with these tough plants as gifts to wives and girlfriends.

According to Pizzetti and Cocker in *Flowers: A Guide for Your Garden,* in 1732 John Dillenius published *Hortus Elthamensis,* with drawings and descriptions of several African geraniums, so by the time Jefferson was gardening and Peale was painting, they were already floral hits.

The leaves assume various shapes, although they usually follow one pattern: They are circular and beautifully scalloped and lobed, with the veins for each lobe radiating from the petiole, or stem, the leaves being velvety above. The petioles are usually long and stiff, and set alternately on the main stem. After the leaves have fallen, these petioles often remain, giving untended plants a rather unkempt look.

When geranium buds first appear, they are nestled in a nest of protecting bracts, each bud enclosed in a protective sepal. But as the flower stalk grows longer and droops a bit, the bracts fall off and the buds begin to open, center first.

Single flowers have five petals. At first glance, they all seem to be the same size, but after a careful look, it's evident that the upper two petals are much narrower at the base and project farther forward than the lower three. And there are evident lines on these upper petals that look as though they were inked in by a steady hand. The lines all point to the center of the flower, where a deep nectar well is found.

If you examine a flower with care, you'll see that this nectar well extends almost the entire length of the stalk, down to a nectar gland that forms a hump at the base of the stalk. If a needle is thrust down the entire length of this nectar tube, you can see from its length that pollination is meant to be carried out by butterflies and moths, for these are the only insects with tongues long enough to reach the bottom.

Nature abhors waste, so when you look at the flowers of double geraniums, where the second level of petals has been formed by changed stamens, there are no nectar glands, because these flowers can never set seed.

The geraniums that led to today's plants were first cultivated by the duchess of Beaufort in 1710. With her horticultural lead, most of the early cultivars were developed in England, many in the nineteenth and twentieth centuries. Germany, too, produced many colorful varieties, where Hillscheid Nurseries introduced eighty new varieties in just three years.

But the heyday of geraniums began with the English Victorians and continued to the beginnings of the First World War. Then development of ornamental plants ceased, because greenhouse heating was banned for the war effort.

The chief chemical found in the oil usually produced by the leaves is geraniol, a compound that possesses strong bactericidal properties and is still used by the pharmaceutical industry. One ton of green is required to produce two and a half pounds of essence. Pelargoniums also are grown for perfume; the first species to be used for this purpose were those imported by the duchess of Beaufort.

THE MAY-APPLE

Podophyllum peltatum

Because of their fruit, May-apples are also known as Devil's apple, hog apple, Indian apple, and wild lemon. Other popular names are the umbrella plant, thanks to the spreading leaf, and goosefoot, thanks to the leaf's shape. Due to its poisonous properties, it's also known as wild jalap (Jalapa being a Mexican town where a purgative root was found) and American mandrake, but don't confuse it with true mandrake *(Mandragora officinarum)*, an unrelated Old World plant with man-shaped roots (the roots were once thought to scream out loud if they were buried beneath a scaffold) used throughout history for medicines and potions.

The scientific name is *Podophyllum peltatum,* with the generic name taken from the Greek word *pous,* for foot, and *phullon,* for leaf, referring to the shape of the leaf.

The plant was well known in colonial gardens and a prominent spring flower of the woods around Monticello. According to *Thomas Jefferson's Flower Garden at Monticello,* which in turn quoted Margaret Bayard Smith writing in *The First Forty Years of Washington Society:* "It was Mr. Jefferson's design to have planted them [May-apples] exclusively with Trees, shrubs and flowers indigenous to our native soil. He had a long list made out in which they were arranged according to their forms and colours and the seasons in which they flourished." Mrs. Smith visited Jefferson both in Washington and at Monticello, and in Charlottesville in the summer of 1809.

In early spring, the plant pushes up a leaf that's folded like an umbrella. This allows it to rise from the earth without damage to its structure. It soon opens on top of a solitary stem that can reach a height of eighteen inches. The leaf is nearly a foot across, rounded, centrally peltate (a botanical way of saying that the leaf is almost circular, with the stem ending in the middle), five- to seven-lobed, dark green above and light green below.

Mature specimens produce a flower at the junction of two umbrellas. It is white, solitary, large, not too attractive to smell, bearing six to nine rounded, flat petals and thick stamens with one pistil at the center.

In July, as the summer advances, the flower's ovary becomes a fruit, a fleshy, yellowish, egg-shaped apple about two inches long. This is the only part of the plant that is not poisonous. And, be warned, although some books describe its taste as being insipidly sweet, I've tried it, and it's sweetly mawkish (*mawk* being an Old English word for worm).

Bebe Miles, in *Wildflower Perennials for Your Garden*, said that you could kill a May-apple by planting it in the direct sun and very dry soil, but other than that, the plant would survive. The leaves and flowers arise from underground stems that are creeping rhizomes and in time produce a very great colony of the plants. It's one of the few wildflowers that can be transplanted in full growth. But if you live with unenriched clay soil, introduce a lot of compost for the May-apples. These plants are fast growers and crowd out most other plants, especially native wildflowers.

Native Americans, who intimately knew the plant life around them, ground the dried roots into a powder as an insecticide for their crops and actually soaked valuable seeds in a prepared liquid to keep mice and other vandals away. They also used the roots to prepare laxatives, and there are reports of some suicides committed by ingesting the roots.

Roots contain an alkaloid called berberine, which can be used to treat fevers (especially malaria) and has been used as an antibiotic. Investigations continue into the possible uses of this plant in contemporary medicine. The purgative action of May-apple rhizome powder is very strong, and the compounds in it are much too toxic to attempt self-medication with this plant. The FDA rates this plant as unsafe. Workers in the extraction process have developed dermatitis.

THE FRAGRANT TUBEROSE

Polianthes tuberosa

Fragrances can reach across the decades like a physical link, reminding us of an eventful time long forgotten. Often floral scents can trigger memory: the faint odor of orange that recalls the mock orange bush that grew next to Grandmother's front porch; the light and citric smell of the evening primrose as it opens its sulfur yellow flowers to the darkening sky; the sweet but cloying scent of tuberoses that my aunt Ida would force into bloom for Thanksgiving dinner.

Jefferson grew tuberoses. And so, in 1736, did John Custis and Peter Collinson. John Bartram had the bulbs in 1761, and son William described tuberoses at a plantation near Baton Rouge as growing "from five to seven feet high in the open ground, the flowers being very large and abundant." In 1765, John Clayton's tuberoses were destroyed by frost. Lady Skipworth grew both the single and double flowers. And in 1807, Bernard M'Mahon sent double tuberoses to Monticello, with their flowering beginning on August 12. On November 9, upon digging up the roots, Jefferson's granddaughter Anne Cary Randolph said, "We shall have plenty of them for the next year."

The tuberose (*Polianthes tuberosa*) derives its generic name from the Greek *polios*, for white, and *anthos*, for flower. There are two explanations for the species name: The first refers to the flower's fragrance, while the second postulates that *tuberosa* is a corruption of the word tuberous. Members of the Agavaceae, they were grown by pre-Columbian Indians of Mexico and have never been known to grow in the wild. The rhizomes were among the first plants to sail back to the Old World, where they were beloved by the Spanish and often found a place in Castilian gardens.

Shelley said that the tuberose was "the sweetest flower for scent that blows," and the Victorians delighted in its sweet, heady fragrance. In *The English Flower Garden*, William Robinson called it a "deliciously fragrant plant" and noted that it often lived through London winters. German ladies called it *Nachtliebste*, and as with the gas plant, there were reports about the flowers giving off sparks of light.

George Moore wrote:

The tuberose, with her silvery light,
That in the gardens of Malay
Is called the Mistress of the Night,
So like a bride, scented and bright,
She comes out when the sun's away.

Unfortunately, because of their strong odor, tuberoses are linked with summer heat and poor air circulation. The odor is so strong that tuberose became popular as a funeral flower and fell out of the public's favor. Today gardeners once again plant a few bulbs in the summer border or underneath the dining-room window so that at night the rich odor can freshen the interior of the house.

Tuberose oil is still used as a classic component of high-quality perfumes. Older references report the plants to have narcotic properties, although one can easily believe that having a few too many glasses of wine on a hot night, then being confronted by the close odor of blooming tuberoses, would have some effect.

There are two varieties: 'Mexican Everblooming', which reaches a height of four feet and bears two-inch-long, waxy, white, extremely fragrant flowers, and 'The Pearl', a shorter plant growing sixteen inches high and bearing two-inch double flowers. The bulblike bases are really rhizomes, as these plants are in the same family as yuccas and agaves. Unless you live in an area where the ground never freezes, store the roots in a warm, dry place over winter. In the north, start the plants indoors about four weeks before the last frost of spring, since they take a long season to bloom. The rhizomes can also be forced for November bloom.

Tuberoses are very erratic with blooming. If you plant a few dozen in spring, a few will bloom in July and a few in August, with perhaps a few left over for a warm September. And once a tuber has flowered, it will never flower again. But future plants are assured from the young tubers that sprout from the parent. They will take at least four years to reach flowering stage.

THE AROMATIC MIGNONETTE

Reseda odorata

Mignonette was introduced to England around 1750 and quickly became so popular that unscrupulous nurseries, unable to keep up with the demand, would substitute *Reseda phyteuma*, another species with a faint musky scent usually described as being foxy. By the first century, the plants were widely grown for their perfume in the Roman and Hellenistic cultures around the Mediterranean Sea. *Reseda phyteuma* was mentioned by Dioscorides as an aphrodisiac, in addition to being an excellent treatment for bruises, so he called it *Reseda*, meaning a healer or restorer.

In 1803, Anne Cary Randolph wrote to Jefferson, "We were so unfortunate as to lose the Mignonette entirely although Mama divided it between Mrs. Lewis Aunt Jane & herself but none of it seeded." In 1811, Jefferson planted this marvelously fragrant plant in an oval bed.

"Linnaeus," said Alice Morse Earle, "thought the perfume of Mignonette the purest ambrosia. Another thinks that Mignonette has a doggy smell, as have several flowers; this is not wholly to their disparagement. Our cocker spaniel is sweeter than some flowers, but he is not a Mignonette."

Napoleon sent the Empress Josephine seeds of this charmer that he collected during his Egyptian campaign in Africa. Having the empress talk about the plant soon gave it that magic touch, and gardeners began growing the plant in pots where they could wander into a garden of fragrance regardless of their station in life.

In literature, the fragrance has been called divine, and in his poem "The Task" (1785) William Cowper (1731–1800), the great English poet, described mignonette as "the fragrant weed, the Frenchman's darling." Cowper is reputed to have christened the plant mignonette.

Also known as garden mignonette, sweet reseda, and bastard rocket, these are fast-growing, branching annuals grown for their sweetly scented flowers. Flowers are not particularly showy but are added to floral arrangements for the scent, which is so captivating that it's grown commercially for an essential oil used in perfumery. The fragrance is not heavy, but still fruity, like a sweet dessert wine.

Plants usually grow about a foot and a half tall, with heavy stems and limp, spatulate leaves. The small flowers are yellow-green to brownish yellow, in dense racemes, and nothing to write home about. But planted by the kitchen door, underneath a dining-room window, or picked for an indoor bouquet, they are wonderful.

Seedlings resent transplanting, so sow them directly outdoors or in pots (pot are especially good, because you can move the fragrance to where you want it). Do not cover the seeds, as they need light for germination. Also provide some shade from the glaring afternoon sun, as these plants prefer the cool. Expect poor growth and flowering during hot weather.

There are a number of cultivars, including 'Ameriorata', great for pots and bearing rose-red flowers; 'Machet', first described in the 1890s as a new dwarf variety from France with bright red flowers; and *Reseda odorata grandiflora*, the best for cultivation, with large floral heads and great scent.

Reseda lutea is more graceful in habit that regular mignonette. Billed as a biennial, plants will flower the first year from seed. They bloom most of the summer on two-and-a-half-foot stems covered with small, light yellow flowers. I built a raised bed of fieldstones and grow *R. lutea* along the top edge, flanked by red coral-bells, and by midsummer they lean over the wall, much like spires of yellow lace.

THE CASTOR BEAN

Ricinus communis

There is one mention of Jefferson planting the castor bean. It's found in *The Garden and Farm Books*, dated May 15, 1811, and says, "Palma Christi. In a row around the nursery." Used since ancient times in Egypt, Persia, Africa, Greece, and Rome (among others), the oil produced by the castor bean plant was known as Palma Christi, or the "Palm of Christ," because the leaf is palmate in shape.

In the King James version of the Bible, Jonah finds himself very uncomfortable as the sun beats down upon his head. Chapter 4, Verse 6 of the book of Jonah reads: "And the Lord God prepared a gourd, and made it to come up over Jonah, that it might be a shadow over his head, to deliver him from his grief. So Jonah was exceeding glad of the gourd." (It should be noted that in the spirit of Jonah's story, the next morning a worm ate through the stem, and Jonah was back again under a hot desert sun.) Many biblical scholars believe that the gourd of Jonah was in reality the castor bean, because it grows so quickly and makes good shade with its very large, attractive leaves.

In fact, the castor bean goes so far back in recorded history that its seeds were found in ancient Egyptian sarcophagi, placed there so that they could accompany the dead in their voyage through the Land of Death.

The scientific name is *Ricinus communis,* and the plant was first described and named by Linnaeus. *Ricinus* means tick in Latin, and the plant was so named because Linnaeus did have a sense of humor and saw a resemblance of the mottled seed to a tick engorged with blood. The species name means common in Latin, because the plant was so common in tropical regions. The popular name of castor bean owes its origin to a mistake on the part of English traders who, upon finding the plant, mistook it for another species, the chaste tree or Monk's pepper tree *(Vitex agnus-castus),* known in Jamaica as agno-casto.

The leaves are stalked, typically with eight radiating leaflets. These are pointed, slightly serrated, and have prominent midribs. Varieties may be green or reddish brown. The flowers are usually green and inconspicuous, but are pink or red in the pigmented varieties. Many stamens are near the base, and branching pistils are near the top of the flower. The soft-spined fruits containing attractively mottled seeds are distinctive features of the plant.

Although commonly referred to as a bean, castor is not a legume. It has also been called the castor oil plant. One of the oldest commercial products, castor oil was used in lamps by the Egyptians more than four thousand years ago. Most authorities consider the plant to be native to tropical Africa, and perhaps it originated in Abyssinia.

Castor oil has been used therapeutically in ancient India. Today it is found in many skin-care products, used as a skin softener and a treatment for lacerations and skin disorders such as psoriasis, as well as for gastrointestinal problems. Children formerly faced a yearly purge using castor oil, because it was thought to rejuvenate youthful bodies after the plagues of winter.

The United States is the largest consumer and importer of castor oil in the world. The oil has been classed as a strategic material critical to our national defense by the Agricultural Materials Act P.L. 98-284, passed by Congress in 1984. An act of Congress requires that sufficient supplies be stored in the United States to meet national defense needs in case of war.

The poison called ricin, taken from castor oil beans, is one of the most potent killers on earth. In its concentrated form, it has remarkably lethal properties. In 1978, Georgi Markov, a Bulgarian journalist, was assassinated in London by being prodded with an umbrella. A tiny ball coated with ricin was lodged on the umbrella's tip. This was wedged in the victim's flesh, and he died a few days later in the hospital.

THE SOAPWORT

Saponaria officinalis

Soapwort, or bouncing Bet *(Saponaria officinalis)*, would be a beloved garden plant if her daytime looks matched her nighttime demeanor. But it's not until late afternoon or evening that her tawdry petals really perk up and her sweet perfume fills the air.

Jefferson is said to have grown soapwort, and he probably did, especially because of the uses ascribed to this plant. And it's listed in most books of the time as a common garden plant. Phillip Miller described soapwort, and copies of his books were in Jefferson's library.

Other common names are legion and include bruisewort, farewell to summer, hedge pink, sweet Betty, wild sweet William, dog cloves, old maid's pink, soap root, saponary, Lady-by-the-gate, crow soap (I'd love to know the derivation of that one), and gill-run-by-the-street. The French word for the plant is *saponaire*, the German is *seifenkraut*, Spanish is *saponella*, and Italian is *saponaria*. Many writers bemoan the most commonly used name of soapwort (*wort* is an Old English word for plant), because even when sprawling, the plant is not unattractive.

Soapwort is an often bent-over perennial, growing up to three feet high but sometimes sprawled in such a manner that one stem holds up another. A jointed rhizome moves through the earth and gives rise to numerous reasonably erect sterile or flower-bearing stems. Flowering stems are sparsely branched with lower leaves and terminate in rich panicles of flowers. The large, five-petaled flowers bloom from late June and on into early October, depending on latitude.

Tubular flowers bloom in a compact inflorescence, in colors ranging from white to pale pink, while the cylindrical calyx is often reddish. There are ten stamens, and the fruit is an oval capsule. While soapwort prefers damp, sandy soil, it's quite adaptable; the only threat (and then only partial) is hot noonday sun in the Southeast. Because this stout plant spreads by a network of rhizomes, it is especially valuable in holding on to the earth in a crumbling slope or bank. Native to Europe and Asia, it has naturalized in North America.

The genus is derived from the Latin *sapo*, or soap, and refers to the mucilaginous juice in the stems, which actually forms a lather with water. Crushed roots produce suds when rubbed in water. It can actually be used as a mild detergent for fine fabrics, and was once added to beer to create a frothy head. The species refers to the plant's use in medicine.

The chemical in soapwort is saponin, found in the saps of many plants. In addition to foaming, this chemical has the faculty of wetting surfaces that are usually difficult to wet. This has led to its use as a wetting agent for spreading fungicides and insecticides where soap is unsuitable. It can actually get waxy surfaces wet without destroying the wax.

Geoffrey Grigson, in his wonderfully informative book *The Englishman's Flora*, suggested that soapwort was used by early medieval fullers, who soaped new cloth with various soaps to thicken the fabric (hence their occupational name) before it went under the stamps of the mill. He also wrote that soapwort was probably one of the ancient sources of lather before the invention of soap.

The lather has been recommended for restoring ancient and delicate fabrics and cleaning old tapestries. Dried plants are placed in muslin bags, then boiled in distilled water, the solution being used cold.

Textile restorers use *Saponaria* that has been boiled in lime-free water to clean and revitalize old, fragile fabrics, and it may also be used as a

gentle wash for damaged hair and sensitive skin. Soapwort is still cultivated for washing woolens in the Middle East. In the Swiss Alps,
sheep used to be washed with it before they were shorn.

In the past, soapwort was also used to produce a head on beer, but
I suspect that any such attempts today would involve some kind of
government action. An old gypsy remedy was to apply a decoction of
the root to a bruise or black eye to quickly get rid of the discoloration.
The eighteenth-century Dutch physician Boerhaeve recommended the
plant as a treatment for jaundice. Mrs. M. Grieve cited its use in vene-
real complaints, especially where the use of mercury had failed, and as
a remedy for the cutaneous troubles resulting from syphilis. In India,
the rhizome is used as a galactagogue. The flowers are sometimes
added to salads or dried for inclusion in potpourri.

In addition to its use as a detergent, the leaves and roots were once
employed as remedies for scrofula and for skin diseases in general.
The early American settlers used it as a wash to counter poison ivy
rash, and today some authorities still name soapwort sap as a possible
relief for the itching of poison ivy.

Researchers have found that soapwort has both antibacterial and
expectorant action: It kills bacteria and loosens phlegm, making it
easier to cough up. But there are warnings about ingesting soapwort,
as saponins can cause irritation to the digestive tract. Disruptive signs
are not noted until you've eaten the plants for several days. Symptoms
include mild depression, vomiting, and diarrhea.

I first realized the evening potential of these plants when I visited
the offices of the *Sullivan County Democrat* in Callicoon, New York.
Across from the newspaper offices are the raised banks of dirt and
cinder that hold the railroad tracks, and these banks are carpeted with
soapwort. During the day, everything was dull on the other side of
the street, the only color being that of parked cars. But we often
worked late hours, and many nights we walked out to be greeted by
the bright blossoms and their sweet perfume.

At dusk, these flowers are busy with the whirring wings of the
sphinx moth, but even during the day, various bees, including the
small halictid bees, come in for nectar. When the blossoms first open,

they reveal five outer stamens that shed pollen on moth and bee alike. Next, the five inner stamens do the same. But the female stigma, capped by two styles, is still protected within the flower's tube, thus preventing self-fertilization. When the stamens finally wither, the stigma emerges to receive pollen brought from younger flowers.

Give these plants full sun in the north and partial shade in the south, but keep them to the edge of the garden, for their afternoon appearance is rather forlorn. They are hardy through USDA Zone 5. 'Rubra Plena' has fragrant double pink flowers on two-foot stems. There is also a white form, 'Alba'.

THE GARDEN SORREL

Rumex acetosa

There are ten entries for sorrel in Jefferson's *Garden and Farm Books*, usually lumped in with other kitchen garden flavors, like tarragon and endive.

Sorrel (*Rumex acetosa*) has been grown in America for a long, long time. A cheerful American traveler named John Josselyn, a man of great curiosity and a pleasing literary style, published in 1672 a book entitled *New England's Rarities Discovered*, and in 1674 another book giving an account of his sea travels. Among his many accomplishments, he compiled a list of all the vegetables he found growing in colonial America. Mixed in with fennel (must be taken up and kept in a warm cellar all winter), clary (never lasts but one summer, as the roots rot with the frost), and sparagus (thrives exceedingly) was garden sorrel.

Rumex is the Greek word for another plant described by Pliny that belonged to this genus, and the species name means acid or sour. Sorrel, with a long history of culinary use, has a lemony flavor produced by the high content of oxalic acid in the leaves. The taste is tart but good. Because of the acid, never use aluminum cookware—a problem not faced by early American cooks or by gourmet French cooks of today, who would never consider using such utensils. Use only stainless steel or enamel, which will not react with the plant juices. Some discretion should be used with sorrel, since it contains so much oxalic acid and tannin. This is one of those plants best used sparingly. Go easy.

A hardy perennial herb, sorrel has been in cultivation for well over five thousand years and grows wild throughout much of Europe and North America. The Egyptians used it in combination with other greens, and the Romans ate salads of lettuce and sorrel in preparation for the heavy meals ahead. By the time of Henry VIII, sorrel was used as a spinach and enjoyed by the entire court. The leaves were ground into a mash, mixed with vinegar and sugar, then used as a sauce for cold meats.

Only the edible sorrel has large, distinctly arrow-shaped leaves about six inches long on a six-inch stalk. Sheep sorrel *(Rumex acetosella)* has thin, small leaves only a few inches long. The flowers bloom in summer and are small and greenish, followed by a fruit, or achene, easily identified by its three wings. The new leaves that emerge from the crown are used for the table.

Sorrel does best in a good, moist soil, in full sun to partial shade. You can grow it in containers if your garden is too small for an unruly plant.

In 1931, writing in her classic volumes called *A Modern Herbal,* Mrs. M. Grieve said that in England, "the leaves are now rarely eaten, unless by children and rustics, to allay thirsts, though in Ireland they are still largely consumed by the peasantry with fish and milk. Our country people used to beat the herb to a mash and take it mixed with cold meats."

Luckily, things have improved for Ireland over the past decades.

The best recipe calls for washing the sorrel in water several times and picking it over carefully, as you would spinach. Then cook it for ten minutes in a little salted water. Drain it as dry as possible, and chop finely. Put it into a pan with a lump of butter. For a pound of sorrel, add a quarter pint of cream and then two beaten eggs. When the purée thickens, it's ready.

Irma Rombauer, in *The Joy of Cooking,* writes that sorrel leaves may be pounded in a mortar with sugar and vinegar to make a delicious tart sauce, or made into a purée, seasoned with tarragon and mustard, for use as a bed for fish.

My wife, Jean, has an old handwritten receipe for a cold sorrel soup that's perfect for a warm summer's evening. Gather four handfuls of washed sorrel leaves. Cut them from either side of the stalks, then chop into small pieces. Simmer in a pan of boiling water for ten minutes. Add one clove of garlic, crushed with some salt, half a cucumber (peeled and sliced), the juice of one lemon, another dash of salt, and a generous amount of black pepper. Beat two eggs. Remove the pan from the stove, and pour a bit of the broth into the beaten eggs, stirring as you go. Return the mixture to the stove, and stir over low heat until it thickens. Add two hard-boiled eggs, finely chopped. Chill the soup in the fridge. Serve cold with some chopped tarragon.

As to medicinal uses, herbals advise that both the seed and the root were used for their astringent properties, and syrups made with the juice of sorrel and the herb fumitory had a reputation for curing the itch. It will supposedly help clear the body of kidney stones and is used as a remedy for jaundice. It's also a good poultice for boils and tumors.

Before cholesterol concerns loomed, I thought we would never get enough sorrel. But now we watch the egg and cream input, so one plant is enough to provide garnishes and flavoring.

Oh, for the days of yore!

THE MANY MARIGOLDS

Tagetes spp.

In 1808, Anne Cary Randolph wrote her grandfather, Jefferson, "We have plenty of the two kinds of Marigolds that you gave us." It was suggested at the time that Monticello saw both the French and the African marigolds in cultivation.

According to *Thomas Jefferson's Flower Garden*, on April 8, 1810, Jefferson sowed seed of the African marigold along the roundabout flower border. And in *The Garden and Farm Books*, he noted the planting of African marigolds in the north and the south flower borders on April 28, 1812.

Ann Leighton wrote that Jefferson sowed marigolds in 1764, but these were most likely calendulas. Until well into the eighteenth century, the name marigold referred to *Calendula officinalis*, the pot marigold. When the so-called African marigolds (*Tagetes erecta*) were discovered in Mexico, they became known as French marigolds and calendulas became pot marigolds. Bernard M'Mahon offered pot marigolds, double African and double French, and quilled African marigolds.

The scientific name *Tagetes* is from the Latin name of Tages, a grandson of Jupiter, who sprang from the plowed earth as a boy and, mythology has it, taught the art of reading weather signs to the Etruscans.

Before the plants received their present official name, they were called the Indian pink (*Caryophyllus indicus*), because many botanists thought they originated in the East Indies.

Originally the genus came from Mexico and Central America. Its recorded history goes back to the Aztecs, who used the plant for the treatment of hiccups or for warding off lightning strikes, or carried the plants in order to cross a river or a body of water in safety. In fact, there is a legend of the marigold, called the Flower of Avenging Death. It is said that before Cortez came to their land of gold and wealth, the flowers were unknown. Then, for each native that was killed, there sprang up great colonies of marigolds as a constant reminder to the generations of Aztecs to avenge the ignoble death of their forefathers.

It was also alleged that the Virgin wore the plant on her bosom, hence the name of Marygold, but another school of thought attributes this name to the marsh marigold and the word *meer*, for pond or lake, and the fact that the flower brightens a damp place with color.

In the 1500s, native marigold seeds were taken to the Spanish Court by explorers and were soon being grown in monastery gardens. From there, the seeds went to France and Africa, and the American native eventually came to be called the African marigold. From Africa, the seeds went to India, where they are still used to brighten up Indian gardens, decorate village gods during harvest festivals, and festoon religious processions of all kinds.

In a seed list printed in a Boston newspaper on March 30, 1760, there was a listing for Lemon African Marigold, our own plant being reintroduced to colonial gardens. It's no wonder the nomenclature became slightly confusing.

In 1683, J. W. Gent, writing in *The Art of Gardening*, maintained, "There are divers sorts besides the common as the African Marigold, a Fair bigge Yellow Flower, But of a very Naughty Smell." The odor becomes especially strong when the stalks begin to decompose in a vase of forgotten flowers, hence one of their common names, the flower of the dead.

Alice Morse Earle (*Old Time Gardens*) was surprised at the unkind remarks about these marigolds and was pleased that Edward FitzGerald (1809–83), who translated *The Rubaiyat of Omar Khayyam* in 1859, loved the African marigold, noting that "its grand color is so comfortable to us Spanish-like Paddies," in a letter he wrote to Fanny Kemble (1809–93), the English actress who wrote about the custom of slavery in America.

The marigold coasted along, always popular, until 1915, when David Burpee took over the William Atlee Burpee Company and began investing money in marigold development. Today there are hundreds of cultivars, and after years of research, Burpee finally developed a white marigold.

Marigolds are used in beds and borders, for edging, in containers and baskets, and even in the vegetable garden, where a chemical found in the marigold root is said to repel certain kinds of nematodes.

The African or American marigold *(Tagetes erecta)* has the largest leaves and flowers. The blossoms are semidouble from three to four and a half inches across, in solid colors of orange, yellow, gold, cream, and the fabled white. According to the cultivar, plants vary from nine-inch dwarfs to over three feet for the larger types.

The French marigolds (*Tagetes patula*, with *patula* meaning spreading in habit) are smaller plants that range in height from six to fourteen inches. Colors are solid or bicolored, with orange, yellow, gold, or mahogany-red combinations. They have been divided into four groups: single flowers; anemone flowers, with rows of overlapping petals surrounding a central disk; carnation flowers, with fully double flowers, and numerous rows of overlapping petals; and crested flowers, with the flower center made of numerous short petals surrounded by either single or double rows of outside petals.

The signet marigolds *(Tagetes tenufolia)*, with *tenufolia* meaning slender leaves, are also smaller plants, reaching only about a foot in height. Blossoms are single, about an inch wide, with a yellow center surrounded by five yellow petals. They are the most charming of the marigolds and are useful as edging in the border.

The cloud plant, or the anise-flavored marigold (*Tagetes lucida*, with *lucida* meaning clear, bright, and shining), is a perennial from Mexico that is usually grown as an annual in the herb garden. Plants can reach a three-foot height, bearing lance-shaped leaves and single, orange-gold flowers that bloom in high summer. The whole plant is sweetly scented, and leaves are used to flavor soups or dried to make herb teas.

Irish lace (*Tagetes filifolia*, with *filifolia* referring to the threadlike leaves) is grown for the leaves and not the flowers. The neat, green balls of fernlike foliage make it a perfect edging plant, while the tiny white flowers blooming in early fall are easily overlooked.

THE COMMON PERIWINKLE

Vinca minor

Jefferson mentions myrtle twice in the "Farm Books." The first time, dated September 30, 1771, it is listed under hardy perennial flowers, and the second time, in 1794, it appears in the list headed "Objects for the garden this year," spelled as perywinkle.

A member of the dogbane family, myrtle, or the common periwinkle *(Vinca minor)*, is a charming, trailing perennial evergreen subshrub. It has shiny leaves and funnel-like, five-petaled flowers. Depending on the cultivar, the flowers may be violet, blue, or white, the species being periwinkle blue. It has both erect flowering stems, from six to eight inches tall, and trailing nonflowering stems that root at the nodes. The evergreen stems contain milky latex.

There are two theories regarding the genus name. The first states that *Vinca* is the classic Latin name and is a shortened form of an old Slavic word, *pervinca,* which comes from the word *pervi,* or first, since this is one of the first flowers of spring. The second points to the Latin word *vincio,* to bind, referring to those long, trailing stems that spread about the ground in tangles of green. Some gardeners of Jefferson's time called it ground ivy, but today that name is generally associated with the European weed *Glechoma hederacea,* which arrived on our shores in ships' ballast.

A much older name, sorcerer's violet, or the French *violette des sorciers*, refers to its color and to its magic properties, as it was a favored flower for making charms and love philters. It was also believed to have powers to exorcise evil, and Apuleius wrote in his *Herbarium* (printed in 1480) that this plant "is of good advantage for many purposes . . . first against devil sickness and demonical possessions and against snakes and wild beasts and against poisons and for various wishes and for envy and for terror . . . and if thou has [this plant] with thee thou shalt be prosperous and ever acceptable." If so, it would be a wondrous addition to the garden.

It was used in garlands in olden times, and according to Mrs. M. Grieve, in her wonderful book of herbal history, *A Modern Herbal*, in 1306, Simon Fraser, after he had been taken prisoner fighting for William Wallace, rode heavily ironed through London to the place of execution, where a garland of periwinkle was placed on his head in mockery.

On a more morbid note, the Italians, in addition to calling myrtle *centocchio*, or hundred eyes, also called it *fiore di morte*, the flower of death, hanging wreaths of myrtle about the necks of people condemned to die. They also placed myrtle garlands on the biers of dead children as a symbol of immortality.

Early settlers often used the plant as a cemetery groundcover, as it was beautiful in growth, lovely in bloom, and required no maintenance once planted, and today their myrtle carpet often reveals the location of overgrown and abandoned cemeteries. My first introduction to this plant was when visiting an old graveyard in the Catskill Mountains, where the last person buried was before the Civil War. Twining around the gravestones, a very healthy planting of myrtle sported glossy green leaves and, on that spring day, sparkling blossoms of periwinkle blue.

In early Anglo-Saxon herbals, periwinkle was known as *parwynke*, and in French, *pervenche*. The periwinkle is considered an emblem of friendship in France, where, after thirty years, Rousseau thought of Madame de Warens, with whom he lived from 1731 until 1740, when he saw myrtle in spring bloom.

In 1939, Liberty Hyde Bailey wrote of his periwinkle in *The Standard Cyclopedia of Horticulture:* "A hardy trailing plant with shining evergreen foliage . . . it forms a dense carpet to the exclusion of other herbs [and] is a capital plant for clothing steep banks, covering rocks, and carpeting groves."

Myrtle has a history of being used in many pharmaceuticals, especially as an astringent, for scurvy, and for sore throats.

Vinca major is a larger plant than *V. minor* and is thought to be an offshoot of the original myrtle, but with a doubling of chromosomes. Of the two, it's the more aggressive and the bigger problem. It's a native of Southern Europe, and it, too, has naturalized in areas of the United States where winters are mild. Once established, it soon crowds out native plants and, unlike *V. minor*, allows no competitor to stand.

The only way to safely rid yourself of either type of myrtle is to remove the plants by hand or to mow them down close to the ground. The leaves have a waxy coating that repels most herbicides, so it's useless even to try spraying them.

A new cultivar on the garden market called 'Illumination' has foliage marked with patches of chartreuse that brighten to a golden yellow, and in the words of that old song, it truly brightens the corner where you are. It blooms in late spring and dislikes hot sun.

SHRUBS

THE EUROPEAN BARBERRY

Berberis vulgaris

A list of woody ornamentals grown by Jefferson includes an amazing number of plants. Some of those included were once high on the horticultural hit parade but today have fallen into disfavor, for a number of reasons, not always esthetic.

Take the European, or common, barberry *(Berberis vulgaris)*. Since medieval times, barberry, because of both its thorns and its medicinal uses, has been an English tradition. Both monks and nuns used cloister gardens to protect these shrubs because they were so valuable. Some of the other common names used over the centuries include the guild tree, woodour, woodsore, and the pipperidge bush, a name of uncertain derivation.

According to Sir John Mandeville (a pseudonym for a French physician who lived from 1338 to 1400 and wrote about travels to Arabia, India, and China), Christ's crown of thorns had four circles each made of a different spiny plant, one of them being barberry. Because the thorns grow in threes, the plant could represent the Trinity. And until knowledge of the wheat rust life cycle was gained through research, barberries were time-honored plants.

The genus name is derived from *berberys,* the Arabian word for the fruit. A few references maintain that the plants are named in honor of

St. Barbara, the patron saint of firearms (an honor bestowed upon Barbara after she was beheaded by her father for being a Christian, and he was then consumed in thunder and lightning).

The inner bark of the common barberry is yellow and, according to the doctrine of signatures (a philosophy of medicine wherein a plant that resembled either a human disease or the organ that suffered was thought to be a cure for that disease), was good for treating jaundice, hence another common name of the jaundice bush. John Parkinson suggested boiling the inner bark or the roots in ale or other drinks as a treatment for that disease. The bark was also used to make both a clothing and a hair dye. Small wooden objects, especially toothpicks, were made from barberry wood because it resisted splitting. The early settlers, who originally brought the plant over from Europe, made a berry tea for the treatment of poor appetites and as an expectorant and a laxative. A root-bark tea was used to promote sweating, and a tincture made from that same root-bark was used to treat arthritis, rheumatism, and sciatica. The whole plant contains berberine, a chemical with possible applications as a bacterial inhibitor. But current books contain warnings on its uses.

From the time that this species was introduced until the late 1800s, everybody gathered barberries to make jams and jellies. They also were often preserved in vinegar, then used to complement both meat and fish.

John Parkinson (1567–1650), writing in *A Garden of Pleasant Flowers*, thought they were a good appetizer "for those that loath their meate," and the famous herbalist Nicholas Culpeper (1616–54) wrote, "They get a man a good stomach to his victuals by strengthening the attractive faculty which is under Mars." My mother talked about barberry jelly—she said it was superior to barberry jam—but I cannot remember her actually making it. The berries are edible when fresh, but are extremely sour.

According to Alice M. Coats in *Garden Shrubs and Their Histories*, the fruit was still being gathered for the table in 1863, at which time five different varieties were available. Not only were the berries used, but the leaves were also employed to make a sour sauce like that of sorrel. But an ominous comment soon appeared in various homemaker magazines and books warning that gathering barberries was a tiring affair.

Jefferson mentioned his wheat crop in 1816, and nobody knew of any dangers then. But the tide turned in 1865, when the rust panic hit. It turns out that barberry leaves serve as hosts to one of the stages in the life cycle of the fungus *Puccinia graminis*, the cause of a devastating disease called wheat rust.

Over the course of many years, the basic solution offered for fighting this rust was to eradicate all the barberries one could find, rather than to simply stop growing barberries in the vicinity of wheat fields. Many states adopted programs to eliminate the plants, and the same held true for Europe. In France and Germany, for example, laws were passed that ordered the destruction of the common barberry, never admitting to the fact that many climates where barberries grow are not suitable to the formation of the disease spores. According to L. H. Bailey, "Destroying the barberry will not check the fungus, as it can grow and spread for years without entering the stage where barberry acts as the host." And destroy it they did. The common barberry was almost eliminated.

The European barberry is a much-branched deciduous shrub growing up to eight feet tall, with simple to three-parted spines, bearing bright red berries in the fall. The dull green leaves are toothed, about two inches long, and borne in groups. The small, yellow, waxy flowers that bloom in the spring have six petals and six petal-like sepals. Thoreau noted that the flower color matched that of the silken robes worn by Tibetan priests.

The flowers also have a heavy foxy smell. To some people, it's mildly unpleasant, but certainly not all that bad. Louise Beebe Wilder thought that "the odor of [barberries] which close at hand is somewhat overpowering, [is] pleasant enough when borne on a wandering breeze from a little distance."

Gertrude Jekyll, that great English gardener, expressed a different opinion:

> There was one flower smell that I always thought odious, that of the common barberry. After a time when I learnt how the wind carries scent I used to approach it cautiously from the windward side. The

smell is not really very bad but of a faint and sickly kind but I remember years when to me it was so odious that it inspired me with a sort of fear, and when I forgot that the barberries were near and walked into the smell without expecting it, I used to run away as fast as I could in a kind of terror.

Believe me, it's not that bad!

To round out the barberry story, we return to the flowers. There are six stamens in a barberry blossom, each capped by six anthers that may be described as little pollen boxes with trapdoors on either side. Each stamen is like a hair trigger on a pistol, and when touched by an insect, it reacts like the wire in a mousetrap, breaking open the trapdoor (a one-time happening), showering the creature with pollen. The action of the barberry stamen led to the belief that the flowers possessed a primitive nervous system, and one Scottish botanist, John Claudius Loudon (1783–1843), actually treated the plants with arsenic and pointed out that the stamens lost their ability to move. But if narcotics like belladonna or opium were used, the stamens became so flaccid, they could be bent at will.

THE SWEETNESS
OF SUMMER

Clethra alnifolia

Jefferson, Washington, and Bartram grew a number of attractive shrubs in their gardens, and high on the approval list was the sweet pepperbush *(Clethra alnifolia)*, or, as often referred to in older books, the alder-leaved clethra. *Klethra* is the Greek name for the alder, hence the scientific name. The common name of sweet refers to the scent of the flowers, for they are extremely fragrant, while the pepperbush came from the fact that ripened seeds resemble peppercorns.

The blossoms are each about a third of an inch across, and they are borne in long, narrow, upright spikes of clustered buds. The individual flowers sport five sepals and five longer petals, with ten protruding stamens and a longer style. The shrub has many branches, each from three to ten feet high, covered with alternate leaves, ovate in shape, and green on both sides. Round, grayish pods, about an eighth inch long, weep over the branches and persist well into winter.

A member of the heath order, this is a great American native that has enjoyed almost as much press as any plant can take, but still it is a rarity in most southern gardens. As with many American natives, except for the gardens of many horticultural students, before finding a home in American backyards, sweet pepperbush was introduced to English gardens, where in 1731, it became an immediate success. Neltje Blanchan observed in *Nature's Garden:*

> Like many another neglected native plant, the beautiful sweet pepper-bush improves under cultivation; and when the departed lilacs, syringa, snowball, blossoming almond, found with almost monotonous frequency in every American garden, leave a blank in the shrubbery at mid-summer, these fleecy white spikes should exhale their spicy breath about our homes.

Louise Beebe Wilder wrote in her charming book *The Fragrant Path:*

> [The] honey-sweet or Sweet Pepper Bush . . . is found chiefly in shaded lanes along the eastern seacoast. The white flowers borne in terminal spikes are so fragrant as to scent all the countryside during the period of their blossoming. About Gloucester, Mass., the Sweet Pepper is called "Sailor's Delight" because the men on incoming ships catch its sweetness when still far at sea. When bruised leaves of the clethra emit a curious odour.

Another clethra opinion is offered by William Robinson, writing in his very famous garden tome, *The English Flower Garden and Home Grounds:*

> The clethra are shrubs and small trees of the Heath Order, the hardy species native of North America. The Alder-leaved Clethra in the wet copses of Virginia reaches a height of 10 ft. or more. With us it grows from 3 to 5 ft., makes a dense bush, bearing in summer white sweet-scented flowers in feathery spikes. It is quite a small tree in the woods of the Alleghenies [and] a valuable shrub for moist peaty places.

The plant is excellent for the back of the border, as it's especially grand when used as a living backdrop for a host of woodland flowers of shorter stature down in front. If you're looking for a shrub that does well in either shade or full sun, here's your plant. The lovely fragrant flowers are the icing on the cake and gilding on the lily.

According to Leonard E. Foote and Samuel B. Jones Jr., in *Native Shrubs and Woody Vines of the Southeast,* it's excellent for landscaping in damp areas, although it tolerates most soils. Plant in groups at the edge of a woods or along the banks of a stream.

Richard Bir, in *Growing and Propagating Showy Native Woody Plants*, recommends the following cultivars: 'Paniculata', which has the largest flowers; 'Rosea', whose flowers begin as pink but fade to white; and 'Hummingbird', a dwarf selection discovered by Fred Galle at Calloway Gardens.

Other available cultivars are 'Ruby Spice', which is reported to have the most consistent pink presently available, and 'Pink Spires', with pink buds that open to white.

Our other native clethra is the mountain sweet pepperbush, or the cinnamon-bark clethra *(Clethra acuminata)*, with pointed leaves that are pale beneath, and spreading to drooping flower spikes. These plants are often found in English gardens, planted at the edges of streams and ponds, but neglected here in their homeland, where they should have a stellar spot in every southern garden. The common name refers to the color of the trunk that appears as the bark peels away.

The beauty of this species is its adaptability, for if found deep in the woods, the individual shrubs become leggy, but when transplanted to a brighter and sunnier spot, the plant responds by becoming a great shrub and sometimes a small tree. Height ranges from eight to twelve feet in average soil and light ranging from sun to moderate shade.

Many plants found in the Appalachian Mountains have Japanese counterparts, and the clethra is no exception. The Japanese clethra *(Clethra barbinervis)* is a shrub to small tree with deep green leaves and five-inch panicles of fragrant, white flowers that bloom in midsummer. The bark is usually smooth and polished, but it often peels off, or exfoliates, making this another great addition to the winter garden.

THE FIG

Ficus carica

There are twelve references to the fig in Jefferson's *Garden and Farm Books*. One dealt with his experimentation with figs imported from France. Another was a notation made on September 5, 1809, about planting eight figs from Dr. Thornton under the southwest end of the wall, about twelve feet apart. A third mentioned covering the figs, along with other tender plants, in November 1813.

Depending on the climate, figs can be large shrubs or spreading trees, having soft wood, fruit that matures in summer and fall, and foliage that is deciduous in winter. In *American Gardens in the Eighteenth Century*, Ann Leighton remarked that figs were the delight of southern gardeners and the source of seasonal correspondence—and envy. And to this day, when these gardeners gather, one of the first subjects to be aired concerns the productivity and survival of the fig.

What we think of as the fruit is actually a hollow, fleshy receptacle with the true fruits, or "seeds," on the inside. In the original fig, there's an opening at the apex of the fruit through which a special gall wasp passes, pollinating the tiny flowers within and bringing about the true fruits. Most of the cultivars do not require a wasp for pollination.

Today most folks think of the fig as being a cookie filling for a creation by some fellow named Newton, an afternoon snack, or a sweetmeat. But thousands of years ago, the Egyptians used fig wood for mummy cases because there was a shortage of good wood in the desert; Judas supposedly hung himself on a fig tree; and it is said that St. Augustine sat under a fig tree when he doubted his beliefs, until a fig spoke to him in a child's voice, telling him to read the Scriptures again—which he did—and his doubts vanished.

Both the common and generic names for the fig refer to the Latin word for the fruit, *ficus*, which in turn stems from the ancient Hebrew *feg*. The species is thought to be a native of Caria, in Asia Minor. Apparently the Greeks imported the fig from Caria, and under Hellenic culture, figs were improved by natural selection, and Attic figs became celebrated throughout the Middle East. Figs were one of the principal foods of the Greeks, being largely used by the Spartans at their public table, and athletes fed almost entirely on figs, believing that they increased strength and swiftness. To that end, figs were such a staple food of the people that a law was passed forbidding the exportation of the best fruit gathered from the best trees.

Nature worshipers are said to have performed spring rites underneath fig tree branches, but most Christians prefer to forget such goings-on. Then again, from the clothing point of view, the fig as the first breechcloth possibly was one of the simplest forms of fashion ever conceived. And many biblical scholars believe that the fig was the original forbidden fruit in the Garden of Eden (others think the quince held that honor). One story proclaims that when Mary sought refuge from the soldiers of Herod, she hid inside the trunk of an old fig tree until the culprits passed her by.

In the Far East, the fig is both a sacred fruit and tree. The banyan, another species of fig, is the huge, sacred tree that Buddha sat underneath. Vishnu is said to have been born under the shade of a gigantic fig. There is, in fact, talk of a fig tree in India that is thought to be over three thousand years old, with a spread of over 920 feet.

In classic myth, the fig owes its beginning to Bacchus, who knew a good thing when he saw it. Supposedly figs were growing at the original site of Rome, and the cradle of Romulus and Remus was suspended beneath a fig tree's branches. In Rome, when Calchas challenged his fellow prophet Mopsus to a test of soothsaying, and the latter,

answering his question, told him, "Yonder fig tree has 9,999 fruits"—
which proved to be true—Calchas, unable to guess anything of equal
importance so nearly, hated himself to death.

The basic substance of figs is dextrose, of which they contain
about 50 percent. Because of this, they have long been used for their
nutritive value, both in the fresh and the dried form, and make up a
large part of the diet of both Western Asia and Southern Europe. A
type of wine was prepared from fermented figs, known to the ancients
and mentioned by Pliny under the name of Sycites.

As to medicines, figs have long been employed for their mild laxative action and are used in a number of syrup preparations. Over
twenty-five hundred years ago, Hezekiah, the king of Judah, used figs
as a remedy for boils.

Jefferson grew three cultivars at Monticello: 'Angelica', 'Brown
Turkey', and 'Marseilles'. 'Brown Turkey' has been a popular, self-pol-
linating cultivar for centuries, but new varieties continue to be found.
Recently the Italian honey fig called 'Lattarula' has appeared on the
fig market. It's self-fertile and doesn't need exceptionally hot summers
for the fruit to mature.

In the United States, figs can be grown as far north as Brooklyn. In
the colder parts of the country, they do well in pots and can winter in
a sunny window or on a sunporch or anywhere the temperature can be
kept above freezing.

Here in Asheville, Sally Rhodes has a marvelous fig tree growing at
the southwest corner of her house, and we think that the sewer pipe
passes below the plant on its way to the street, hence the roots, whatever the season, are always warm. I have a 'Brown Turkey' growing up
against the western stone wall of our house, but unless I bend it to the
ground and mulch it well, it always takes at least two years to recover
from winter's chill. Just a few blocks away from our house, David
Hurand dutifully bends his fig tree to the earth, and it bears fruit.

THE GARDENIA

Gardenia jasminoides

Gardenias, or as they were called in the 1700s, Cape jasmines, were favorites in eighteenth-century America. Jefferson grew them; in fact, everybody who could grow plants had gardenias in the garden or in pots.

The scientific name of the plant was often confused. At one time, the gardenia was thought to be a fothergilla, especially when Lafayette's gardening aunt, the countess de Noailles, thought that was the case and made that point at many societal dinners. The English botanist John Ellis (1711–76) was a friend of Linnaeus and asked that the gardenia be named in honor of Dr. Alexander Garden (1730–91) of Charleston, South Carolina. Linnaeus did so, confusing things further by making the species *jasminoides*. In 1793, Dr. Moses Marshall listed his fothergillas as *Fothergilla gardeni* and sent plants to Bartram labeled as gardenias. Bartram also wanted to honor Dr. Garden, and somehow Linnaeus did so but also honored the Cape jasmine.

Confusion reigned because the fragrance of a gardenia is nothing like the fragrance of jasmine, and the plant has no connection with the Cape of Good Hope. Nobody knows for sure, but they first came from China or the East Indies.

Around 1761, when *Gardenia jasminoides* was introduced into Europe, they were usually grown in greenhouses, as most nurserymen and horticulturists thought the plants were too tender to grow outdoors. Gardenias can actually take temperatures as low as eighteen degrees F and do quite well in USDA Zone 7.

When it comes to buttonholes and corsages, camellias and gardenias have long been rivals. They're also rivals in the garden, because they both require about the same growing conditions. In many cases, the gardenia outpaced the camellia, because camellias have no scent.

Gardenias need an acid soil and require a lot of water when in active growth. In dry summers, they benefit from occasional spritzings with water. The six-foot shrubs are covered with bright green, glossy leaves and begin to bloom from late spring to summer, with fragrant white, waxy flowers whose petals yellow as they age.

Temperature usually controls gardenia bloom. At night temperatures above sixty-five degrees F, buds will not form, but once the buds are there, night temperatures must be above sixty-five degrees F or they drop. Ideal temperatures are between sixty-five and seventy degrees F during the day and sixty to sixty-two degrees F at night. The flowering response requires fourteen hours in that temperature range.

If you grow them in pots and provide all the correct growing conditions, but they do not bloom, stick a folded-up wire clothes hanger in the pot. Trust me, they will bloom. As to the explanation, your guess is as good as mine.

Now back to the countess de Noailles. As Marie Antoinette's lady advisor, not only was she a good-hearted woman with great respect for the protocol and a wish to preserve the greatness of the French court, but she was also a power in her own right. She also knew that her nephew, the Marquis de Lafayette (1757–1834) had many reasons to come to America and fight in the Revolution. After all, he wanted revenge against Great Britain for the death of his father and the loss of French possessions in America.

In June 1776, Lafayette presented his credentials to the Continental Congress, which opposed granting any more commissions to foreign mercenaries, reasoning that only American officers who had proved themselves in battle should be promoted to general. But Lafayette agreed to serve without a salary, so Congress relented and commissioned the young man a major general—at just nineteen years old.

Years later, on November 2, 1824, Lafayette stayed with former President Thomas Jefferson at Monticello. He was a guest at a banquet held at the University of Virginia at Charlottesville. At dinner, the marquis was seated between former presidents Jefferson and James Madison. Lafayette must have made a good impression, because he was Jefferson's guest for nine days, until he left to visit Fredericksburg, where a parade and dinner were held in his honor.

Perhaps they talked about the countess and gardenias.

RHODODENDRONS
AND AZALEAS

Rhododendron spp.

On March 21, 1810, Jefferson planted seven rhododendrons in four oval beds in each corner of the house. They probably were *Rhododendron maximum*, called the great laurel, or the rosebay rhododendron. Popular at that time as well was the rhodora rhododendron (*R. canadense*), a small shrub that French friends asked Jefferson to send over to Europe. Jefferson was also fond of the pinxter flower (*R. periclymenoides* [*R. nudiflorum*]), also known as the honeysuckle azalea.

Sir George Sitwell (1860–1943), the father of all the slightly fey Sitwells, had a passion for rhododendrons, but only the leaves. He thought the flowers were a distasteful distraction, so when they appeared, they were promptly removed.

The genus *Rhododendron* represents some eight hundred species of usually evergreen, sometimes semievergreen, and often deciduous shrubs—rarely, but sometimes, small trees—found in the Northern Hemisphere, chiefly in the Himalayas, Southeast Asia, and the mountains of Malaysia, but in fact almost everywhere except the continents of Africa and South America. All of the plants discussed in this chapter are American natives.

Horticulturists who deal with these popular plants have divided them into various categories based on botanical differences. But for most purposes, it's only necessary to know that there are two major divisions in the group: rhododendrons and azaleas. Both belong to the same genus, but azaleas are either evergreen or deciduous and have flowers shaped like funnels, whereas rhododendrons are usually ever-green and have bell-shaped flowers.

Fossil remains of these plants point to a long existence. As a genus, rhododendrons date back to the Miocene era, a time of warmer global climates from twenty-three to five million years ago.

The generic name is from the Greek *rhodon*, or rose, and *dendron*, tree. In 1583, Andrea Cesalpino, a professor of medicine at Pisa and personal physician to Pope Clement VIII, published *De Plantis*, the first important taxonomic system proposed since antiquity. In fact, 150 years later, his system of classifying plants in a hierarchical order provided the starting point for Linnaeus's system of classification.

In 1753, Linnaeus recognized the rhododendrons and, at the same time, created another genus for azaleas. This second genus led to end-less confusion, and in 1796, botanists pointed out that it was too complicated to maintain azaleas and rhododendrons as distinct gen-era. In 1834, rhododendrons were divided into eight divisions still recognized today, with azaleas taking two of these sections.

Few of the rhododendrons are listed as pharmaceuticals, but there are stories of poisoning by feeding victims honey made from rhodo-dendron blossoms. Greek legends report famished soldiers eating wild honeycombs and immediately taking ill with stomach cramps, diar-rhea, delirium, and great stomach upheaval, some actually dying from the food. Some rhododendrons found in Central Asia are reputed to have toxic smoke when the wood is burned, as those who inhale it act as if poisoned.

In 1736, John Bartram found the great laurel, or rosebay rhododen-dron *(R. maximum)* on the banks of the Schuylkill River. It was the first of the evergreen species, and when Peter Collinson heard about these shrubs, he asked for plants, not seeds, so transplants were shipped over six at a time. Collinson reported that upon reaching his garden, they did well but didn't bloom. They had been planted in soil that lacked the necessary acidity, and they never flowered until 1756.

The great laurel rhododendron, the hardiest native broad-leaved rhododendron in North America, was interesting to collectors because it flowered later than most others, and it also had greater interest as a foliage plant. In nature, these shrubs can reach a height of thirty feet; in gardens, they do not grow as high, but they form a great backdrop to the other plants and do very well in full shade.

The shrubs flower in June and July. The flowers vary from a pale to a deep purple-pink, with greenish yellow spots on the upper surface of the corolla that probably function as nectar guides for pollinating insects. While the flowers are attractive, they're often covered by the leaves. But the strength of these plants is not to be ignored.

R. maximum has been hybridized, with one of the results of crossing with *R. cinnamomeum* being 'Cunningham's White', named for the man who made the cross in 1850.

John Fraser, a Scottish linen draper and hosier in Chelsea, upon visiting the Chelsea Physic Garden, took a great interest in botany and became a great plant collector. In 1796, he visited Russia and was appointed botanical collector to their majesties Paul and Maria. He returned to collect plants in America with his elder son, John, and in 1809 sent the first species of *R. catawbiense,* our mountain rhododendron, to English gardens.

This species grows to a twenty-foot height, is an evergreen shrub, and with age can become a small tree. The green, six-inch-long, oval leaves are glossy above. Clusters of lilac-purple bell-shaped flowers bloom in late spring. This species is the parent of many Catawba hybrids.

Shortly after its arrival in England, this rhododendron was crossed with some tender species such as *R. arboreum* from the Himalayas, and today, while the original species still enjoys a place in gardens, it's led to some of the hardiest and most dependable cultivars for gardens in the Northeast. It's also used as a stock plant for grafting hybrids and has a long history of being used in the development of various contemporary hybrids.

A few of the available Catawbiense hybrids (all hardy in USDA Zone 5) are 'Arno', with double flowers of white with a purple edge; 'President Lincoln', with flowers of an amaranth rose with reddish orange markings; and 'Purpureum Grandiflorum', bearing flowers of imperial purple with reddish orange markings.

The Carolina rhododendron (*R. carolinianum*) is a native of North Carolina that is evergreen in habit (the leaves are brown beneath) and reaches a height of about six feet. The flowers are a light pinkish purple. This species, also introduced into England by John Fraser, was thought to be a relative of *R. minus*. It was promptly lost to the trade, but in 1895, it was reintroduced from a nursery in North Carolina. In 1912, it was reclassified as a distinct species. This plant is a star in my garden.

The Piedmont rhododendron (*R. minus*), or dwarf rhododendron, occurs from North Carolina south to Georgia, primarily in the inner coastal plains and the lower mountains. It grows as a small, rounded shrub from three to six feet tall. These plants will tolerate some sun but will also take shade and are great plants for naturalizing an area. The evergreen leaves are oval in shape. Rose-pink to white flowers bloom in terminal bunches, usually in June.

Azaleas are among the most colorful of all flowering shrubs, bearing three- to six-inch clusters of red, yellow, orange, pink, white, or purple flowers in spring and early summer. One species, *Rhododendron prunifolia*, usually blooms in late August to September. In many cases, azaleas sport brilliantly hued autumn leaves. The deciduous species are usually grown in the North, and the evergreens from USDA Zone 6 and south.

The sweet azalea (*R. aborescens*) grows up to six feet tall and in late spring to early summer bears clusters of very fragrant (especially at night) two-inch flowers that are white or white tinted with rose. These plants do best in a moist soil, and even if you never saw the flowers, they are worth growing for the fragrance alone.

The flame azalea (*R. calendulaceum*) was another introduction of John Fraser. It's an incredible native shrub bearing large clusters of two-inch flowers in early summer. The fragrant blossoms range from bright scarlet to pure orange to bright yellow, all on five- to nine-foot plants.

This is a special plant for American gardens of USDA Zone 5 and higher, as the flowers can bloom in the sun and still remain beautiful for up to two weeks. When gardeners grow a number of seedlings, there is tremendous variation in flower color. The three-inch leaves drop in the fall.

The pinxter azalea, or the wild honeysuckle *(R. periclymenoides)*, grows up to six feet tall and bears faintly scented pale pink to white flowers, about an inch and a half in diameter, in late spring.

The roseshell azalea *(R. prinophyllum)* is similar to the pinxter, except that the flowers are larger and more fragrant, and the plants grow about a foot taller.

A new introduction from the National Arboretum, 'Pyrored', may not yet be widely available but is one to watch for. Its glowing red flowers and small evergreen leaves are particularly wonderful when paired with white flowering dogwood. Two Robin Hill hybrids, 'Sir Robert' and 'Nancy of Robin Hill', both offer large, frilly, pastel pink flowers on low, spreading, semideciduous plants. They are reliably winter-hardy. *R. kempferi* 'Othello' flowers profusely, the blossoms a soft, warm pink with a lot of orange. The plant has good autumn color. Many of the Exbury hybrids, such as 'Salmon Orange', are spectacular two-tone blends. 'Gibraltar' is an especially good glowing orange. These hybrids look wonderful when planted near other flowers in related colors.

Many older azalea cultivars are also quite lovely and are veteran performers in the garden, but they may be difficult to find in commercial nurseries. For interested gardeners, they are worth the search. Two of the choice old Glenn Dale hybrids are 'Kobold', evergreen with rich burgundy blossoms in midseason, delightful against a white background; and 'Tomboy', with profuse flowers of pink or pink and white.

Cultural requirements for rhododendrons and azaleas are basically the same: a well-drained, acidic soil composed of leaf mold combined with sphagnum peat moss. Heavy clay and alkaline soils mean slow death to the whole group. When planted next to a masonry wall of brick or stone, over the years lime is leached out of the wall by the action of rain, and eventually the soil becomes alkaline and the plants suffer. Adding ferrous sulfate should rectify the situation for a time, but consult your local extension agent for a correct reading of the soil pH and the right amount of chemical to add. Do not be tempted to use aluminum sulfate—it can have an adverse effect on the plants.

Rhododendrons and azaleas prefer a location that protects them from both the continuous heat of the summer sun and harsh winds in summer and winter. Though some species are quite hardy (to minus twenty-five degrees F) even when exposed to bitter winter winds in the northern part of the country, most prefer winter temperatures that remain above zero degrees F. Both plants need a soil that remains continually moist, as their root systems are shallow and thinly branched.

Rhododendrons and azaleas generally should be planted out in the early spring; the plants are waking from winter slumber and ready to shoot into growth and flowering. This schedule is especially important in the North, since it gives plants adequate time for settling in before the next winter. In warmer climates, rhododendrons can be moved most of the year.

Planting preparations are much the same as for other balled-and-burlapped or container-grown shrubs: The hole must be large enough for the roots to spread out. If the plant has been packaged without extra soil on top of the roots—that is, with the top of the root ball near the soil surface—set the root ball so that the crown is at the same depth as it was in the container. Fill the hole with a mixture of peat moss and compost, three parts to one. Mix the soil lovingly around the roots to remove large air pockets. Firm it, but don't pack it so hard that you compact the soil. Water thoroughly after planting. Keep the soil moist, and follow a careful watering schedule for the remainder of the growing season. Unlike most evergreens, rhododendrons and azaleas can be moved with relative ease since their root systems are shallow and so close to the stems. Be careful to take enough soil, and use plenty of water to settle the new plants in.

May is the best month for rhododendron and azalea displays, but a lot of the dwarfs bloom in April. Remove spent blossoms to prevent seed formation and channel the plant's effort into next year's crop of blooms.

Prune rhododendrons and azaleas in early spring so that new growth has a chance to harden before winter sets in. Cut off the new leaf shoots or trim back to a small bud. These buds are sometimes so small that they are easily missed. Do not cut off any branches without leaving a bud below the cut, or you will not get new growth.

If there is a dead branch on a plant, prune it back to live wood; new shoots will then emerge. On old, overgrown plants, branches should generally be cut back to one foot in length to encourage compact growth. These plants have been butchered with a knife and saw, yet they put forth new growth, and in a few years, one would never know they had been attacked.

THE LILAC

Syringa vulgaris

"**W**hen lilacs last in the dooryard bloomed . . . ," wrote Walt Whitman in the mid-1800s. But there have been lilacs in the dooryards of America since the middle 1600s, when colonists brought the common lilac *(Syringa vulgaris)* over from Europe and England. *Syringa vulgaris* was the first lilac species to be introduced into Europe, arriving from Turkey in the sixteenth century. Lilac, by the by, is an Old English word derived from the Arabic *laylak,* or bluish, and the Persian *nilak,* this last from *nil,* meaning blue.

In a letter of 1737, Peter Collinson, the English Quaker botanist, wrote to John Bartram, the famous plant explorer: "I wonder that thou should be sorry to see such a bundle of white and blue lilacs. That wonder might have soon ceased, by throwing them away if you had them already." So by then they must have been common enough to consider throwing them out.

In 1767, Thomas Jefferson recorded planting lilacs in his garden book. On March 3, 1785, George Washington wrote that he had transplanted existing lilacs in his garden.

Several years ago, I spoke with a lilac expert at the Brooklyn Botanic Garden, Daniel Ryniec, who shared his insights on lilacs. He told me that there are twenty-three distinct species, with about two thousand named cultivars in seven different colors—white, violet, lilac, blue, pink, purple, and red. Another color, a yellow-white was introduced in 1949 with *Syringa vulgaris* 'Primrose', but purists consider it to be a shade of white. The cultivars include both single and double flowers.

The hundreds of lilacs on the nursery market today include *Syringa vulgaris* cultivars 'President Lincoln' (single blue flowers), 'Firmament' (single blue), 'Mme. Lemoine' (double white), 'Sensation' (single purple with white edge), 'Sarah Sands' (single purple), 'Charles Joly' (double magenta), 'Lucie Baltet' (single pink), 'Romance' (single pink), and 'Victor Lemoine' (double lilac); *S. hyacinthiflora* 'Annabel' (double pink); *S. reflexa* (single pink); *S. reticulata* (single white); and *S. patula* 'Miss Kim' (single purple), this last lilac especially recommended for planting in warmer climates.

There are only two tree forms. *Syringa pekinensis* grows to thirty feet, and *S. reticulata* reaches a height of sixty feet. They do fine in USDA Zone 3, which means that most American gardeners can enjoy them. The most unusual lilac is *S. pinnatifolia*, from China, which has pinnate leaves and white flowers without much fragrance.

Through careful observation and hybridizing, future trends will be toward dwarf, disease-tolerant varieties. Cultivars that flower well in warmer climates, such as California and the South, are also becoming available.

Pests that affect lilacs can usually be controlled by good cultural practices such as proper fertilizing, pruning, careful plant selection, and if necessary, applications of horticultural oils and soaps.

Powdery mildew, lilac borers, viruses, mites, and girdling from European hornets are common problems with lilacs. Powdery mildew late in the season may not need to be treated, but if your lilacs get it in June and it keeps coming back year in and year out, it will eventually weaken the plant. Farther south, where it is more humid, you may need to spray your plants with a fungicide such as Bordeaux mixture or summer horticultural oil.

Lilacs need full sun. Those in partial shade will bloom, but not to their best advantage. They also need a reasonably fertile, well-drained garden soil, preferably with a good organic matter content. Alternate yearly applications of 5-10-5 fertilizer and horticultural limestone usually satisfy nutrient and pH requirements. A layer of organic mulch will conserve soil moisture, reduce weeds, and protect the plants from mechanical injury.

As far as pruning is concerned, many lilacs left to their own devices in the overgrown gardens of abandoned farms bloom year after year. But to maintain the best flower quality, cut out diseased canes plus the suckers that grow around the base, beginning the pruning process after flowering is over. Drastic pruning on older lilacs will result in fewer flowers in the coming year, but after that the plant will be fuller and healthier.

Lilacs should be dead-headed, both to save the shrub energy and for cosmetic purposes. Be careful when dead-heading not to remove next year's flower buds, which are located on the two branches just below the dead flower heads.

I grew up in Buffalo, New York, a place of harsh winters with many feet of snow. Just about sixty miles to the east was Rochester, on the shores of Lake Ontario, now the lilac capital of the world. Its love of lilacs dates back to 1892, when Highland Park horticulturist John Dunbar planted twenty varieties on the sunny southern slopes of the park. Today the park is the scene of an annual, two-week-long Lilac Festival, with over half a million people attending the event each year. The park grows over five hundred varieties of lilacs, and more than twelve hundred lilac bushes dot its 155 acres.

One of the sadder things about lilacs is their persistence in the landscape, as noted when driving past long-neglected American farmhouses and seeing houses in ruins (or just old foundations), but there, close to where the front door once opened, lilacs still bloom with only birds and insects in attendance.

TREES

THE SERVICE TREE

Amelanchier canadensis

At Jefferson's Monticello, the service trees *(Amelanchier canadensis)* began to bloom in late March to early April. The early spring blooms of the shadbush or serviceberry have always gladdened hearts weighed down with memories of winter snow and ice. In full bloom, the hundreds of white blossoms look like thousands of long pieces of pure white tissue paper, with every five individual pieces affixed to a common center.

While Jefferson called it the service tree, it is more commonly known as the shadbush, because in the Northeast, about the time when its first blossoms open, the inland waters flow free after a winter's freeze, and American shad *(Alosa sapidissima)* run up the streams and rivers. Other common names include Juneberry, serviceberry, sarviceberry, Maycherry, Saskatoon, shadblow, Indian pear, sugar pear, sweet pear, grape pear, sugar plum currant tree, and western serviceberry.

Dick Bir, in his book *Growing and Propagating Showy Native Woody Plants*, notes of hearing that "service" or "sarvice" referred to the fact that with the winter ground frozen solid, anyone who died in the winter had to wait for the thawing of the earth for burial, and that often occurred when the shadbush bloomed. Another interpretation is that the tree that bears also serves, hence service tree and serviceberry.

In reality, this plant's name has English roots. The *Amelanchiers* of America and the service trees of England both bloomed in May and both had usable fruit. The American trees were thought to be close relatives of the wild service tree *(Sorbus torminalis)* and the service tree *(S. domestica)*. The first originally came to England from Europe and North Africa, with fruit described as being best used for settling the stomach, colic, or "green sickness" in virgins, a malady I've not been able to pinpoint. The second service tree was also introduced to England, this one brought by John Tradescant from the Mediterranean region. The bark was originally used for tanning leather, and after being touched with frost, the fruits are still used as food. So service came from *serves*, from the Old English word *syrfe*, which is from the Latin *sorbus*. The derivation of the scientific name is far simpler, coming from the Provençal French name of the European species, *Amelanchier ovalis*.

When we lived in the Catskill Mountains at an elevation of nine hundred feet, our trees would usually bloom toward the end of April. Along the Neversink Gorge, at the same elevation but with the Neversink River helping to warm the area, serviceberries began to bloom about the third week in April. Farther up in Forestburgh, at an elevation of twelve hundred feet, the blooming was delayed until April 27. Here at the Botanical Gardens in Asheville, at an elevation of twenty-four hundred feet, the trees bloom between April 7 and April 30, depending on the severity of the winter.

I have fond memories of walking a narrow pathway that once delineated the boundaries of a field in the late 1800s, where a twenty-five-foot-high serviceberry grew in a large clump, its gray bark echoed in the many stones that lay about, remnants of a wall that tumbled many years ago. Even in midwinter, when the sky was a darker shade than the bark of that tree, it was a beautiful sight, especially when the many branches were viewed through a cloud of snowflakes. But coming upon that blooming tree in spring was like approaching a burst of galaxies at universe center: shining white lights surrounded by nothing.

In many parts of the country, the blooming time of shadbush is too early for wild or domestic honeybees, so the flowers are generally polli-

nated by little dark brown or black female bees of the *Andrena* tribe.
They live in burrows rather than hives, some digging numerous branched
tunnels and some content to dwell in a simple straight tunnel.

As to gathering the fruits of the serviceberry, it's far easier described
than done. The dark red to purple, round pomes (the correct name for
the fruits of related members of the rose family) have a sweet and
pleasant odor and taste that are attractive to both people and birds—
not to mention chipmunks, squirrels, deer, and mountain goats—and
unless you net the trees, the animals usually get there first. The pomes
usually ripen in June; at higher elevations (above twenty-five hundred
feet), in mid-July; or farther North, even in August. If you're lucky
with your netting, a superior jelly and jam can be made from the fruits,
not to mention great pies and sauces. Unlike many wild foods, serviceberries are very good to eat and do not taste like a mawkish pasteboard
with seeds.

A U.S. Department of Agriculture booklet entitled *Food Plants of
the North American Indians* says that the Native Americans used the fruit
of service trees and bushes both fresh and dried, the pomes being
boiled and eaten with meat or added to pemmican, sun-dried, thin
slices of pounded buffalo or venison meat packed with animal fat. A
tea was made from the dried leaves. Sometimes the berries were dried
for winter use. Also, the Chippewa used a root-bark tea of serviceberry mixed with other herbs as a tonic for the digestion or excessive
menstrual bleeding.

One more use of the service tree clan should be mentioned. *The
Oxford English Dictionary* notes that in Scotland in the late 1700s, service tree branches were fixed above the stakes of tied cattle to protect
from the evils of elves and witches.

There are several different species in addition to the common serviceberry *(Amelanchier canadensis)*. *A. lamarckii* has white flowers, tinged
with pink, and can reach a height of thirty feet. *A. arborea* is usually a
tall shrub but can reach a height of thirty-three feet. *A. laevis*, the
Allegheny serviceberry, can attain fifty feet, is good for Zones 4 to 8,
and has lovely white flowers with foliage that has a purple cast when
young. This species includes the cultivars 'Rosea', with pink flowers,
and 'Prince William', a form with multiple stems and blue fruits. *A.*

alnifolia, the Saskatoon serviceberry, is a smaller species, growing to about fifteen feet high. It tolerates alkaline soil (pH 5.0 to 6.0) and is hardy to Zone 6.

The job of nomenclature regarding serviceberries has not improved over the years, and in order to cut down on confusion, many nurseries have created their own species. Today catalogs often speak of *Amelanchier grandiflora* or, if they are more careful nursery folk, *Amelanchier* x *grandiflora,* signifying that all these new varieties are hybrids of one kind or another. Among the most popular are 'Robin Hill', with pink flower buds and yellow-red fall color, and 'Cole's Select', with white flowers and red fall foliage. They are hardy to Zone 5.

DOGWOODS

Cornus spp.

THE COMMON DOGWOOD
Cornus florida

On April 17, 1779, Monticello suffered a terrible freeze, with "every leaf being killed on the hardiest trees." However, Jefferson wrote, "Dogwoods & other early budding trees escaped." In 1817, he noted that the dogwoods *(Cornus florida)* were in bloom on April 3 to 22.

In *Travels of William Bartram,* on his way to western Florida in 1774, Bartram wrote:

> We now entered a very remarkable grove of Dog wood trees (Cornus Florida), which continued nine or ten miles unalterable, except here and there a towering Magnolia grandiflora. . . . These trees were about twelve feet high, spreading horizontally; their limbs meeting and inter-locking with each other, formed one vast, shady cool grove, so dense and humid as to exclude the sun-beams, and prevent the intrusion of almost every other vegetable, affording us a most desirable shelter from the fervid sun-beams at noon-day. This admirable grove by way of eminence has acquired the name of the Dog woods.

Dogwoods are beautiful trees year-round: in spring when in blos-som, in summer for their shade, in fall for their scarlet berries, and in winter when their interlocking branches form highways and byways on which squirrels travel about, never touching the ground. Indeed, many gardeners consider dogwoods to be the most beautiful native trees in the eastern part of America.

Cornus florida is the flowering dogwood. *Cornus* is from the Latin word for horn, referring to the toughness of the wood; *florida* means to flower freely. Dogwood is one of those unfortunate popular names given for a reason that had nothing to do with the real merits of the plant. Back in merry old England, it was the practice to steep the bark of dogwoods to make an astringent decoction used to wash mangy dogs. There was also another belief that the berries were a cure for rabies.

The glorious dogwoods generally grow to a height of thirty feet with a twenty-foot spread, but they have been known to reach over forty feet. Back in 1934, the largest recorded flowering dogwood in the Carolinas grew near Harbison Spring, on the south side of Mount Satulah in Macon County, North Carolina. This handsome tree was forty feet high with a spread of fifty-three feet and a diameter of one foot measured three feet from the ground.

The flowering dogwood is a deciduous tree with an interesting horizontal branch structure that causes the trees to have a distinctive flat top. Four-inch oval leaves come to a sharp point. They turn a number of reddish and bronzy colors in the fall, but chiefly scarlet.

Flower clusters consist of small, petalless, tubular blossoms set inside four large, showy, white (sometimes pink) bracts with a notch out of each tip. These bracts, which are really modified leaves, attract small insects like *Andrena*, the mining bee, which seek the nectar in the floral tubes. It's because of those bracts that bloom lasts for weeks instead of days.

Red berries follow in autumn. Though considered too bitter for human consumption, they are especially valuable for wildlife. In addition to gray squirrels, deer, chipmunks, mice, and even beavers, numerous birds quickly clear the trees of their fruits. They are particularly important to the American robin.

The bark on mature trees is broken up into small, square blocks, making dogwoods attractive even in winter. The wood is very hard and once had value for items such as commercial loom shuttles and spindles and tool handles. In the mountains of North Carolina, the wood was once used for flooring. Golf club heads also have been made from this wood. But today many states have placed the flowering dogwood on the protected list.

In colonial America, a tea brewed from the bark was said to reduce fevers, and the powdered bark was made into a toothpaste. The bark of the roots yields a scarlet dye, and a distillate has served as a quinine substitute. Though their age is rarely discussed, a specimen that is well sited, with plenty of water and air circulation, can live far in excess of one hundred years.

Flowering dogwoods are found from central Florida northward to southwestern Maine, extending westward through southern Ontario to central Michigan, central Illinois, Missouri, southeastern Kansas, eastern Oklahoma, and eastern Texas.

Many of our native dogwoods are dying as a result of a plant disease called dogwood anthracnose, caused by several types of fungi and recognized since the late 1970s. It attacks trees both out in the woods and in home gardens, although the disease is worse to woodland plants because the environment is cooler and wetter there, whereas trees in home gardens usually receive more sunlight and thus are better at surviving. The first symptoms are spots on the leaves, followed by leaf scorching. Soon the leaves die yet remain hanging on the tree, carrying infection. Sometimes an infected tree will grow a number of vertical branches, or water sprouts, and these sprouts will carry the disease back into the bark. The bark then gets cankers, like localized dead spots. So trees can be under a two-way attack. The disease is also worse as a result of wet springs.

To prevent the disease, practice good sanitation and maintenance. This includes pruning off dead twigs that carry the spores; watering trees during extended dry spells (since they are shallow-rooted); and fertilizing every year in spring or late fall. Spray the trees with a fungicide when the young leaves appear in spring, and twice more at two-week intervals. Replace any lost trees with the Chinese dogwood (*Cornus kousa*), a tree that is not immune but is resistant.

THE CHINESE DOGWOOD
Cornus kousa

The Chinese or Japanese dogwood *(Cornus kousa)* grows about twenty-five feet tall. It's an upright deciduous tree with a spreading form. Leaves are oval, and as on our native trees, the flower clusters are surrounded by large, showy, white, pointed bracts followed by berrylike fruits attractive to birds. These trees grow in full sun in cooler climates but tolerate open shade, too. They need light, well-drained soil rich in organic matter, preferably with an acidic pH.

THE CORNELIAN CHERRY
Cornus mas

Jefferson also grew the cornelian cherry, or as he called it, Ciriege corniole. The scientific name is *Cornus mas.* It's a small deciduous shrub or tree up to twenty-five feet high, of open habit.

Apparently at the beginnings of European civilization, everybody thought that the cornelian cherry was the male form and the swamp dogwood the female form of the same plant, hence the species name of *mas,* for male or robust. Christian legend stated that the European dogwood provided the timber for Christ's cross, especially because the four leafy bracts are in the shape of a cross and the berries are red.

In very early spring, before the leaves emerge, small yellow flowers bloom in umbels, the umbels surrounded by (as in all the dogwoods) four small greenish bracts. Around the end of the average spring, small oval drupes develop, eventually ripening to a shiny dark scarlet.

When properly limbed up, these are elegant trees, once held in high fashion after their introduction from Central Europe to English gardens back in 1551. Initially grown as fruit trees (the berries had astringent properties and made an adequate jelly), in a short time they migrated from the orchard to the flower garden. They are hardy to USDA Zone 4.

'Golden Glory' is a cultivar with a more upright and formal growth habit, maturing at twenty-five feet tall with a fifteen-foot width, with denser flowering. It's available in single-trunk or multistemmed forms.

THE SWAMP DOGWOOD

Cornus sanguinea

Jefferson also grew the swamp dogwood *(Cornus sanguinea)*, a twelve-foot-high shrub with red or purple berries known in seventeenth-century trade as the dogberry. Humphrey Marshall, another colonial who traded seeds with England, called it the American red-rod Cornus. Other common names in England included prickwood, skewerwood, and snakes' cherries.

The flowers of this European native are not that attractive and are reputed to have an unpleasant smell, but the autumn berries make an attractive addition to the wild garden. At one time, the timber of this shrub was used to make spikes, ramrods, pipe stems, arrows, and toothpicks.

THE MIGHTY WALNUT

Juglans nigra

Among the many trees that Jefferson knew and grew, he was quite familiar with the American black walnut *(Juglans nigra)*. In 1734, Peter Collinson asked John Bartram to collect forest tree seeds for shipment to England. Bartram immediately began collecting, and in the winter of 1735–36, the following seeds arrived on foreign shores: a peck and three-quarters of dogwood berries, thirty-two hundred swamp Spanish acorns, two pecks of red cedar berries, and three thousand black walnuts. Of all the seeds in that particular collection, the most important were the black walnuts.

The amazing thing about the black walnut family is that with some twenty species of trees, there are no black sheep, no invasive species that take over when planted or become threats to their surroundings. They are truly magnificent trees.

The genus *Juglans* is an ancient name taken from *Jovis glans*, or Jupiter's acorn, a name used by Pliny for the Persian walnut *(Juglans regia)*. The Greeks, who knew the walnut as the Persian walnut, dedicated the tree to Diana, and wherever possible, her feasts were held beneath those branches. Unscrupulous fortune tellers used the nuts to tell a person's fate, and the rumor was that spirits of evil lurked in the branches and exercised undue influences over everyone who stood beneath them. In fact, rumor had it that one particular walnut in Old Rome was so full of impish spirits at night that it became a public scandal, and eventually it was cut down and the Church of Santa Maria del Popolo was built on the site.

The Lithuanians have a legend about a great flood, believing that the Deity was eating walnuts as the waters overcame the earth, whereupon the righteous, climbing into the shells as they fell upon the surface of the sea, found in each shell an ark, and so were able to escape the death planned for the world's wicked.

In America, the black walnut is a majestic tree from 80 to 150 feet high. The tall trunk has a diameter up to six feet. The bark is dark brown, scaly, and furrowed, and the wood is a dark purple-brown with a silvery luster. It is very hard, durable, and strong, with a fine grain.

The leaves of the walnut are alternate, up to two feet long, feather-like in shape, with thirteen to twenty-five individual leaflets on a stem. They are yellow-green in color, turning yellow in the fall, and are spicy scented when crushed.

The leaves of a black walnut look a great deal like the infamous, invasive Chinese tree of heaven (*Ailanthus altissima*), except that the walnut has white woolly buds and serrate leaves with one leaflet missing at the tip, while the tree of heaven has woolly brown buds and smooth leaves with a leaflet at the tip.

The trees flower in May, with greenish, staminate catkins up to six inches long on old wood. The nuts are large, up to two inches in diameter, with a hard shell. The shell is convoluted, as is the nutmeat, which is oily, sweet, and edible.

It was inevitable that the settlers and farmers of the sixteenth and seventeenth centuries would soon find that the wood of the black walnut was great for gunstocks, and trees were sacrificed by the thousands. At that time, nature did most of the replanting. Today, the trees are distributed from southern Ontario to Florida and west to Texas and Nebraska.

The wood continues to be in great demand for veneers, interior finishing, gunstocks, and cabinetmaking. The bark is used for tanning.

At one time, the nut husks were crushed, then used to stupefy fish, but today this is an illegal act. Everybody from mice to squirrels to humans eats the nuts.

Black walnut shells are almost as tough to crack as an Agatha Christie mystery novel. My father used a hammer. Other inventive folks drive over the nuts in a truck. No matter what method you use, the shells are enclosed in a mushy, greenish yellow husk that stains everything touched by the juice. Black walnuts are more strongly flavored than Persian walnuts, and higher in protein. They are commonly used in cookies and cakes, and some recipes use walnuts as a meat substitute.

One problem with black walnuts is familiar to anybody who has ever gardened in the shade of these trees. Black walnuts, and to a lesser extent other walnut species, produce a plant poison. The roots and nuts contain a chemical called juglone, which is toxic to many plant species. The chemical is thought to inhibit cell respiration.

Some plants exhibit stunted growth when planted within the drip line of a black walnut, whereas others, like the members of the tomato or nightshade family, will not grow at all. Shallow-rooted plants seem to do better than those with deep roots. There are, however, hundreds of plants that will grow in company with black walnut roots; consult your local extension service for a list of plants impervious to juglone.

THE TULIP POPLAR

Liriodendron tulipifera

In Ann Leighton's book on American gardens, under the heading of "Plants Most Frequently Cultivated," the entry for the tulip tree (*Liriodendron tulipifera*) simply states: "Universally acclaimed. Catesby. Collinson. Bartram's. Prince's (Prince being The Long-Island Nursery of William Prince at Flushing Landing where he sold tulip poplars seedlings for 20 shillings each)."

That Washington and Jefferson grew this magnificent tree just adds one more star to its already illustrious biography. It's rare that a tree that sends up such fast-growing seedlings would become one of the finest symbols of our natural heritage. The tulip tree is the state tree of Indiana and Tennessee. Some historians claim that Daniel Boone built a sixty-foot dugout boat called a pirogue from a single tulip tree trunk, and used it to carry his family down the Ohio River from Kentucky out to the western frontier.

This tree has many common names, including yellow poplar, blue poplar, tulip poplar, tulip tree, and yellow wood. Most gardeners, including Jefferson, have called it the tulip poplar, although it's not a poplar at all, but a member of the magnolia family. The genus name is from the Greek *leiron*, for lily (referring to the flowers), and *dendron*, for tree. The species name means tulip-bearing.

There are only two species in the genus, one in America and one in China *(Liriodendron chinense).* The American species grows taller and has larger flowers. Fast-growing and able to live over three hundred years, with a trunk that approaches five to ten feet in diameter, it inhabits eastern North America, ranging from Vermont west through southern Ontario and Michigan, south to Louisiana, and east to northern Florida.

One of the best-known tulip poplars was the tree to which George Washington tied his horse when he worshiped at Falls Church, Virginia, before the Revolutionary War. At that time, the tree was at least three hundred years old. Another tulip poplar was planted in 1785 by Washington at Mount Vernon, since designated the site's official bicentennial tree. The historic Davie Poplar on the University of North Carolina campus is yet another of the oldest tulip poplars in the country. It was under this tree that Gen. William Richardson Davie took lunch when, in 1789, he and his committee selected Chapel Hill as the seat of the university. This massive tree has been struck by lightning and survived several hurricanes. Davie Poplar Jr., grown from a cutting, and Davie Poplar III, grown from the eldest tree's seed, are planted nearby.

Because the tulip poplar flowers bloom only at treetop—and most bees fly only fifty feet or so in the air—since 1989 the National Arboretum has been manually pollinating these flowers using a lift bucket and Q-tips. Seedlings of this tree were sent to replace tulip poplars destroyed in the 1999 hurricane at the palace at Versailles.

The bark of the tulip poplar is gray and closely ridged. The leaves are truncate with four lobes and shallowly notched at the end, a smooth, dark green above and light green below, turning a beautiful yellow in the fall. In silhouette, the leaves suggest a tulip. The trunks of old trees are often branchless for quite a distance up. The specimen in my front yard shoots straight up, with the first lateral branch about twenty feet in the air.

And the flowers! They are showy and handsome, with orange tints brushed over greenish yellow corollas, marked to attract bees. One of John James Audubon's great bird lithographs portrays the upper reaches of a blooming tulip poplar with a flock of Baltimore orioles flying about a nest, surrounded by attractive leaves and two glorious flowers. The blossoms look like those of magnolias until the central spike splits open to reveal the seeds. Upon maturity, magnolia seed-pods open up the back, but tulip poplar fruits are dry and don't open. A flat wing rises above the seedbox, and the contraption flies away on the autumn breezes.

The wood has long been held in high regard for construction lumber and for plywood. The grain is straight, there's little shrinkage, and it has excellent gluing qualities. In Jefferson's time, it was used for carriage bodies and shingles; today it's used for cabinets, furniture, and pulp.

Deer browse on the seedlings, and birds and small animals feed on the winged fruits, called samaras, few of which are fertile. It's a favorite nesting tree for many birds, and the flowers are a marvelous nectar source for hummingbirds. According to the honey industry, the flowers from a twenty-year-old tree produce enough nectar to make four pounds of honey. Tiger swallowtail butterflies use the leaves. Even bears occasionally spend the winter sleeping in the huge hollows that often develop in old trees.

In the 1800s, a heart stimulant was extracted from the inner bark of the roots, and a rheumatism tonic came from the stem bark.

Second only to sycamores in trunk diameter, tulip poplars are difficult to transplant. They should be moved only when young saplings and in active growth, taking as much root as possible.

This is a noble lawn and shade tree and probably has a better reputation in Europe than here. As others have opined about the tulip poplar, "There is no season when the tree is not full of interest and beauty, no matter what its age."

THE UMBRELLA MAGNOLIA

Magnolia tripetala

Jefferson was familiar with at least five species of magnolias, including the cucumber tree *(Magnolia acuminata)*, the large southern magnolia *(M. grandiflora)*, the sweet bay magnolia *(M. virginiana)*, and my favorite of them all, the umbrella magnolia *(M. tripetala)*, which was seeded at Monticello in 1810.

The name *Magnolia* honors the French botanist and horticulturist Pierre Magnol, and *tripetala* refers to the three large petaloid sepals that enclose the numerous petals, which are smaller than the sepals.

Umbrella magnolias are not large trees, the usual height being between thirty and forty feet. They have an irregular habit and stoutly contorted branches and twigs. The thin bark is gray and smooth, with bristly warts. They grow near streams and in damp, rich soil in Virginia, the Carolinas, and western Georgia, and from southern Michigan to central Illinois, then south to the Florida panhandle and Mississippi; in fact, wherever tulip trees *(Liriodendron tulipifera)* are present, you might find the umbrella tree.

The common name refers to the umbrellalike whorls of leaves that surround each flower. The twigs have the habit of sticking out at right angles from an erect branch, then turning up parallel with the parent branch, so that the entire tree itself suggests an umbrella. The leaves are sixteen to twenty-four inches long and slightly oval, being broader above the middle than below and tapering narrowly to the stout petiole. They are dark green in summer, turning a yellow-brown in autumn. This is an exotic-looking tree that looks more like a denizen of a rubber plantation than an eastern woodland.

The spring-blooming flowers are very large and showy. The inner petals are a creamy white with a purplish base and up to five inches long, while the outer petals (really sepals) are a greenish white. When the blooms are smelled from a distance, the gardener tends to be kind and calls the fragrance interesting, but up close, the odor is piercing, sharp, and very unpleasant. These flowers are pollinated by beetles instead of bees.

The conelike fruits are five to six inches long. They start out looking like green cucumbers, but turn a bright rose color when mature, later turning brown, and contain individual seeds that are pink to red. The fruits mature in August to September. They are composed of numerous follicles that split open in late summer, each releasing two seeds.

One of the most beautiful early hand-color engravings of American plants is Mark Catesby's portrayal of the umbrella tree in the book *The Natural History of Carolina, Florida and the Bahama Islands*, published between 1730 and 1747. In this illustration, as in many of Catesby's, the magnolia flowers stand out almost like sculptures against a background of dark green, sometimes matte black, that throws the white flowers into relief.

The caterpillar stage of the tulip tree moth *(Callosamia angulifera)*, one of the giant silkworm moths, with a wingspan up to four and a half inches, feeds only on the umbrella magnolia, tulip tree *(Liriodendron tulipifera)*, wild black cherry *(Prunus serotina)*, and sassafras tree *(Sassafras albidum)*.

Umbrella magnolias rarely live more than a century, with most individuals surviving about forty years. Although rarely used by landscapers, it's very effective as a specimen plant, especially in a small garden, because of its exotic look and fast growth habits.

THE MAGNIFICENT
HEMLOCKS

Tsuga canadensis

On April 12, 1804, Jefferson noted in *The Garden and Farm Books* that forty-odd hemlocks *(Tsuga canadensis)* and Weymouth pines were planted near the aspen thicket. Weymouth pine, a name commonly used in Europe, refers to Lord Weymouth, who planted numbers of white pines *(Pinus strobus)* shortly after their introduction to Europe in 1705.

One of the most beautiful of the American evergreen trees, mature specimens often reach heights of one hundred feet or more, with trunks up to four feet in diameter. The leaves are linear, dark green, and very finely toothed, from a quarter to two-thirds of an inch long, with two whitish bands beneath. They persist until the third season. The flowers are negligible, but the fruits are ovoid cones from one-half to three-quarters of an inch long. Both in the garden and in the landscape, hemlocks are truly great trees.

They tolerate most conditions but do best in a cool, moist, acid soil in full sun or some high, open shade. Shallow roots make them easy to transplant and fast-growing. They can be sheared for a formal hedge but are not happy in hot climates.

Back in the 1700s, a physician and philosopher named Dr. Christopher Witt made his home in Germantown, Pennsylvania. He is thought to have established the first botanical garden in the colonies and numbered among his good friends Peter Collinson, the great garden enthusiast in London. Sometime before 1730, Witt sent some hemlocks, or "small firs," to Collinson, who planted them in his garden at Perkham in Surrey. In 1749, Collinson's collection, including the hemlocks, was moved to Mill Hill at Hendon, some eight miles northwest of London, an event that took two years. Mill Hill eventually became a boarding school for boys, and some two hundred years later, the Witt hemlock was still growing. Measurements made in 1835 showed the tree to have two trunks, each a foot in diameter and about fifty feet high.

In a 1932 letter to Charles F. Jenkins, the curator and founder of the Hemlock Arboretum at Far Country, in Germantown, Maj. N. G. Brett-James, author of a biography of Collinson, wrote: "The hemlock spruce is still in good health and is not changed in size from when Dr. H. Harris measured it in my company for Dr. Hingston Fox in 1923, and so it is almost exactly the same as in 1835. It's undoubtedly the oldest *Tsuga canadensis* growing in Great Britain." Such fidelity to a tree shows how much hemlocks are admired by both the garden and arboretum communities.

There are now fourteen hemlock species, of which ten are Asiatic and two native to the Pacific states and adjacent Canada, one extending north to Alaska. In the early days of scientific nomenclature, the first hemlock was included with the pines and labeled *Pinus canadensis* by Linnaeus in 1763. In 1796, André Michaux moved the hemlock to the fir category, calling it *Picea canadensis*. It was the celebrated Austrian botanist Stephen Ladislaus Endlicher (1804–49) who, in 1847, first used the name *Tsuga*, the Japanese name for the hemlock. He added the tree to a section of his genus *Pinus*. The Japanese apparently had no written language of their own until writing was introduced from China about 400 A.D. According to some scholars, the Chinese character thought to describe the hemlock means tree with hanging branches, an accurate description. Other specialists think the word *Tsuga*, which in Japanese means tree mother, came before the Chinese introduced writing. In 1855, the French botanist Elie Abel Carriere (1816–96) classified all hemlocks into a separate family group under

the generic name *Tsuga.* So in the great tradition of botanical termi-
nology, a great North American tree bears a Japanese name that could
be originally Chinese, conferred by an Austrian, confirmed by a
Frenchman, and now accepted around the world.

The eastern hemlock once covered vast acres in the mountains of
New England and New York, spilling over into Pennsylvania, north
through Canada to Nova Scotia, west to Minnesota, and south along
the Appalachians to the north of Alabama. Its first, and so far only,
glory came after tannin was discovered in the bark, and a gigantic
tanning industry arose around the virgin hemlock forests. The shoes
of Civil War troops were made supple with the trees from the Catskill
Mountains. Hemlock groves were felled until the German chemical
industry discovered a substitute. By the end of the nineteenth century, all the virgin hemlocks were gone, and a vast industry died along
with them.

As witnessed in the woods that surrounded our country house in
Sullivan County, New York, the soil wants of hemlocks are slight. An
acid soil is needed, and in times of extreme dryness, needles will turn
yellow and fall. If this happens, immediately give them a good soaking, and they will recover.

Finding and growing hemlock seedlings that germinate on the forest floor can be a fascinating hobby. These little trees exhibit a great
many variations in color, needle and tree size, and the general shape of
the tree itself. Since hemlocks produce numerous seedlings, the ground
that supports a hemlock grove will be covered with plants in various
stages of growth. All that is needed is a sharp eye to pick out the one
tree that is different from the rest and move it to a better spot. If left
to mature on their home ground, the mutations will usually die out
because they cannot compete with their larger, more typical brethren
for light, water, and soil nutrients.

Hemlock seedlings are also surprising because of the patience they
show. These little trees will remain small for decades, shadowed by the
mature trees around them. Then, when disaster strikes and a big tree
dies or is felled in a storm, the seedlings in the best spot for increased
light will suddenly take hold and eventually be forced to fight it out
for the survival of the strongest.

The Museum at the Royal Botanical Garden at Kew has a sample of bread made in 1793 from the inner bark of the California mountain hemlock *(Tsuga mertensiana)*. The explorer Alexander Mackenzie, for whom the Mackenzie River is named, received the bread as a gift from a Northwest Indian tribe. This food was considered a great delicacy. It consisted of the hemlock's inner bark, shaped into cakes about fifteen inches long and five inches deep, then sliced and dipped in salmon oil. Outside of casual mentions of hemlock tea used by lumbermen when no other drink was available, it's the only report I've found of the tree used as a food.

Linnaeus once made an extended trip to northern Scandinavia and came to a place where large numbers of reindeer were dying from a mysterious cause. He discovered that they were eating cowbane *(Cicuta maculata)*, a first cousin of poison hemlock *(Conium maculatum)*. A concoction made from the leaves and roots of this last plant is thought to have been the fatal drink that ended the life of Socrates. Because the spreading branches of *Tsuga canadensis* resemble the highly pinnate leaves of *Conium,* early botanists got the plants mixed up.

Native Americans used a tea made from the new needles of the Canadian hemlock for kidney ailments. They added leafy branches to steam baths for the treatment of rheumatism, colds, or coughs, and to induce sweating. The inner bark was steeped for a tea used to treat colds, diarrhea, fevers, coughs, scurvy, and various stomach problems. Solutions were also used to stop bleeding. Because of the tannin content, the bark is very astringent.

VINES

THE VIRGIN'S BOWER

Clematis virginiana

Jefferson grew the Virgin's bower *(Clematis virginiana)*, which had a number of other popular names, including woodbine, leather flower (although this usually refers to *C. viorna*), devil's-darning-needle, traveller's joy, and old-man's beard, this last referring to the plumed seedpods. Virgin's bower, the most popular common name, really hearkens back to the European clematis *(C. vitalba)*, which looks a great deal like its American cousin when going to seed. When Europeans saw our native clematis, they gave it the same name. The reason for the name is evident when you see the vine rambling through a thicket in the fall, the slanting rays of the sun hitting the feathery plumes on the seeds, and all lighting up like a halo. Traveller's joy is another English common name, this one saluting the walking tourist, because from early leaves to bursting blossoms to feathery seedpods, this plant exuberantly shows the passing of the seasons.

The ancient Romans believed that clematis rambling up the walls of their houses would protect the homes from thunderstorms, while the Germans believed the plant would attract lightning. But there's another, less attractive legend associated with the European plant. In France, it's called *herbe au gueux*, meaning beggar's plant, because French beggars were said to crush the leaves into a fine dust, which they then applied to their skin to raise ulcers, meant to generate compassion in the public. Hence today, in the language of flowers, clematis is a symbol of artifice. Another little-known common name is shepherd's delight, as poor folks would smoke cigar lengths of the dry stems because they drew well and didn't burst into flames.

The name *Clematis* is from the Greek word *klema*, or vine-twig, although the plants are not really vines, but clambering subshrubs. They are all members of the buttercup family, Ranunculaceae.

The plants love to grow at the edges of thickets or along streambanks where they can ramble through the branches of other plants, reaching up to the light but still keeping their roots shaded and cool. The Virgin's bower will grow in most well-drained soils, in full sun or partial shade. The vines will easily climb fences, shrubs, and small trees. The white, one-inch-wide flowers have four petals and bloom in clusters. The seedpods bear many two- to three-inch, feathery, and glistening silky threads.

Our native vine is sometimes confused with the sweet autumn clematis (*Clematis terniflora* or *C. paniculata*, or as it's now called, *C. maximow-icziana*), an Asian vine that has escaped from gardens. The two vines are easily distinguished by examining their leaves: On the Virgin's bower, almost all leaves have jagged teeth, whereas on the sweet autumn clematis, the leaves are rounded and most are untoothed.

THE HYACINTH BEAN

Dolichos lablab

I visited Monticello one sunny afternoon in early fall to take photographs for a lecture to the College for Seniors at the University of North Carolina at Asheville. And few memories I have are sharper than the sight of arbors at the southwest corner of Jefferson's thousand-foot-long vegetable garden terrace, entwined from toe to tip with the boundless blooms and seedpods of that glorious climber the hyacinth bean *(Dolichos lablab)*.

For the year 1812, Jefferson's *Garden Book* mentions the vines as "Arbor beans white, scarlet, crimson, purple . . . on the long walk of the garden." Although not specifically referred to by Jefferson, this tender perennial vine is such a show-stopper (not to overlook its worldwide importance as a vegetable crop) that it must have been on the estate, especially because his favorite nurseryman, Bernard M'Mahon, listed the seeds in his collection.

The genus name *Dolichos* is the Latin word for long, referring to the stems, and *lablab* is the Egyptian name for the beans. Common names for the hyacinth bean include dolichos bean, Egyptian bean, Zaramdaja, lablab, bonavista or bovanist bean, seim (or sem) bean, Indian bean, frijoles caballero, Chinese flowering bean, Pharaoh's bean, and in many parts of China, pig's-ears, referring to the shape of the leaves. Originally from tropical Africa, the plants are now cultivated around the world, usually as a food plant, but often as an ornamental. It's a very popular plant in China, where it has been grown on backyard fences and trellises for centuries.

Many seed catalogs incorrectly list it as an annual vine, but it's a true perennial and, as many tropical perennials do, blooms the first year from seed. This twining vine has purplish stems and alternate, pinnately divided leaves with three large leaflets. It can grow twenty feet in a good season. The white, pink, or purple pea-shaped flowers are fragrant and grow in elongated clusters. They are followed by fragrant fruits with the color of a rare violin, usually maroon to mahogany in color. These open to reveal three to five black seeds with a conspicuous white hilum, the elongate scar on the edge of the bean where it was attached to the inside of the pod.

Several cultivars have been selected, including some with white flowers and pale green pods; some with red flowers; some with long, thin, cylindrical pods; and some dwarf forms. Many are day-length neutral, but the majority of selections still flower as day length shortens, hence they are stellar additions to the late summer garden. Well-planted vines will produce hundreds of spikes, each crowded with the lavender flowers and leading to a crop of hundreds of pods. The distinctive, long-lasting pods are suitable for the cut flower industry.

The young pods and beans are used in the production of many oriental foods, but they should be avoided by gardeners without the knowledge of just how to prepare them. The beans have an unpleasant odor when cooking, at least to most western noses. The purple color disappears during cooking. Some books claim that young leaves are eaten raw in salads while older leaves must be cooked like spinach. The large, starchy root tubers can be boiled and baked. The dried, mature seeds must be boiled in two changes of water before eating because they contain toxic levels of cyanogenic glucosides. In Asia, the mature seeds are made into tofu and fermented for tempeh. They are also used for growing bean sprouts and as livestock fodder.

Hyacinth beans are easy to grow, but unless you live in a very warm climate, start seeds about eight weeks before the last frost by putting three beans in a four-inch peat pot. When seedlings are about six inches high, pull up the two weakest plants. When planting out, do not disturb the root ball, and provide full sun. Alternatively, set out seeds directly when the soil is above sixty-five degrees F. These climbers need a good tilth, and do best in alkaline or calcareous soil. If planting them out in an acid soil, first add some lime to the soil. Once established, like most tropical vines, they need occasional feedings with a good liquid fertilizer.

THE YELLOW JESSAMINE

Gelsemium sempervirens

Carolina jessamine *(Gelsemium sempervirens)* is the native flower of South Carolina and certainly deserves the honor. Jefferson also called it jessamine. Ann Leighton states that Jefferson called *Bignonia capreolata* the Virginia yellow jasmine, also known as the cross vine—somewhat confusing.

The genus name is taken from the Latin word for jessamine, and the species refers to the evergreen habit of the vine. Common names include mail-box vine, Carolina wild woodbine, evening trumpet flower, wood vine, yellow false jessamine, and in Mexico, madreselva.

This twining vine with thin, wiry stems reaches a height of about twenty feet, but the spread can be just about any size, depending on the space. The growth becomes stockier with adequate sunlight. The leaves are up to three inches long and a lustrous dark green. Fragrant, yellow, trumpetlike flowers bloom in clusters, each blossom about an inch and a half long. The fruit is made up of two joined sections, each containing a great many winged seeds.

In the wild, this lovely vine grows throughout southeastern North America, from Florida to Texas and north to Arkansas and Virginia. Habitat varies from sand dunes to thickets, and from dry areas to wet woods. In early spring, these vines are seen blooming along the interstates, where they twine through open fences and through and around shrubbery.

In addition to growing as a vine, Carolina jessamine makes a great groundcover and can be used to cover banks and other areas where many plants refuse to grow. Mow groundcovers every few years to maintain density. The plant will also do well in a container.

There are some new cultivars for this vine. The first is 'Lemon Drop', a small, rounding groundcover that matures to a two-foot height and a three-foot spread. The plant is covered with flowers in the spring and is great as a garden accent or for mass plantings. It prefers a good, well-drained soil with organic matter and can adapt to a slightly alkaline soil. 'Butterscotch' blooms about two weeks earlier than the species and again in the fall. It's much smaller than the species and would be great on a small patio or deck. 'Pride of Augusta' is a double-flowered cultivar.

As to soils, this is a tolerant vine. There are few pest problems, and pruning should be carried out after flowering. Older vines that become top-heavy or sparse can be pruned back to a few feet above ground level after flowering. Remove dead or broken branches, and shape the plant each year after bloom.

All parts of the Carolina jessamine plant are toxic, containing chemicals called gelsemine and gelseminine, which act as motor nerve depressants and are related to strychnine. If ingested, symptoms include dizziness, visual disturbances, and general spasms. Accidental poisoning is very rare because of the plant's extremely bitter taste. It's one of the few plants that deer will avoid.

THE BALSAM APPLE

Momordica balsamina

On April 18, 1810, Jefferson planted balsam apples *(Momordica bal-samina)* in the flower borders along with larkspurs and poppies. These plants are great additions to the garden for many reasons. The balsam apple is a fast-growing tropical vine cultivated for its ornamental leaves, pretty flowers, and fruits.

The scientific name is derived from the Latin *mordio,* to bite, so called from the bitten appearance of the fruit, and *balsamina,* referring to the use of the pulp as a liniment.

Originally from Africa and Australia, these perennial vines are treated as annuals in many northern gardens, climbing up small trunks, trellises, or through shrubbery using grasping tendrils. The deeply palmately lobed, ivylike leaves are light green and have an intense, sometimes unpleasant smell.

Flowering begins about a month after planting seeds. The small axillary flowers range from creamy white to light yellow and have black centers. After fertilizing, the fruits, which have an upside-down drop shape, turn from green to deep orange.

When the fruits are mature, they split along three sides, much like the pods in recent horror films, revealing a red interior and large white seeds. These vines make excellent screens and are great for covering rock piles or old stumps in the garden. They need a long growing season for the fruits to mature, about sixteen weeks after sowing, so start seeds indoors at least eight weeks before the last frost.

The immature fruits are known as bitter melons or bitter gourds. Unpeeled bitter melons, with their spongy white interior pulp and seeds, are sliced for use as a vegetable in various Asian dishes, or the fruits may be stuffed or pickled, but they must be properly prepared, including parboiling or soaking them in salted water to remove the bitterness. The *AMA Handbook of Poisonous and Injurious Plants* specifies that they contain momordin, a plant lectin (toxalbumin) that interferes with protein synthesis in the intestinal wall, so eat them at your own risk. I will continue to use them for decorative purposes only.

A liniment made by adding pulped fruit to almond oil is useful for chapped hands and burns. Using some fruits from a previous harvest, my wife mixed a bit of this salve and found that it does indeed promote healing skin.

The balsam pear *(Momordica charantia)* is another perennial vine used as an annual screen. It grows up to twelve feet in a good season, eventually producing large, spindle-shaped fruits that taper from the middle to either end. The orange-yellow fruits, about eight inches long, burst open at maturity to reveal white seeds and scarlet linings.

POISON IVY AND
ITS RELATIVES

Rhus spp.

There is a trail from Monticello to Jefferson's Rock. It passes fields of poison ivy that wander through pits and ditches that are remnants of the busy charcoal-producing days of the 1800s. As you walk, you descend into an attractive forest of maples and hardy oaks that grow above an understory of dogwoods.

The Rock is beyond the trail that leads to the Harper Cemetery. Legend claims that the flat stone supported by pillars is not the rock that Jefferson stood upon. No, a company of soldiers angered by his 1800 campaign to cut defense spending was said to have pushed the rock bearing Jefferson's name over the cliff. While most historians agree that he visited this rock formation, which rock he stood (or sat) upon and which one rolled down the hill isn't known.

But Jefferson knew all about poison ivy, having described it as an ornamental. John Bartram actually sold poison ivy by the pot at his Philadelphia nursery. Gardeners in those days all wanted one of these vines to climb a tree in the backyard, for when the leaves turned golden in the fall, they brought another touch of the exotic to the garden.

"Leaflets three, let them be" is one of those old saws that we first hear from a relative who's suffered from meeting this vine head-on, or from savvy suburban or rural schoolteachers who happen to live in areas where this vine grows well.

Hikers, home owners, and gardeners usually meet three toxic members of this infamous tribe: poison ivy, also called poison oak, cowitch, or markry *(Rhus radicans)*; poison oak *(R. diversiloba)*; poison oak or poison ivy *(R. toxicodendron)*; and poison sumac, also known as swamp sumac, poison elder, or poison dogwood *(R. vernix)*.

The scientific name of poison ivy has been *Rhus radicans* for decades, with *Rhus* being an ancient Greek name for the genus and *radicans* meaning rooting, which they certainly do. But the genus of these plants was recently changed from *Rhus* to *Toxicodendron*. (*Toxicodendron radicans* means poison tree that roots.) Most books still used *Rhus*, however, and I will, too. These poisonous plants are all members of the cashew family. And all parts of the plants described below are poisonous to the touch.

Poison oak *(Rhus diversiloba)* grows as a shrub to eight feet and often climbs wooden supports, either posts or trees. The toothed or lobed compound leaves grow in threes and are about three inches long. The flowers are greenish and the fruits are clusters of white berries. The plants are common from British Columbia to Baja California.

The second poison oak *(R. toxicodendron)* is basically a creeping shrub to about six feet, bearing three leaflets, each lobed or bluntly rounded, and spreading by creeping runners. Flowers are greenish, blooming in panicles, and the fruits are white. It grows throughout eastern North America.

Poison sumac *(R. vernix)* is a shrub or small tree, reaching about twenty feet in height. The leaves are compound but grow with seven to thirteen leaflets instead of three. The flowers are greenish, as are the hanging bunches of fruit. The leaves turn a brilliant crimson in the fall.

With age, poison ivy *(Rhus radicans)* vines can get very thick. I've found noble vines over two inches in diameter clinging to the sides of trees, notably apples. The amazing thing about this ivy is its ability to grow along the woods floor for years, appearing to be a rambling and weak-stemmed vine that acts as a groundcover and creeper. The infamous three leaves in this stage are bright green and rather small, usually under six inches long—but still poison to the touch.

But suddenly this ivy will start to climb a tree, producing a vine of such girth that Tarzan could probably swing with it if he were immune to the vine's itch. The leaves can then reach ten inches in length and become quite attractive in their own right. Over many years, the vines grow larger, until they become as thick as a transatlantic cable. Tiny rootlets on either side, wiry projections that work their way into the tree's bark, provide added support to the vine and give it a decidedly hairy look. And they are strong.

On the plus side, poison ivy provides valuable winter forage for wildlife. The fruits are eaten by many birds, which suffer no ill effects. If the ivy has vined up a tree in a part of your wild garden where you can keep visitors away from it, let it be, for in the fall, the leaves turn a beautiful golden yellow. In fact, if the plant were not poisonous, we would all be growing it in the backyard.

The problem with these plants is that all of its parts—roots, stems, leaves, berries, and flowers—contain volatile oils that cause severe skin inflammation, itching, and blisters because they act on the histamine found in the cells of the human body. Legend says that Native Americans rubbed leaves on an existing rash for treatment, and homeopathic physicians use tiny doses to treat allergies, but the dose used is so small that only a trained physician can handle the job properly—and I'm still a skeptic about that particular cure.

The name of the compound in poison ivy sap that causes all the trouble is urushiol. It is rendered inactive by water, but the chemical can persist for months or years on shoes, on clothing that hasn't been washed, or on dead ivy roots buried in the ground. The rash that one gets is a reaction to the oil, and typically, by the time the victim begins to itch, the urushiol is gone.

The skin that first contacts the urushiol and has the largest dose of the oil will usually break out with a rash the first time around. Then, soon after brushing against poison ivy, the victim can spread this oil by touch. Even when directly exposed, the palm of the hand never reacts. But if the oil reaches the face, a rash can break out in hours. The skin on the inner arm is also very tender, but a rash takes longer to develop with the thicker skin on the lower arm. Sometimes a part of the body that has not been directly exposed will break out, usually because the skin has been sensitized by a previous attack.

And woe to the person who burns the ivy and inhales the smoke. The irritant rides on the smoke particles, and the inside of your respiratory system reacts just like your skin. In fact, smoke from burned plant specimens over one hundred years old can still cause dermatitis, inside the body or out. Imported lacquerware is often coated with a finish that contains sap from the Asiatic species *(Toxicodendron vernici-flua)*, and just touching the surface can cause problems for highly susceptible people.

Washing thoroughly with water and laundry soap (not hand or bath soap, as the oils they contain easily spread the urushiol), or swabbing the infected spots with alcohol within five to ten minutes of exposure, usually (but not always) removes the oil-based irritant and generally prevents the rash. The problem with that approach is knowing when you have been exposed. A commercial preparation called Tecnu is available at most drugstores, and it works like a charm. Also if your dog or cat wanders through a patch and then you pet the animal, you may break out.

There are a few chemicals that can kill poison ivy, but even a dead and dried plant or its roots can cause a reaction. Heavy, tree-climbing vines can be cut at the base, but as the sap also causes problems, wear gloves. If pulling vines out of the garden, wear gloves and a long-sleeved shirt, and wash all your clothes after use. The safest thing to do with the collected plants is to let them air dry until dead and then bury them. Glyphosate herbicides will kill poison ivy, and this method of removal is very effective if you are only killing the plants and not planning on gardening the area.

So my advice is to buy a few giant packs of rubber gloves—the kind doctors use—sold at most drugstores, and wear long pants that reach down and over your shoe tops plus a sweatshirt that covers your wrists with the ends tucked under the gloves. Then stop every so often to change gloves, carefully pulling them off with the same attentions you would follow if working in the Black Hole of Calcutta during the time that *Journal of the Plague Year* was published.

BIBLIOGRAPHY

Anshutz, Edward Pollock, ed. *New, Old and Forgotten Remedies*. Philadelphia, 1900.

Bailey, Liberty Hyde. *The Standard Cyclopedia of Horticulture*. New York: Macmillan, 1944.

Banister, John. *A Catalogue of Plants Observed by Me in Virginia*. In *Historia Plantarum*, Vol. 2, edited by John Ray. London, 1688.

Barton, Benjamin Smith. *Elements of Botany; or, Outlines of the Natural History of Vegetables*. Philadelphia, 1803.

Bartram, William. *Travels of William Bartram*. Edited by Mark Van Doren. New York: Dover Publications, n.d.

The Bernard E. Harkness Seedlist Handbook. 2nd ed. Portland, OR: Timber Press, 1993.

Betts, Edwin M., and Hazlehurst Bolton Perkins. *Thomas Jefferson's Flower Garden at Monticello*. Revised and enlarged by Peter J. Hatch. Charlottesville, VA: University Press of Virginia, 1986.

Bir, Richard. *Growing and Propagating Showy Native Woody Plants*. Chapel Hill: University of North Carolina Press, 1992.

Blanchan, Neltje. *Nature's Garden: An Aid to Knowledge of Our Wild Flowers and Their Insect Visitors*. New York: Doubleday, Page & Co., 1904.

Breck, Joseph. *The Flower Garden; or, Breck's Book of Flowers*. New York: Orange Judd & Co., 1865.

Brett-James, Norman G. *The Life of Peter Collinson*. London: privately printed, 1935.

Bulfinch, Thomas. *Bulfinch's Mythology*. New York: Thomas Y. Crowell Company, 1913.

Burke, Edmund. *On Taste / On the Sublime and Beautiful / Reflections on the French Revolution / A Letter to a Noble Lord*. New York: P. F. Collier & Son, 1969.

Burr, Fearing. *The Field and Garden Vegetables of America*. Reprint. Chillicothe, IL: American Botanist, 1988.

Catesby, Mark. *The Natural History of Carolina, Florida and the Bahama Islands*. 2 vols. London, 1729–47.

Chambers, Sir William. *Plans, Elevations, Selections and Perspective Views of the Gardens and Buildings at Kew in Surrey, the Seat of Her Royal Highness the Princess Dowager of Wales*. London: J. Haberkorn, 1763.

Clusius, Carolus. *Rariorum plantarum historia*. Antwerp: Joannes Moretus, Officina Plantiniana, 1601.

Coats, Alice M. *Garden Shrubs and Their Histories*. New York: Simon and Schuster, 1992.

———. *The Plant Hunters*. New York: McGraw-Hill Book Company, 1969.

Cornett Newcomb, Peggy. *Popular Annuals of Eastern North America, 1865–1914*. Washington, DC: Dumbarton Oaks, 1985.

Culpepper, Nicholas. *The English Physician Enlarged with 369 Medicines Made of English Herbs*. London: S. Ballard, L. Hawes, and Company, 1765.

Earle, Alice Morse. *Old Time Gardens*. New York: Macmillan Company, 1901.

Earle, Mrs. C. W. *More Pot-Pourri from a Surrey Garden*. New York: Macmillan Company, 1899.

Earnest, Ernest. *John and William Bartram*. Philadelphia: University of Pennsylvania Press, 1940.

Ellacombe, Henry N. *In a Gloucestershire Garden*. London: Edward Arnold Publishers, 1896.

Ewan, Joseph, and Nesta Ewan. *John Banister and His Natural History of Virginia, 1678–1692*. Urbana: University of Illinois Press, 1970.

Fletcher, H. L. V. *Popular Flowering Plants*. London: Garden Book Club, 1970.

Foote, Leonard E., and Samuel B. Jones Jr. *Native Shrubs and Woody Vines of the Southeast*. Portland, OR: Timber Press, 1989.

Genders, Roy. *Bulbs: A Complete Handbook*. Indianapolis: Bobbs-Merrill Company, 1973.

Gent, J. W. *John Worlidge: Systema horti-culturae; or, The Art of Gardening in Three Books . . . Illustrated with Sculptures, Representing the Form of Gardens,*

According to the Newest Models. London: printed for Tho. Burrel and W. Hensman, 1677.

Gerard's Herbal: John Gerard's Historie of Plants. Edited by Marcus Woodward. United Kingdom: Senate, 1998.

Gleason, Henry A. *The New Britton and Brown Illustrated Flora of the Northeastern United States and Adjacent Canada.* New York: Hafner Publishing Company, 1963.

Grieve, Mrs. M. *A Modern Herbal.* 2 vols. New York: Dover Publications, 1971.

Grigson, Geoffrey. *The Englishman's Flora.* London: Phoenix House, 1955.

Hanmer, Sir Thomas. *The Garden Book of Sir Thomas Hamner.* London, 1933.

Hedrick, Ulysses Prentiss. *A History of Horticulture in America to 1860.* New York: Oxford University Press, 1950.

Hill, Sir John. *A British Herbal.* London, 1756.

Hogarth, William. *The Analysis of Beauty.* London, 1753. Reprint. Edited by Joseph Burke. Oxford: Clarendon Press, 1955.

Home, Henry (Lord Kames). *Elements of Criticism (Gardening and Architecture).* New York: Collins & Hannay, 1829.

Hottes, Alfred C. *Garden Facts and Fancies.* New York: Dodd, Mead & Company, 1949.

Jefferson, Thomas. *The Garden and Farm Books.* Edited by Robert C. Baron. Golden, CO: Fulcrum, 1988.

Jekyll, Gertrude. *Children and Gardens.* London: Country Life, 1908.

Johnson, C. Pierpont, and J. E. Sowerby. *The Useful Plants of Great Britain.* London: Robert Hardwicke, 1862.

Josselyn, John. *New England's Rarities Discovered.* Reprint. Massachusetts Historical Society, 1972.

Lampe, Dr. Kenneth F., and Mary Ann McCann. *AMA Handbook of Poisonous and Injurious Plants.* Chicago: American Medical Association, 1985.

Lawson, John. *A New Voyage to Carolina.* Reprint. Chapel Hill: University of North Carolina Press, 1967.

Leighton, Ann. *American Gardens in the Eighteenth Century: "For Use or for Delight."* Boston: Houghton Mifflin Company, 1976.

Lloyd, Francis Ernest. *The Carnivorous Plants.* New York: Dover Publications, 1976.

Loewer, Peter. *Thoreau's Garden: Native Plants for the American Landscape.* Mechanicsburg, PA: Stackpole Books, 1996.

————. *The Wild Gardener: On Flowers and Foliage for the Natural Border.* Mechanicsburg, PA: Stackpole Books, 1991.

Main, Thomas. *Directions for the Transplantation and Management of Young Thorn or Other Hedge Plants, Preparative to Their Being Set in Hedges.* Washington, DC, 1807.

Mason, William. *The English Garden: A Poem in Four Books.* A corrected edition with notes by W. Burgh. York, England: A. Ward, 1783.

McClintock, David, and R. S. R. Fitter. *The Pocket Guide to Wild Flowers.* London: Collins, 1956.

Miles, Bebe. *Wildflower Perennials for Your Garden.* Mechanicsburg, PA: Stackpole Books, 1996.

Miller, Philip. *The Gardener's Dictionary.* 8th ed. London, 1768.

M'Mahon, Bernard. *The American Gardener's Calendar.* Philadelphia, 1806.

Nichols, Beverley. *Merry Hall.* New York: E. P. Dutton & Co., 1953.

Nichols, Frederick Doveton, and Ralph E. Griswold. *Thomas Jefferson Landscape Architect.* Charlottesville: University Press of Virginia, 1978.

Ohwi, Jisaburo. *Flora of Japan.* Washingon, DC: Smithsonian Institution, 1965.

The Oxford Companion to Gardens. New York: Oxford University Press, 1986.

Parkinson, John. *A Garden of Pleasant Flowers (Paradisi in Sole: Paradisus Terrestris).* New York: Dover Publications, 1976.

Parsons, Frances Theodora. *How to Know the Ferns.* New York: Charles Scribner's Sons, 1927.

Pizzetti, Ippolito, and Henry Cocker. *Flowers: A Guide for Your Garden.* New York: Harry N. Abrams, 1968.

Pursh, Frederick Traugott. *Flora Americae Septentrionalis; or, A Systematic Arrangement and Description of the Plants of North America.* London: Richard & Arthur Taylor for White, Cochrane, & Co., 1814.

Redouté, Pierre Joseph. *Lilies and Related Flowers.* Woodstock, NY: Overlook Press, 1982.

Robinson, William. *The English Flower Garden and Home Grounds.* London: John Murray, Albemarle Street, 1901.

Rombauer, Irma, and Marion Rombauer Becker. *The Joy of Cooking.* Indianapolis: Bobbs-Merrill Company, 1964.

Sieveking, F. S. A., and Albert Forbes. *Gardens Ancient and Modern: An Epitome of the Literature of the Garden-Art.* London: J. M. Dent & Co., 1899.

Sitwell, Sir George. *On the Making of Gardens.* New York: Charles Scribner's Sons, 1951.

Skinner, Charles M. *Myths and Legends of Flowers, Trees, Fruits, and Plants.* Philadelphia: J. B. Lippincott Company, 1925.

Smith, Margaret Bayard. *The First Forty Years of Washington Society.* New York: Frederick Ungar Publishers, 1965.

Stearn, William T. *Botanical Latin.* North Pomfret, VT: David & Charles, 1987.

Steyermark, Julian A. *Spring Flora of Missouri.* St. Louis: Missouri Botanical Gardens, 1940.

Taylor, Norman. *The Practical Encyclopedia of Gardening in Dictionary Form.* Garden City: Halcyon House, 1942.

Tice, Patricia M. *Gardening in America.* Rochester, NY: Strong Museum, 1984.

Torrey, John, and Asa Gray. *A Flora of North America.* New York: Wiley & Putnam, 1838–43.

U.S. Department of Agriculture. *Food Plants of the North American Indians.* Misc. Publication 237. Washington, DC: U.S. Department of Agriculture, n.d.

Van Ravenswaay, Charles. *A Nineteenth-Century Garden.* New York: Universe Books, 1977.

Whately, Thomas. *Observations on Modern Gardening.* 3rd ed. London: Payne, 1771.

Wilder, Louise Beebe. *The Fragrant Path.* New York: Macmillan Company, 1932.

INDEX